£10

D1476402

WITHDRAWN

Birmingham: the First Manufacturing Town in the World 1760–1840

by the same author

Britain in the Widening World
A Social History of the English Working Classes 1815–1945

BIRMINGHAM

The First Manufacturing Town in the World 1760–1840

ERIC HOPKINS

WEIDENFELD & NICOLSON
LONDON

First published in Great Britain in 1989 by
George Weidenfeld & Nicolson Ltd
91 Clapham High Street, London SW4 7TA

British Library Cataloguing in Publication Data

Hopkins, Eric
Birmingham : The First Manufacturing
Town in the World 1760–1840.
I. West Midlands. (Metropolitan County) –
Birmingham – Industrialization. 1770–1860
I. Title
338′.09424′96

ISBN 0 297 79473 6

Photoset by Deltatype Ltd, Ellesmere Port, Cheshire
Printed in Great Britain by
Butler & Tanner Ltd
Frome and London

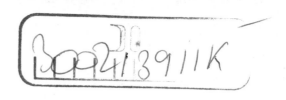

In memory of Barbara Joan Hopkins 1919–86

For you abide,
A singing rib within my dreaming side.

Alun Lewis

Contents

Illustrations

East View of Birmingham, 1779 (Mary Evans Picture Library)
The Bull Ring, 1812 (Mary Evans Picture Library)
Christchurch, c. 1830 (Mary Evans Picture Library)
Birmingham Town Hall, 1834 (Mary Evans Picture Library)
Memorial to Boulton, Watt and Murdock by William Wloye
View of Aston Flint Glass Works, 1842 (Birmingham Reference
    Library)
Elevation and plans of back-to back houses, Great Russell Street,
    Chadwick Report, 1842 (Birmingham Reference Library)
Plans of two new courts, Bradford Street, Chadwick Report, 1842
    (Birmingham Reference Library)
Elevations of houses in new courts, Bradford Street, Chadwick
    Report, 1842 (Birmingham Reference Library)
New Street, 1838 (Mary Evans Picture Library)
High Street Market, early nineteenth century (Birmingham Reference
    Library)
William Hutton 1723–1815 (Birmingham Reference Library)
Thomas Attwood 1783–1856 (Birmingham Reference Library)
Pen grinding room, Hicks, Wells & Co., 1851 (Mansell Collection)
The Gun Proof House, 1851 (Mansell Collection)
Boulton & Watt's Soho Works, late eighteenth century (Mary Evans
    Picture Library)

Introduction

This book is essentially a synthesis, a bringing together of material relating to the economic and social history of Birmingham during the Industrial Revolution, a period covering the years from the mid-eighteenth century to about 1840. Although secondary material is extensively used, the book also incorporates a good deal of primary source material resulting from my own research, some of which has already appeared in print. It is in no sense a complete account of economic and social change in Birmingham, 1760–1840, which would be impossible to achieve in a book this size; but guidance is given in the text, footnotes and bibliography as to further sources of information.

Above all, the book seeks to place Birmingham firmly in the context of the great national changes in economy and society which are associated with the Industrial Revolution, and to demonstrate that Birmingham should be seen as the norm in this connection, and not merely as a rather dull and boring exception to the exciting tale of change in the cotton industry. Much of industry was *not* transformed in the period up to 1840, even though industry itself expanded greatly in relation to agriculture. As Professor Crafts has observed recently, the main feature of British industrialization involved getting a lot of workers into the industrial sector, rather than getting a high level of output per worker once they were there. All the same, much depends on what is meant by a 'high level of output': in the case of Birmingham, division of labour had in fact gone far by 1760, so that output was already relatively high in terms of labour productivity. The essential point is that the great economic achievements of the successive decades were based not on massive technological break-throughs, as in the cotton industry, but on existing modes of production, and principally on the small workshop with its hand machinery. Only in the 1830s did steam power begin to be used on any significant scale, and only then were larger work units becoming more common and more prominent. There was thus a gradual and undramatic change to more modern means of production, in a town which was already industrialized by 1760. By 1840 the larger workplace and the traditional small workshop existed side by side, but with the latter predominating numerically. The major aspects of these economic changes are traced in the first four chapters.

Inevitably, economic growth was accompanied by social change, and this forms the subject of the succeeding five chapters. Here the story is again of organic development from the mid-eighteenth century onwards. Society in Birmingham was subjected to all the strains of expanding urbanization which were manifested generally in industrial towns, and the response of Birmingham's middle classes to emerging social problems was in many ways typical of what happened elsewhere. Town improvement was originally on a limited scale, and directed for the most part to removing obstacles to marketing and trade. Only later in the period was there a growing sense of civic identity and responsibility, characterized by the activities of the Birmingham Political Union, and culminating in the incorporation of the borough in 1838. Earlier on, as happened in other towns, simple provision was made for the sick and for the poor in the form of hospitals and a new poor law system. Later on still, more schools, churches and chapels were established.

As for the great majority of Birmingham's population, the working classes – those people with dirty faces and no names, as one eighteenth-century observer slightingly put it – they got on as best they could, but with a wide social gap separating the more skilled in regular employment from the unskilled labourer. Their lives at work and away from work are surveyed in chapters 6, 7, and 9, but without revealing any great discontinuities with the past. Relationships with employers have also been re-examined, and the conclusion reached largely confirms (with minor reservations) the conventional view of class co-operation rather than of class conflict.

Since this is a work of economic and social history, political activities have been excluded for the most part, though some reference to politics has been unavoidable in attempting to assess the role of the middle classes in the town. Inevitably there are references to Chartism but, somewhat reluctantly, this topic has been excluded, partly because of the decision to end the book at about 1840, and partly because the subject of Chartism in Birmingham would really require a book on its own.

As is customary, this Introduction has been written last, and it is at this point that the author is more uncomfortably aware than ever of possible shortcomings. It would have been helpful, for instance, to have provided a detailed survey of the various industries firm by firm, coupled with a quantitative assessment of the growth in size of work units, and an analysis of the workings of individual firms over a period of time. Unfortunately, the scarcity of source material makes this kind of approach impossible, as Professor Court noted as long ago as 1946, and his hope that the examination of business archives would supply some of the missing detail remains unfulfilled, principally because so few business records have survived. Again, the sheer size of Birmingham by the 1840s has made it difficult to undertake the kind of micro-study possible, for example, in the smaller towns of the Black Country.

I am grateful to my colleagues in the Department of Economic and Social History, University of Birmingham, for the comments on drafts of the earlier chapters, and especially to Professor J. R. Harris and to Mr Peter Cain for their wise advice on the first three chapters. Needless to say, they bear no responsibility whatsoever for any errors, omissions or misconceptions which may remain in spite of their good offices and their patient attempts to guide me into the paths of better historiography. Lastly, my thanks are due to the departmental secretaries, Sue Kennedy and Diane Martin, for their much appreciated help in typing the final drafts of this book.

E.H.
Stourbridge

PART 1

The Mid-Eighteenth Century Scene

I

Birmingham Economy and Society in the Mid-Eighteenth Century

By the mid-eighteenth century Birmingham had long been an industrial centre specializing in metal work. In the Tudor period Leland commented on the number of smiths of various kinds when he visited the town about 1538:

> There be many smiths in the town, that used to make knives and all mannour of cuttinge tooles, and many lorimers, that make bittes, and a great many naylors. So that a great part of the towne is maintained by smiths, who have their iron and sea-cole out of Staffordshire.[1]

Later in the same century Camden referred to the metal workers of Birmingham, which town he described as 'full of inhabitants, and resounding with hammers and anvils, for the most part of them are smiths'.[2] In the following century the emphasis was still on swords, edgetools and nails, together with two new industries, the manufacture of guns and of brass. The hearth tax returns of 1683 show a total of 202 forges in the town, over half of them concentrated in Digbeth, Edgbaston Street and Deritend, all in the lower part of the town near the River Rea.[3] The division of the town into a lower, industrial area and an upper, more residential part, was described in 1755 by a visitor who

> reconnoitred the town, which is another *London* in miniature: it stands on the Side of a Hill, forming a Half-moon; the lower part is filled with the Workshops and Ware-houses of the manufacturers, and consists chiefly of old Buildings; the Upper Part of the Town, like *St James's*, contains a Number of new, regular streets, and a handsome square, all well-built and well-inhabited . . .[4]

⚹ The original reason for this concentration on the metal industries is clear enough: as mentioned by Leland, it was the availability of iron ore and coal close at hand on the South Staffordshire and East Worcestershire coalfield. It has also been argued that plentiful supplies of wood for converting into charcoal were easily obtainable from the woods of north-east Warwickshire, and that this explains why metal industries developed in Birmingham rather than exclusively on the coalfield to the west.[5] Be that as it may, it is clear that by the eighteenth century Birmingham industries formed a vital part of the widespread iron industry in the Midlands. This industry was based on furnaces and forges in an area stretching from the Forest of Dean and South Wales to the West Midlands, North Midlands and Cheshire, most of the works being under the control of three major partnerships. The largest partnership, the Iron Works in Partnership, formed in 1692, controlled fourteen active ironworks in the Forest of Dean and the Stour Valley. The next largest concern, the Staffordshire Works, controlled most of the ironworks within and to the north of the Trent Valley in Staffordshire. Although pig iron was produced in the Midlands, the local forge capacity exceeded the furnace production, so that crude pig iron was transported into the area, either up the Severn from the Forest of Dean to Bewdley and thence by road to Birmingham and the Black Country, or overland to the central area from Cheshire and North Staffordshire. The focal point of this network of furnaces and forges was Birmingham and district. By the early eighteenth century Birmingham thus provided essential markets not only for ironworks close at hand in South Staffordshire, but also for works at a far greater distance in the south-west and the north-west.[6]

Why did Birmingham develop in this way, even before the onset of the Industrial Revolution? A number of explanations have been put forward, none of them of sufficient weight when taken separately, and all of them requiring qualification to a greater or lesser extent. One of the most important causes of Birmingham's growth, it is said, is the fact that Birmingham was not an incorporated borough until 1838. Since it lacked a charter, it was not subject to the restrictions of the Clarendon Code, so that dissenters could freely settle there. The consequence was (or so it was alleged) that it attracted a vigorous and independently-minded class of immigrant who had much to contribute to industrial growth; and certainly Dissenters, particularly Quaker employers, were prominent in Birmingham in the eighteenth century. Further, the lack of a charter meant that there were no guilds with long-established privileges and exclusive apprenticeship regulations which could fetter both industry and trade. The way was therefore open for the display of initiative and enterprise. In these two respects Birmingham was in a favoured position. In the words of its historian, William Hutton: 'A town without a charter is a town without a shackle', and the result was a place where men went about their business with a quickened step. Hutton's description of his first impression of Birmingham on his visit in 1741 is well-known:

> I was surprised at the place, but more so at the people. They possessed a vivacity I had never beheld. I had been among dreamers, but now I saw men awake. Their very step along the streets showed alacrity. Every man seemed to know what he was about. , . .[7]

Persuasive as these arguments may seem, it would be unwise to place too much emphasis upon them. Although Birmingham's freedom to attract Dissenters and to develop without gilds may well have had important results for the growth of its industries, it must be remembered that other industrial towns such as Wolverhampton had similar advantages, yet failed to develop so rapidly. Further, not all chartered boroughs were slow to grow industrially, and some had significant numbers of Dissenters in spite of the legislation of the 1660s; Coventry is a case in point.[8] Other factors must have played their part, and Professor Allen has suggested that the availability of a supply of good drinking water permitted the settlement of a large population close to the South Staffordshire coalfield.[9] Clearly, no single explanation can account for Birmingham's growth in the early eighteenth century, and other historians have preferred to stress the tradition of working in iron (which was easily extended to working in brass and steel), the trading connections with London, and the growth of a demand for small articles such as shoe buckles and metal buttons which the fashionable world of the early eighteenth century required.[10] To this list of causes may be added the fact that Birmingham's central position gave the town a wide hinterland from which to recruit immigrant labour. An analysis of nearly 700 settlement certificates for the years 1686–1726 shows that over 500 immigrants came from the counties of Warwickshire, Staffordshire, and Worcestershire.[11] It remains true that the fundamental cause of the growth of Birmingham's metal industries must be the availability of local supplies of iron ore and coal, but the pace at which development took place must have depended on the influence of the factors already discussed operating over a period of time. Certainly the development of the toy trade in the early eighteenth century illustrates the way in which industrial expansion took place. The Birmingham toy trade comprised many different small articles of iron, brass, and steel, such as buckles, buttons, snuff-boxes, and trinkets of all kinds. The firm of Boulton & Fothergill, for example, were manufacturing a variety of such articles in 1763, including the following:

> chapes, inlaid buckles, buttons platina, Coat, Breast, & Sleeve Buttons platina, Watch Chains, bell locks, Watch Keys, watch hooks, tapestry hooks com(mon), met(al) buttons, steel watch chains, platina buckles, steel . . . & en(amelled) Butt(on)s.[12]

Later Boulton introduced silver-plating and ormolu work, together with tableware, candelabra, vases, statuary and other artistic productions. The importance of the toy trade was explained to a House of Commons Committee in 1759 by two leading manufacturers, John Taylor and Samuel Garbett. They claimed that the town had increased by at least a half since the toy trade had begun, and that it employed at least 20,000 in Birmingham and the neighbouring towns, of whom 6,000 were using gold and silver in the course of manufacture. The trade amounted to about £600,000 per year, of which about £500,000 was exported.[13]

The growth of this trade depended partly upon the imports of brass into the area – brass itself was not made in the town until 1740[14] – and partly on the skill with which Birmingham ironworkers could adapt their traditional techniques to new purposes. There seems to have been no difficulty about the redirection of skills, and indeed some Birmingham wares acquired the reputation of being both cheap and nasty; the old saying was that given a guinea and a copper kettle, a Birmingham workman could make a hundred pounds' worth of jewellery. Nevertheless, the testimony to ingenuity is obvious, and production in the toy trade was greatly improved by the division of labour. This appeared most marked at the large establishment of John Taylor, who was the most important button and snuff-box manufacturer at the mid-century. The same London visitor to Birmingham in 1755 observed that 'The Multitude of Hands each Button goes thro' before it is sent to the Market is likewise surprising; you will perhaps think it incredible when I tell you they go thro' 70 different Operations of 70 different Work-folk.'[15]

The modern reader may well find this difficult to believe, but a decade or so later Lord Shelburne considered that the great rise of Birmingham was due partly to the discovery of mixed metals, and partly to the subdivision of labour. According to him, a button would pass through fifty hands, and each hand would pass perhaps a thousand buttons a day. Work then became so simple that '5 times in 6, children of 6 or 7 years old do it as well as men'.[16]

As important as the division of labour was the use of advanced hand technology in the form of small, hand-operated machines. Thus, Taylor and Garbett informed the Committee of the House of Commons in 1759 that many of Birmingham's goods were made with the help of machines or engines invented by the people of Birmingham, which 'lessens the manual labour and enables boys to do men's work'. At the end of 1770, Matthew Boulton wrote to the Earl of Warwick, making strong claims for the efficiency of production in his Soho factory:

> . . . although in many places they have as good and as cheap materials as we have, and have labour cent per cent cheaper, yet nevertheless by the superactivity of our people and by the many mechanical contrivances and extensive apparatus wh we are possess'd of, our men are enabled to do from twice to ten times the work that can be done without the help of such contrivances & even women and children to do more than men can do without them.[17]

His claims are echoed in the Introduction to *The Birmingham Directory* (*1777*) which refers to the facility and dispatch with which things are made, 'principally owing to the engines, etc., employed in the fabrication thereof, which other countries are, in a great measure, deprived of'.[18]

The machines referred to here are principally the stamp, the press, the lathe, and the drawbench.[19] It is commonly said that the stamp was invented in 1766 by John Pickering, a toymaker of London, and was speedily adapted by Richard Ford of Birmingham for the shaping of hollowware.[20] Be this as it may, a form of stamp was in use for the minting of coins in Tudor times, and stamps were certainly used in the button trade in Birmingham before 1766. A Swedish visitor to the town in 1749 described the kind of stamp employed for shaping buttons:

The afore-mentioned small blanks which are cast are then stamped in steel moulds to the shape of buttons as required. The second mould is concave and engraved with the pattern, the upper mould is convex and is fixed in a sufficiently large iron weight, which is hoisted up with a rope and block and by its own weight it moulds the blanks to buttons when it falls down. The weight passes between two posts and in this way it falls straight. A man hoists the weight, holding the rope in his hand and with his foot in a piece of iron resembling a stirrup at the end of the rope.[21]

The blanks mentioned here were punched out in a press. According to the same source, this press

. . . is composed of a smooth cylindrical punch of steel, which is pressed by the screw into a hole, corresponding in size to the stamp. In this way a small circular disc is pressed out and this disc falls through the hole into a container placed beneath. . . . Bigger and smaller punches may be put into this machine depending on the task.[22]

The lathe, a treadle-operated machine dating back many centuries, performed an essential service in the metal industries by producing engine-turned parts in round or oval section. In the button trade, its use included the trimming of buttons taken from the stamp:

From here the buttons are taken to another workshop, where the edge which is a result of the punching is trimmed off in a lathe. This lathe has two irons. Their points fit each other, one is concave and the other convex corresponding in size to the various buttons. Between the aforesaid two irons the button which is to be trimmed is put in, and after it is trimmed, which takes a second, it falls out by itself, when the man pushes a spring with his elbow whereby the aforesaid two irons come apart a little, but they soon come together again, when another button is put in and the man withdraws his elbow.[23]

Lastly, the drawbench, a simple machine for drawing out wire to a uniform thickness throughout, was often used in pin-making, and dated from the previous century.

These four machines were vital to efficient production in the toy trade. It is impossible, of course, to say how widespread their use was in Birmingham, but the indications from advertisements in the local press are that they were very commonly employed by medium-sized firms, and usually took specialized forms and sizes appropriate to the work undertaken. Although it is often assumed that hand technology before the advent of steam-powered machinery was usually simple and crude in nature, in fact the 1749 account quoted from above makes it clear that manufacturing processes in Birmingham at the time were surprisingly complex and refined. Further, there is an interesting parallel to be drawn with the employment of children in the early textile mills later on in the century in that teams of children were used to keep the Birmingham machines working. For example, on the stamp:

> . . . a small boy makes the blanks red-hot in a small furnace. Another boy puts them under the punch, one by one. The third picks them out of the punch and greases the upper mould between each punching with a greased brush. All this goes quite quickly.[24]

Writing in 1836, Hawkes Smith pointed out that these machines by no means superseded human labour, but rather supplemented it by supplying more force than could be wielded by the arm and the tools of the workman alone, 'still leaving his skills and experience of head, hand, and eye in full exercise'. It was for this reason that he considered that Birmingham had suffered infinitely less from the introduction of machinery than those towns where machinery was an actual substitute for human labour, though he did not comment on the use of the child labour which was essential to its employment.[25]

Closely associated with the toy trade was the jewellery trade (really a specialized branch of the toy trade), and the use of japanning finishes which was to develop further with the manufacture of papier-mâché in the second half of the eighteenth century. Pin-making also commenced at the mid-century when it was started by the Ryland family in New Street.[26] It was to become a major industry by the nineteenth century. Meanwhile the manufacture of swords and guns continued to flourish, the gun industry becoming highly specialized, with individual firms concentrating on making particular parts of guns.

The Swedish visitor of 1749 provides a remarkable illustration of the skills used in one particular workshop for drilling touchholes in gun barrels:

> At Mr Th. Hadley's workshop another person, a Mr Born, made golden touchholes in two fine steelbarrels in the following way.

Using a common spiral drill he drilled the touchhole to this calibre, but with another blunt drill made the hole outwardly wider in this fashion. In the hole he made screw threads. . . . From a golden rod, beaten to the width of the hole, there was also made a screw with a matching thread. . . . This golden screw was screwed flush in the hole and was beaten with a hammer so that the outwardly wider hole was filled up. Then an average touchhole was drilled with a finer drill through the centre of the golden rod. . . . At the drilling through the gold as well as the making of the threads fresh cream was used instead of oil. It has a better effect. . . . The advantage of a golden touchhole is that it never rusts, nor is it attacked by the air or by the sulphur and the nitric acid which are in the powder, but consequently keeps its constant diameter which is not the case with iron touchholes.[27]

Sketchley's Birmingham Directory (1767) classifies separately gun- and pistol-makers (thirty-five), gun-barrel makers and filers (eight), gun-barrel polishers and finishers (five), gun-lock makers, forgers, finishers and filers (eleven), and gun-swivel makers and stockers (three). The same directory lists the numbers in each of fifty-five different metal trades. There is no doubt that by the mid-eighteenth century Birmingham had become a town to be visited by the curious for the wide range of its industries. When Lady Shelburne spent three days there in 1766, she paid visits to all the most famous establishments and witnessed the manufacture of buttons, buckles, snuff boxes, guns, papier-mâché boxes, and the melting, painting and stamping of glass.[28]

The sizes of the largest firms at this time are well-known. John Taylor was termed 'the most considerable maker of gilt-metal buttons, and enamell'd snuff-boxes' by the London visitor of 1755, who continued: 'we were assured that he employes 500 persons in those two branches, and when we had seen his workshop, we had no scruple in believing it.'[29] When Matthew Boulton entered into partnership in 1762 with John Fothergill, he set about building his famous manufactory at Soho, Birmingham, where by 1771 he claimed to employ 700 hands; the year after he said he had to feed 1,000 mouths weekly.[30] Even before this he regarded himself as being in charge of 'the largest Hardware Manufactory in the World'.[31] However, these two establishments of Taylor and of Boulton & Fothergill must have been exceptional, and records have not survived of any other firms of comparable size in the 1760s, though the other works visited by Lady Shelburne in 1766, such as those of Samuel Garbett, John Baskerville, and 'the quaker gunsmiths' (probably Farmer & Galton) must have employed considerable numbers. Not until the early nineteenth century is it possible to gain a better idea of the size of firms below the scale of the very largest establishments;[32] but even then it is clear that the majority of firms were still those of small masters or garret masters, employing only members of their own family together with one or two journeymen. It is therefore a fair assumption that the typical workshop unit was still very small in the mid-eighteenth century.

Working conditions in Birmingham industry are also largely undocumented before the nineteenth century, but from what is known of the keeping of St Monday in the first half of that century it seems likely that a flexible working week of the kind traditional within a small-master economy was the norm. This pattern of work meant that emphasis was laid upon the production of certain quantities of manufactured goods rather than rigid adherence to set working hours. Payment was usually by the piece rather than by the day or week. Workers could therefore determine their own hours within broad limits, often doing little or no work on Mondays but working very long hours towards the end of the week in order to earn a living wage. This is not to say that working hours in the aggregate were not very long, a daily average being perhaps twelve to fourteen hours; but a number of factors all made for a constantly changing work pattern very different from that dictated by factory discipline in its classic form – the availability or otherwise of raw material (itself affected by transport problems caused by the weather), the keeping of traditional holidays and, above all, the ebb and flow of demand. In the larger works the unreliability of water power in the summer months was also an important consideration.[33]

Even in Matthew Boulton's Soho works in the 1760s where one might perhaps expect a discipline comparable to that of the new cotton spinning mills, the regime seems to have been surprisingly lacking in vigour.[34] Certainly Boulton's workers took off all the traditional holidays at Christmas, Easter and Whitsun. In December 1764 the stocktaking which was planned to take a fortnight actually took nearly a month during which no work was done. In April of the next year little work was performed generally in Birmingham during Easter Week, and Boulton complained later that 'it was impossible for us to make one of our workmen do any business for the full Whitsun week'.[35]

There was also the problem of drunkenness at work. As we have seen, Boulton boasted of the 'superactivity of our people', but he had to admit that there were times when workmen were too drunk to work:

> . . . our workmen in the plated way have very few of them been at work this week past having been drunk all the while, and it was not in our power to persuade them to set to work again while they had any money left, a vexatious circumstance we are frequently subjected to when we have the greatest need of their dilligence.

A week later, Boulton had to confess to a customer that he had been unable to fulfil orders 'owing to the insolence and drunkenness of our workmen'. Early in the next year Boulton complained that the workmen wanted to keep holidays (presumably at Christmas, when stocktaking was carried out) for three weeks 'in which there is scarcely one scrap of work done'.[36]

It is therefore a reasonable assumption that the working week was by no means uniform throughout the year in mid eighteenth-century Birmingham. Not that this was at all unusual elsewhere, of course. It was common practice in England at the time, and the failure of workmen to apply themselves steadily to their work was often remarked upon in the early eighteenth century, and especially their tendency to do only enough work to pay for immediate needs rather than to save for the future.[37]

Domestic trade must certainly have been expanding in the Birmingham area during the first half of the eighteenth century as the toy trade grew in response to the demands of fashion and as part of the national increase in prosperity. This expansion of the domestic market can be seen in a variety of ways; for example, the increase in road traffic led to frequent complaints about the state of the main roads into Birmingham. In 1707 the Bristol Road was said to be almost impassable due to the heavy traffic in iron, coal, and salt (this road communicated with the salt works at Droitwich). Between Birmingham and Evesham, eighty pack-horses a day were carrying vegetables and fruit to meet the needs of an industrial population.[38] In 1726, a petition to the House of Commons for permission to introduce a turnpike bill alleged that a ten-mile stretch of road between Birmingham and Wolverhampton had become 'dangerous and almost impassable by reason of the great number of carriages constantly employed in carrying of iron, and iron goods, and coal'. Witnesses confirmed this, and stated that the king's carriages used for transporting soldiers could not pass through that winter, and that at Wednesbury the ruts were deep enough to damage the foundations of houses.[39] In the same year the first Birmingham Turnpike Act was obtained for the Stratford and Warwick roads. In 1727 further Acts were passed for the roads to Wednesbury, Bromsgrove and Dudley.[40] By 1731 there was a weekly service of carriages and waggons to London, with additional coaches in operation by 1741.[41] Other indications of the growth of trade may be found in the increasing number of inns providing accommodation for travellers and in the widespread circulation of Birmingham's first permanent newspaper, *Aris's Birmingham Gazette*, in the early 1740s. An advertisement in the *Gazette* might be booked outside Birmingham in several towns some distance away, such as Shrewsbury, Bridgnorth, Worcester, Leominster, Warwick and Wolverhampton.[42]

A further illustration of the way in which domestic trade was growing is to be seen in the increasing importance of the middleman or factor. Such a person had a valuable part to play in marketing the products of the workshop, or in bringing together the output of several workshops in order to market one composite product as in the gun trade. Given the very large number of small workshops and the amount of subcontracting in Birmingham, the factor had a vital role to perform if trade was to continue to expand. In his evidence before the House of Commons in 1759, Taylor commented on the economic function of the factor as a link in what might be an elaborate chain extending from the workshop to the humblest village shop: 'The master workmen sell to the factor, the factor to the merchant, the merchant to country dealers or shopkeepers in the large towns, who sell to the shopkeepers of inferior rank in small towns and villages.'[43]

Certainly the factor might promote Birmingham goods nationwide. Hutton was well aware of this. Though he appears to have thought – wrongly – that the function of the factor or merchant was of only recent origin, it is still significant that he should have emphasized the wide-ranging marketing of Birmingham products:

> The practice of the Birmingham manufacturer, for perhaps a hundred generations, was to keep within the warmth of his own forge. The foreign customer therefore applied to him for the

execution of orders, and regularly made his appearance twice a year; and though this mode of business is not totally extinguished, yet a very different one is adopted. The merchant stands at the head of the manufacturer, purchases his produce, and travels the whole island to promote the sale; a practice that would have astonished our forefathers.[44]

Boulton spent a good deal of his time in making business contacts in London, where he worked through agents so as to bypass the London jewellers and sell direct to the nobility and gentry. He also planned to open his own shop in London.[45] Less well-known, earlier Birmingham figures such as Tobias Bellaers, the ironmonger, travelled extensively in selling their wares.[46]

In this relatively complex web of commercial relationships, it is not surprising that the sale of goods on credit, and the use of instruments of credit, such as bills of exchange, were commonplace. This is very apparent in the business records of Boulton & Fothergill at the mid-century. In 1762 the credit given on articles of their own manufacture was six months, and three months on articles purchased by them for resale. No doubt these terms were varied to suit the degree of importance of the customer, and in 1764 one customer, Erhlich & Co, were informed somewhat stiffly that the firm's general terms were no more than three months' credit, with a discount of 2½ per cent, and goods free of carriage to London. It was also put to them that

> If you have six months' credit from the Commissioners [i.e. factors or agents] of this place, they are far more able to comply with those terms than ourselves by reason we have no credit in a manufactory as all our material and workmen's wages are obliged to be discharged every Saturday throughout the year.[47]

In fact, this has to be taken with a pinch of salt, for Boulton & Fothergill often lived very precariously on credit, having a massive running debt (the Bill Account) based on numerous bills of exchange which were used not only to raise cash to pay for materials supplied on credit, but also to pay instalments on loans.[48]

One other sign of the increasing commercial activity at the mid-century was the establishment in 1752 of a Court of Requests, or small debts court, which facilitated the recovery of debts under forty shillings. Seventy-two commissioners were appointed by local Act of Parliament, three to constitute a quorum. This court sat every Friday

morning in the chamber over the Old Cross, and according to
Hutton, there usually appeared before the court between eighty and a
hundred cases to be determined.[49] Bankruptcies occurred from time
to time, and it was not uncommon for disputes to be carried to the
London courts. Disagreements over contracts and the break-up of
partnerships are to be found in complaints from button-makers,
japanners, brassfounders and other manufacturers in Exchequer Bills
and Answers from 1750 onwards.[50]

It is difficult to take this sketch of the Birmingham home market
much further, given the paucity of surviving information as to its
detailed working. Nevertheless, it is certain that both industry and
commerce were thriving, and the business records of Boulton &
Fothergill show a modernity of spirit which would not be out of place
today. Their letter books reveal a concern with such matters as the
recording and dispatch of orders, the credit-worthiness of new
customers, excuses for delayed or non-delivery of goods, problems of
cash flow, attempts to raise more loans, the progress of stocktaking,
difficulties with the workmen, and so on. All this has a familiar ring
today, even down to Boulton's complaints, following a visit to Lord
Shelburne, about the way Bentley, the warehouse manager, was
failing to carry out his duties ('reading newspapers and magazines, or
perhaps writing out a love-song') whenever Boulton went into the
warehouse.[51]

So far as foreign trade is concerned, it is reasonable to assume that it
was of less importance than domestic trade to Birmingham manufacturers in the mid-eighteenth century, but it was certainly not
negligible. For example, the gun-making firm of Farmer & Galton
was the principal supplier of guns, cutlasses and knives to the
Company of Merchants trading to Africa, thus playing a leading role
in providing guns for the slave trade. This firm also sold to three of the
biggest firms trading with North America, and to France. There was
an important trade with Portugal, and alarm was expressed at the
news of the Lisbon earthquake in 1755, which it was said, 'hath very
affectingly alarmed the inhabitants of this town, a great quantity of
our manufacturing being sold there'.[52]

The earlier letter-books of Boulton & Fothergill certainly indicate a
widespread trade in Europe, with customers scattered throughout
Holland, France, Germany, Italy, Switzerland, Austria and Turkey.
In 1767 Matthew Boulton claimed that 'more than half the letters we

receive are wrote in the German language'. This was at a time when his partner John Fothergill was spending two years abroad, making contacts with European customers.[53] It has been said that by concentrating on goods which were valuable in relation to their size and weight, Birmingham had gained world-wide markets before most other inland centres.[54] It is highly likely that the toy trade enjoyed a flourishing export trade, though it would be surprising if as much as five-sixths of production in value was actually exported, as claimed by Taylor and Garbett in 1759.

It is impossible, of course, to assess accurately the extent of Birmingham's foreign trade, given the complete lack of figures on which to base calculations. Although it has been estimated that nationally exported manufacturers, other than textiles, more than doubled between 1699–1701 and 1752–4 (from 12 per cent to 29 per cent), yet woollen textiles still constituted 47 per cent of all domestic exports by value in 1752–4.[55] The great days of cotton-manufactured exports still lay in the future. Further, although Farmer & Galton undoubtedly had a valuable connection with the Africa Company, only 7 per cent of their guns out of an annual production of 12,000 went to the company in the mid-eighteenth century, while the average value of the gun cargo of a slaving ship was only between a quarter and a fifth of the total value of the cargo.[56] Again, Boulton & Fothergill obviously made considerable efforts to increase their sales overseas, yet it has been argued that a major reason why the partnership lost money was the serious losses resulting from foreign trade.[57] Customers abroad often delayed payments until the exchanges were in their favour, and it was extremely difficult if not impossible to recover bad debts in European countries. When a representative of the firm was sent to Russia and Poland, he secured orders amounting to several thousand pounds, but they were never paid for, and his travelling expenses came to £1,200. Boulton remarked that it was the same old story, a lack of remittances from abroad.[58] As this was in the early 1780s, it seems likely that problems of this kind were not unknown earlier in the century, and that foreign trade was still relatively hazardous. Though not in itself without risk, the safer market was undoubtedly at home.

How wealthy were Birmingham's leading manufacturers at the mid-century? It is clear that the most prominent industrialists lived very comfortably. When Lady Shelburne paid her visit to Birmingham in

1766, she was received by Matthew Boulton at Soho House, where he was accustomed to entertain noble visitors, and she had tea with John Taylor, the button king, at his villa ('a very handsome house'). Afterwards she visited Mr Baskerville's residence ('also a very pretty place out of the town').[59] Taylor, certainly the most important button maker, is reputed to have left £200,000 when he died nine years later. His will, dated 1767, gives no hint of wealth on this scale, though he did leave substantial legacies of £8,000 each to his two sons William and Charles, and £10,000 to his daughter Mary on her marriage, together with an annuity to his wife of £400.

As for the smaller manufacturers, their names appear fleetingly in the pages of the local newspaper *Aris's Gazette*, and in the local directories, but there is little evidence surviving which permits safe generalization about them at the mid-century. No doubt many of them were self-made men who had started with little or no capital of their own. The presenters of the petition to the House of Commons in 1759 claimed that they knew at least a hundred persons who had begun trade without any fortune, but had raised themselves by their own ingenuity and industry.[60] Of course, similar claims might be made for other manufacturing areas, but the numbers of small masters in Birmingham and the variety of metal trades, which permitted a change from one trade to another as their prosperity waxed or waned, make the claim feasible enough.

A survey of Birmingham insurance policies issued by the Sun Insurance Company of London in the year 1765 helps to establish the economic standing of some of the smaller manufacturers and retailers.[61] The largest single policy taken out was for £2,000 by William Welch, Joseph Williamson and John Startin, toymen and ironmongers of Snow Hill, insuring their warehouse for £250 and their stock for £1,750.[62] Other large policies include two for £1,000 each, taken out by Isaac and Nathaniel Whitehead, thread-makers, the first policy covering a house (£80), and household goods (£100), two rooms (£30), three houses (£150, £300, £130), and two other houses at £80 and £130. The second insured a house (£130), household goods (£100), three houses (£80, £20, £30), three stables (£70), another nine houses (£540 in all), and a shop (£30).[63] Charles Tompson, a corkscrew-maker, took out three policies (£800, £500, £500), covering thirty-six houses in all, together with three shops, stables and brewhouses.[64] The value of the houses ranged from £100 down to £15, the last figure presumably representing a very small and probably decayed building.

Other larger policies were issued to Edward Thomason, a buckle-maker, for £1,000, to Henry Venour and Abel Humphreys, drapers, for £1,500 and to William Harold, also a draper, for £1,500.[65] Edward Thomason clearly put his money into rather larger and more valuable property. The details of his policy are:

Dwelling house	200
Household goods	80
A warehouse	50
Stock therein	50
A large shop	50
House ajoining	150
Another house	170
Another house	100
Two other houses	150
	£1,000

The policy issued to Venour and Humphreys covered a house for £300, and stock for £1,200; while Harold's policy insured his stock and dwelling house in Moor Street together at £1,500. Of the seventy-six policies surveyed for the year 1765, eight were for sums between £1,000 and £2,000 (not counting Tompson's three linked policies), and twenty-four for amounts between £500 and £1,000. Thus, just under half were for sums between £500 and £2,000.

In commenting on these figures, it must be acknowledged that they are not very large when compared with some of the biggest policies issued to London sugar refineries or breweries in the same year which might reach £20,000. Further, there is no reference in the insurance registers for 1765 to what were probably the largest works in Birmingham at the time, Boulton's Soho works which cost £10,000 to build: presumably they were insured when they were completed in 1765.[66] Nevertheless, the Birmingham policies obviously represent only a proportion of the properties insured in the 1760s in the town as a whole, and do not necessarily indicate the total property holdings of each policy holder. For example, one small policy taken out by Joseph Tirebuck of the Windmill Inn was for £300, giving cover of £100 on his house, £100 on his household goods, and £100 on his stables (a relatively large sum), but nothing on his stock, which may of course have been covered by another policy in a previous year.[67] It should also be noted that none of the policies included insurance for machinery, or fixtures and fittings, some of which might have considerable value. On the whole, this sample of Birmingham policies demonstrates the importance of the button, gun, and toy trades (thirty-three of the seventy-six policies relate to these trades), and also shows that the larger policy holders had businesses which might fairly be termed substantial. Further, it is very noticeable that many of them had invested money in house property. An outstanding example here is provided by Charles Tompson, the corkscrew-maker, with buildings and houses insured to the tune of £1,560. Even smaller policy holders often insured a number of houses. Interesting examples here are two bricklayers, Henry Gough and James Day. The former insured four houses for £220, and a further four houses (let to a button-maker, chain-maker, butcher and nailer) for £170 – in all, £390. The latter insured eleven houses and a schoolhouse, their values ranging from £65 to £15.[68] In these two cases, it might well be that their stated occupations are misleading, and that they were on the way to becoming jobbing builders – a useful illustration, perhaps, of the possibilities of advancement mentioned by the petitioners of 1759. Thus, even before the beginnings of national industrial expansion in the last quarter of the eighteenth century, Birmingham possessed an impressive corps of medium and small businessmen with substantial property investments, and it will come as no surprise that Birmingham's first bank – Taylor & Lloyd – was established in 1765.

It is not by chance, of course, that so many of the Sun policy holders of 1765 had invested in property. At a time of rapidly expanding population there were ample opportunities for the erection or purchase of houses, and investment in property was perhaps the safest form of investment at the time. Hutton, who was a stationer and bookseller by occupation, was constantly buying both land and houses, thereby acquiring a useful additional form of income. In his journal for the year 1769, he congratulated himself on his successful property dealing: 'The purchase of land was a delight, a study, a profit. I have acquired by it more than £10,000. We saved this year £479.'[69]

There can be no doubt that by the mid-eighteenth century Birmingham was well-placed for a massive development of industry. On the supply side there was the ready availability of finished iron from the Black Country, with mineral fuel close at hand, and long-established skills in the working of metal, whether iron, brass or steel. On the demand side, the markets for the products of the toy trade were

growing, as fashionable society indulged its taste for showy orna-
ments; while the gun trade met the less fanciful requirements of
overseas expansion and the slave trade. Unlike the textile industries,
the metalware trades of Birmingham did not suffer from technological bottlenecks in their mode of production. There were no
problems comparable with the need for faster spinning, or the
production of strong yet fine cotton thread. Indeed, Birmingham's
use of stamps, presses, drawbenches and lathes made the town pre-
eminent not only in the Midlands but in Europe. The French, for
example, may have excelled in the theoretical description of
machinery and manufacturing methods, but in practice they were far
behind Birmingham industrialists and welcomed their help. In 1756
the Birmingham button-maker Michael Alcock, set up a button
factory at La Charité, and subsequently his sons were to establish
another factory at Roanne. Alcock has even been regarded as the
founder of French light engineering.[70] It is clear that the prosperity
of Birmingham industry before the Industrial Revolution owed
much to an advanced hand technology utilizing basic machine tools.

This prosperity must have been on a substantial scale. It is not
merely that Birmingham was obviously drawing attention to itself as
a centre of thriving industry; it can also be argued that it was the
fastest growing industrial town in the country at the mid-eighteenth
century. During the preceding half-century Birmingham had
increased in population from between 5,000 and 7,000 in 1700 to
23,688 in 1750 – that is, it had at least trebled and possibly
quadrupled in size, and this at a time when the population of England
had increased by only 14 per cent. By way of comparison, Leeds had
about doubled in the same period, so had Manchester and Salford.
Only Sheffield could match the growth of Birmingham, increasing
from less than 3,500 in 1700 to 12,001 in 1757. It is no wonder that it
was claimed in Birmingham in 1750 that 'this place has been for a
long series of years increasing in its buildings'.[71] Not all of this
expansion can be attributed, of course, to industrial prosperity, for
the town was an increasingly important regional centre, providing
trading facilities for a wide area and becoming an important cultural
and professional centre.[72] Nevertheless, at the heart of Birmingham's success lay iυ technological expertise, expressing itself in a
variety of machines and processes, including the setting-up in 1746
of an important plant by John Roebuck and Samuel Garbett for the
manufacture of commercial sulphuric acid, termed by the historians

of the chemical industry 'a pivotal event in eighteenth-century economic history'.[73]

As a consequence of these advances, expansion could take place after 1750 without further technological innovation. This is not to say that there was no need to improve communications, or to extend the use of steam power from the mine to the workshop, or to improve the supply of iron – all matters to be discussed in the next chapter. Any reference to the changes in the second half of the century make it easy to see how Birmingham's industrial productive methods in the 1750s might appear to stand in need of improvement – the familiar argument from hindsight; but none of the changes which actually occurred appears to have been an urgent necessity, or was of so fundamental a nature as to transform Birmingham industry overnight. Industry in Birmingham was already firmly based on efficient productive methods, geared to expanding markets. It did not require a technological revolution for it to enjoy a prosperous future later in the century. When Boulton and Watt developed the improved steam engine in the 1770s it was first employed on any scale in the Cornish mines – not in Birmingham. Thus, although Birmingham became the home of one of the greatest agents for change in the Industrial Revolution, it was not immediately put to use in Birmingham itself because there was no great call for its services. In fact, as will be seen in the next chapter and in chapter 3, steam power was not an important feature of Birmingham industry until the 1830s at the earliest. This lack of striking technological change in industry in Birmingham may account for the comparative neglect by historians of the town's industrial growth in the eighteenth and nineteenth centuries. Attention is too often focused on the textile industries of Lancashire and Yorkshire where industrial change and growth are so much more spectacular, and may be more readily traced in documentary evidence. Yet between 1750 and 1775, before mechanized spinning had begun to create the modern Lancashire cotton industry, Birmingham moved from being the fifth largest town in England and Wales to being the third largest, with a population of about 40,000; only London (775,000) and Bristol (55,000) were larger.[74] To put this another way, since Bristol was a port as well as a centre for industry, it may fairly be claimed that by 1775 Birmingham was the largest industrial town outside London. Little recognition is given to this fact in the conventional textbooks. So Birmingham's industry not only stood poised for expansion in the 1750s but was developing fast in the following decade even before the beginnings of the Industrial Revolution in the Lancashire textile industry in the 1770s. As the national economy subsequently grew and was transformed, Birmingham was able to play a full part in that transformation, already possessing a well-established and fast-growing industrial base, and becoming a formidable rival to the better-known industrial towns of the North.

PART 2

The Economy 1760–1840

2

Forces for Change

In the last decades of the eighteenth century, the British economy was affected by the new industrialization which was associated with the increasing use of power-driven machinery. Not only did industry itself begin to undergo radical change, but more and more it replaced agriculture as the most important sector of the economy, until by the mid-nineteenth century Britain had become the first industrial nation. The cause of this transformation has been the subject of lengthy debate, but whatever emphasis is given to one or other of the various factors which are commonly held to have contributed to the final outcome – and few historians today would be content to single out any one predominant cause – it remains true that technological innovation was an important aspect of industrialization. Certainly it is hard to think of the Industrial Revolution without attributing great importance to the role of new machinery in the textile industry, to the new processes in the production of wrought iron, and to the widespread use of the new Boulton & Watt steam engine. But what then can be said of the causes of industrial growth in Birmingham before 1800? How can the extraordinary industrial development of the town in the second half of the eighteenth century be accounted for, given the fact that there were no major technological innovations in Birmingham industry in this period?

The main aim of this chapter is to survey the forces of change in Birmingham industry in the period up to 1800, but before examining these in detail, it must be emphasized again that the Industrial Revolution was not exclusively the consequence of change in the textile and iron industries. Too much prominence has been given in the past to the role of the textile industry, in particular. Important as it was as the exemplar of an industry based on steam-driven machinery, less than a fifth of all industrial workers in 1851 were engaged in mechanized industry. The new industrial towns of Lancashire and Yorkshire were in one sense anomalous in the economic developments of the time, the majority of workers in industry still being employed in workshops rather than in factories in the mid-nineteenth century. Thus Birmingham constitutes the norm and not the exception in experiencing industrial growth in the second half of the eighteenth century without the development of the factory system, and what happened there was typical of the work experience of the majority of industrial workers nationwide. As a result there were plenty of towns which were industrialized in 1851 but which lacked large-scale mechanized industry (for example, Sheffield, population 135,000; Newcastle, 88,000), while others had only limited industry, but were still of a considerable size (for example, Bristol, 137,000; Plymouth, 90,000; Hull 85,000; and Brighton, 66,000). All this may be common knowledge, but it is surprising how often the implications fail to sink in, such is the power of stereotypical thinking and of historical images rather than historical realities. It follows that urbanization was not synonymous with industrialization, and that industrialization up to 1851 and even later was not synonymous with mechanization, whatever changes were wrought in the second half of the nineteenth century by the increased use of machinery.

That Birmingham had become a great industrial centre by 1800 is undeniable. Arthur Young's description of the town in 1791 as 'the first manufacturing town in the world' bears striking testimony to this fact. However, there is the problem of disentangling cause from effect when attempting to account for the rapid growth of industry. It is quite possible to identify as a cause something which originally was merely a consequence of prior growth, and subsequently an accompaniment of growth, and of assistance to it, being essentially both cause *and* effect. For example, the development of a banking system in Birmingham was certainly of great benefit to Birmingham businessmen, but banking grew in the 1760s (as we shall see later in this chapter) when the informal methods of raising capital locally stood in need of supplementing and were finally replaced by a more specialized banking service. Industry, trade and services all developed in mutual interdependence, the growth of any one sector both initiating and at the same time responding to growth in the other sectors in a complex system of economic relationships.

It has been suggested that what was required for further industrial development after 1750 was an improvement in communications, and a greater availability of capital.[1] Additional forces of change include the continued growth of population, technological change in the Black Country, and minor improvements in the hand machines already widely employed in the town. It will also be necessary to comment briefly on the use of steam power in the period up to the 1830s. This approach is highly traditional in nature, but is likely to prove more effective than any attempt at a more sophisticated analysis based on econometric methods, given the lack of statistical material on which to base models of growth.

Birmingham's central position in the Midlands made an adequate road system essential, the nearest major river, the Severn, being twenty miles away at Bewdley. It has already been mentioned that in 1726 the first Turnpike Act was obtained for the Stratford and Warwick roads.[2] In 1727 the road to Wolverhampton via West Bromwich and Wednesbury was turnpiked, and then in 1760 the other road to Wolverhampton by way of Smethwick.[3] On the south side, the roads to markets in London and the southern provincial towns were of no less importance; in 1772 the Bristol road to Bromsgrove had £5,000 spent on its first four miles out of Birmingham.[4] Yet another road to the Black Country and its supplies of coal, the Halesowen road which went on to Kidderminster, was turnpiked in 1753.[5] Such was the importance of road communications to Birmingham that roads were turnpiked even after the canal era had begun; for example, the Walsall and Hampstead road (1788), the Handsworth road (1809), and the Pershore road (1828).

These improvements in the Birmingham road system certainly encouraged carriers to provide more services. By 1777 a local directory listed as many as seventeen waggon services to London, together with three to Walsall, three to Wolverhampton, two to Dudley, and one to Edinburgh. Altogether 130 named places were served, the furthest afield being Appleby, Brecon, Bristol, Edinburgh, London, Southampton, St Ives, Welshpool, and York.[6] At the same time, coach services also improved. In 1767 there seems to have been only one regular London coach, three times a week, together with two fly services. By 1785 the number of London services had increased to six, and there was a total of twenty-eight services running from seven separate inns.[7] During the course of the second half of the eighteenth century, the speed of the London to Birmingham coaches improved, so that a journey which in 1752 had taken two days in summer and three days in winter took only nineteen hours in summer and twenty-two hours in winter by 1782.[8] All this is not to say that road services had become uniformly good. In 1763 the Birmingham–London carriers are said to have increased their charges on the grounds that the deterioration of the roads had increased their costs.[9] Two decades or so later Hutton thought the Walsall road 'rather below indifferent', and the Dudley road 'despicable beyond description'.[10] Nevertheless, the increase in road traffic is unmistakable, and it provides an excellent indication not only of the great expansion of the transport of raw materials and manufactured goods but also of the greater volume of passenger traffic. Businessmen such as Boulton were frequently on the move, a fact to which his letters and diaries bear witness. But there remained the problem of cheap transportation of raw materials, such as coal and finished iron, which were still moved by waggon or by packhorses.

This problem was largely solved by the building of canals. The Birmingham Canal Act, 1768, authorized the construction of the Birmingham canal through the Black Country to Aldersley, north of Wolverhampton, where it joined the Staffordshire and Worcestershire canal. This canal in turn allowed connections to be made to the south at Stourport on the river Severn (and then on to Bristol), and to the north to the Trent and Mersey canal, and so on to Hull and Liverpool. The first cargo was carried on the canal in 1770, and its construction was completed in 1772. According to Hutton, coal which had previously been brought into Birmingham by road at a cost of about 13s per ton, was now sold at 7s per ton, being conveyed in boats carrying about twenty-five tons, 'each drawn by something like a skeleton of a horse, covered in skin'. (Hutton disliked the cruelty with which canal horses were treated.) Certainly the canal was a commercial success, the capital required being about £70,000, divided into shares of £140 each, limited to ten per purchaser. By the 1780s these shares were selling for about £370 each.[11] The canal proved a valuable means of transporting heavy materials in addition to coal. As Hutton put it:

This watery passage, exclusive of loading the proprietors with wealth, tends greatly to the improvement of some branches of trade, by introducing heavy materials at a small expense, such as pig iron for the foundries, limestone, articles for the manufacture of brass and steel, also stone, brick, slate, timber, etc.[12]

Other canals were built following the success of the Birmingham canal. The Birmingham to Fazeley canal (1783) provided a much shorter route to Hull than via Aldersley. Transport to the west was improved by a connection between the Birmingham canal through the Dudley canal to the Dudley–Stourbridge canal, which joined the Staffordshire–Worcestershire canal at Stourton. To the south a canal was begun in 1793 to join Birmingham and Worcester, but was not completed until 1815. This canal passed through a long tunnel under the Wast Hills before entering the famous flight of thirty locks at Tardebigge. In his rhyming directory of 1800, Bisset refers to this section of the canal:

> Now gently to the right your eyes incline,
> And mark you where barges float along yon line,
> Till disappearing in the dark profound
> They sail some thousand yards beneath the ground.
> From thence emerging, swiftly on they glide
> To reach the confines of the Severn's tide.

Writing in 1800, Bisset was not to know that the thirty locks subsequently built would hardly permit a swift glide to the Severn at Worcester. Another link between this canal and the Dudley canal was provided by the building of the Lapal Tunnel (1801). Other Acts for canals to the south were also passed in 1793 for the Warwick and Birmingham canal, and the Stratford canal. The former joined the Fazeley canal at Digbeth, and was completed in 1799; the latter joined the Birmingham and Worcester canal at King's Norton.[13]

Thus Birmingham became the centre of a network of canals which spread over the West Midlands, giving cheap transport for heavy goods and raw materials. In the rather odd words of a standard authority: 'Birmingham was becoming the Kremlin from which canals radiated in all directions.'[14] There can be no doubt of the importance of this improvement in transport facilities for Birmingham's economic growth. Nevertheless, it must be kept in perspective. There is nothing to show that local industry was hampered more seriously by poor transport before the canal era than industry elsewhere. Canal building accelerated rather than created industrial growth in the Birmingham area; industrial activity was already substantial before the construction of the canals. The major service provided by them lay in the cheapening of the cost of carrying coal and other raw materials, as Hutton noted, rather than in carrying the output from Birmingham's myriad workshops. The well-known drawbacks of canal transport – the slow speed of travel, the difficulties of transhipping goods from one canal to another, the problems caused by the freezing or drying up of canals – all took effect in Birmingham as much as anywhere else. It was not until the coming of the railways in the 1830s that a speedy and punctual service became available for Birmingham products. Until then, the benefits of the canal system were limited to the cheaper transport of raw materials, especially coal, rather than the transport of goods or passengers.

Another factor for change was certainly the increased availability of capital made possible by the growth of a banking system. Banking facilities of a simple kind were provided in the early eighteenth century by the more prosperous tradesmen. Hutton claimed that 'about every tenth trader was a banker, or retailer of cash. At the head of whom were marshalled the whole train of drapers and grocers.'[15]

It was pointed out in chapter 1 that a firm of drapers, Henry Venour and Abel Humphreys, was among the largest Sun insurance policy holders in 1765. In that year the first Birmingham bank was established by two of the wealthiest local businessmen, John Taylor, the button manufacturer, and Sampson Lloyd II, the ironmaster. They were joined in the enterprise by their two sons, John Taylor the younger, and Sampson Lloyd III, each contributing a capital of £2,000, that is, £8,000 in all. At first Taylor & Lloyd were represented in London by the banking firm of Smith & Payne, late of Nottingham, but in 1770 their own branch was opened in Lombard Street with a capital of £20,000.[16] In the first ten years of its existence the firm is said to have made annual profits averaging 45 per cent of its capital. Later on, in the twenty years from 1780 to 1800, the rate of profit on a larger capital of £30,000 moved from about 16 per cent to 25 per cent. By the early 1790s other banks had entered the field in Birmingham – Coate's, Goodhall's, and Spooner's – so that Taylor & Lloyd no longer had a monopoly. In their earlier days they became treasurers for the Birmingham Canal Company, and for the general hospital which opened in 1779.[17]

There can be little doubt that Taylor & Lloyd and their successors. facilitated the recruitment of capital locally, but, although the first bank in Birmingham itself, it has been suggested that there were already as many as 150 banks outside London by 1776.[18] Further, it has been noted that banks like Taylor & Lloyd may be seen as indicators of local prosperity at the time of their founding, rather than as direct creators of it. The raising of loans through local tradesmen and the provision of credit by means of bills of exchange, both of which preceded the beginning of banking in Birmingham, must have continued to flourish for some time after 1765 as they had before. London remained the centre of the banking world in England in the 1760s and 1770s, and Matthew Boulton raised major loans in this period both in London and Amsterdam.[19] Thus it would be unwise to place too much emphasis on the establishment of professional banking in Birmingham in 1765 as a principal factor leading to industrial growth. Clearly it helped to increase the pace of development and demonstrates the vitality of local industry and trade without in itself initiating a new phase in industrial expansion.

How far did the growth of the population in Birmingham during the second half of the eighteenth century contribute to the growth of industry? All population figures before the official census of 1801 are estimates, of course, but a number of figures are available for Birmingham to show the general trend:[20]

Year	Population
1750	23,688
1778	42,250
1785	52,250
1801	73,670

If these figures are anywhere near correct, they show that Birmingham's population roughly trebled between 1750 and 1801. This increase was due partly to the national growth of population of the time (about 50 per cent), and partly, and much more significantly, to immigration into the town. It will be recalled that John Taylor and Samuel Garbett claimed in 1759 that the population of the town had increased by at least 50 per cent since the toy trade had begun, and doubtless the growth of industry had attracted immigrant labour before the mid-century, so that Birmingham's population was getting larger well before the upswing of the national population during the second half of the century.

It remains a matter for speculation how far this growth in numbers stimulated trade and industry. On the one hand, it can be argued that mere immigration simply indicates that industry is already expanding, and that jobs are available for labour coming from outside the town. On the other hand, it may be suggested that the ready availability of labour permitted industry and trade to expand, and in turn provided additional local demand, given the relatively high level of wages for skilled men, so that population increase can be regarded as a direct cause of economic growth. Certainly it contributed to a marked increase in retailing, and to a building boom, especially in the 1770s and 1780s.[21] On the whole, it seems safer to associate the enlarged urban population with concrete examples on the demand side such as these – it can hardly be denied that immigration resulted in an increased need for housing and retailing – rather than with supply side factors. Labour had always been relatively plentiful in the surrounding countryside (as noted in chapter 1), and the level of agricultural wages at any one time in relation to urban wages was necessarily an important element in determining the strength of movements into the towns. All these arguments have force, and relevance, though clearly the absence of adequate wage data makes it impossible to assess their importance in any quantitative sense.

One further important cause of industrial growth was the cheaper iron made available by technological innovation in the Black Country iron industry. After the mid-eighteenth century the increasing use of mineral fuel (that is, coke rather than charcoal) in the blast furnace meant that cheaper and better pig could be supplied, while local changes in the production of wrought iron by the potting and stamping process, and then finally by Cort's puddling and rolling process, resulted in the Black Country becoming the second largest producer of finished iron in the United Kingdom.[22] At the beginning of the eighteenth century the Black Country was already of prime importance in forge work, but as explained in chapter 1, pig and bar iron were brought into the area to supply the forges. By the end of the century the Black Country was producing its own primary iron on or near the coalfield itself, utilizing both the new methods of producing wrought iron and the steam power of the Boulton & Watt engine. Thus, as demand grew for the products of Birmingham industry, the raw material for the gun trade and the toy trade became more and more easily obtainable a short distance away in the Black Country.

Indeed, the two industrial areas of Birmingham and the Black Country grew rapidly side by side, each supplying valuable markets to the other.

There is, however, an interesting contrast between the economic changes in the two areas. In the Black Country, technological innovation (mineral fuel, puddling and rolling, and steam power) transformed the iron industry by 1800, so that something like a revolution occurred in what was the most important industry in the region. In Birmingham, as we have already seen, technological change in the thousands of small workshops was on a different scale, and the division of labour and hand-operated machines were widely employed in the middle decades of the eighteenth century, well before the onset of the Industrial Revolution. The great expansion in Birmingham industry which began before 1750 and continued during the second half of the century owed little to large-scale technological change. Unlike the Lancashire spinning industry, Birmingham industry in 1800 was certainly not based on water or steam-driven machinery housed in factories. There was no technological revolution in Birmingham in the eighteenth century, though it may be allowed that Birmingham profited indirectly from the use of steam power in the Black Country iron industry, and perhaps from more efficient pumping engines in Black Country coal pits.

This is not to say, of course, that following the adoption of the stamp, and the use of the press, lathe and drawbench from the 1750s onwards, there were no technological improvements of any kind in the Birmingham area for the next fifty years. On the contrary, many improvements in existing machinery were made, but they were all on a minor scale and not comparable with the major inventions such as the Crompton mule. By 1800, according to Prosser, ninety patents for inventions had been granted to Birmingham inventors, as compared with only twenty-seven to Manchester; he also claims that up to 1852, 'Birmingham stood first among the provincial towns as regards the numbers of grants of letters patent.'[23] No doubt this was common knowledge in Birmingham at the end of the eighteenth century, for Bisset says of Birmingham inventions:

Inventions courious, various kinds of toys,
Engage the time of women, men, and boys,
And Royal patents here are found in scores
For articles minute – or pond'rous ores.[24]

Patent evidence can easily be misleading, but it seems safe to say that with the exception of Watt's momentous patents for the steam engine, none of the Birmingham patents was of revolutionary significance, though they must have helped to improve the efficiency of existing methods. Many of the patents of the 1780s, for example, were to do with buckles and buttons.[25] Yet steam power in itself was of relatively small importance till the 1830s, at the earliest, even though water power in the town was very limited in nature.[26]

Indeed, it is doubtful whether steam power can be considered to have had any direct influence at all upon the growth of Birmingham before 1800; and even before 1830 its use was very limited. In 1815 there were only about forty engines in use in the town. By 1830 this number seems to have risen to 120, and from then on, the rate of increase quickened, one authority giving a total of 169 by 1835, and another 240 by 1838.[27] Thus, between 1830 and 1838 the number of engines had doubled, and there appears to have been a considerable increase in numbers between 1835 and 1838. Yet this expansion comes only at the very end of the period covered by this book, and long after the major era of growth in the second half of the eighteenth century under examination in this chapter. Moreover, even in the 1830s the size of the engines might be quite small. According to the evidence given before the Factory Enquiry Commission in 1833, Phipsons, the pin-makers, used only four horse power, hired from an adjoining engine. Thomas Ledsam & Sons, button manufacturers, also hired 'a small portion of steam' from an engine next door. Only one witness, Jenkins, used a comparatively large engine, one of 100 horse power.[28] The total horse power employed by the 169 engines in 1835 amounted to only 2,700 horse power, that is, a notional average of 16 horse power. Many of the more recently erected engines must have been of less than 16 horse power – for example, the eight engines put up in 1833 had a total power of only 57 horse power, and the seventeen erected in 1834 a total of only 157 horse power.[29] It is therefore clear that, however significant the increased use of steam might have been in the 1830s – and it obviously must have improved productivity in the early Victorian period – steam power was not a cause of industrial expansion in Birmingham before 1800.

The reasons for this slow adoption of steam power in Birmingham are not difficult to find. The nature of industry in the town at the time with its many hundreds of small workshops and its skilled labour force precluded any immediate employment of steam power on a substantial scale: gun-makers, jewellery workers, toy-makers, and glass-makers made virtually no use of it – it was simply inapplicable to their mode of production. Button-makers and pin-makers used it on only the smallest scale. Only in the primary metal industries were steam engines useful for hammering, rolling, and blowing purposes, and as the iron and brass industries did not begin their really significant period of expansion till the 1830s (see chapter 3), it was not until then that steam power was used on a considerable scale. Thus the only witness before the Factory Commission of 1833 who utilized a large engine of 100 horse power, the Mr Jenkins just mentioned, was a brass founder. By 1839, the most important use of steam power within the borough was for rolling copper, brass, and other metals (570 horse power), followed by its employment in iron forges, foundries, and wrought iron mills (363 horse power), and then for drawing wire (150 horse power). Ten years later in 1849, the total engine power available was still only about 5,400 horse power, though doubtless by then its use was spreading beyond the metal industries.[30]

This discussion of the various factors influencing the growth of industry in Birmingham in the second half of the eighteenth century makes it clear that industrial expansion was not the result of any one predominant factor. The growth of trade, the improvement in transport facilities, the beginning of professional banking, the growth of population, and the development of the Black Country iron industry all took effect on a vigorous local economy which was already developing fast by 1750. For this reason it may well be maintained that whatever happened to the national economy between 1760 and 1830, the word 'revolution' is inappropriate as a description of industrial change in Birmingham in this period. Admittedly, industry expanded vastly, but not on the basis of technological innovation. A thriving manufacturing industry simply responded to the growth of the national economy, but (as we have seen) without resort to the factory system which became so characteristic of the cotton industry.

It is not easy to determine which aspect of the growth of the national economy had the greatest significance for Birmingham industry. Indeed, to ask this question raises many thorny problems relating to the causes of the Industrial Revolution. Nevertheless, it may at least be asked whether it was an increase in trading nationally which resulted in such a striking growth of Birmingham's industry after 1750, and it is tempting at first to attribute that growth to the increase in foreign trade, an increase which some historians in the past have regarded as the basic cause of industrialization.[31] As we have seen in chapter 1, great claims were made in 1759 for the importance of overseas trade in the toy trade. Matthew Boulton was clearly very interested in the possibilities of increasing the European trade of Boulton & Fothergill. Hutton himself thought that foreign trade was very important for Birmingham traders: 'for the West Indies, and the American world, are intimately acquainted with the Birmingham merchant; and nothing but the exclusive command of the East India Company over the Asiatic trade prevents our riders from treading upon the heels of each other in the streets of Calcutta'.[32] He added, significantly: 'To this modern conduct of Birmingham in sending her sons to the foreign market, I ascribe the chief cause of her rapid increase.'[33]

There is the further point that in the early nineteenth century foreign trade was still considered highly important in Birmingham, and a succession of witnesses before the Committee of the House of Commons appointed to consider petitions against the Orders in Council in 1812 were emphatic on this matter. Allowance must be made of course for some exaggeration, as all the Birmingham witnesses were solidly against the Orders as being deeply injurious to foreign trade (even though it transpired early on that they had not all read the petitions they had signed); but the high proportion of Birmingham's trade given to foreign markets was stressed again and again. It was stated that 'Our trade to the United States of America would be about equal to what we call our home trade, England, Ireland and Scotland.' It was also alleged that perhaps two-thirds of Birmingham manufacturers depended on foreign markets, home trade accounting for about a third of total sales.[34]

On the other hand, this evidence is not conclusive, and the figures for national exports for the third quarter of the eighteenth century do not suggest a great boom in exports. Admittedly these figures have their imperfections, but it seems that exports of non-ferrous metals and manufactures rose only modestly in the 1760s after 1762, and thereafter remained stable before declining positively during the War of American Independence.[35] It was not until the conclusion of that war that the figures picked up again and forged ahead at the end of the 1780s. The same may be said of exports of wrought iron and hardware.[36] The 1780s are the first decade in which British exports began a really fast and sustained growth, the earlier period of 1760–81 being one of stagnation and of an actual decline in the volume of exports, something unique in the history of British trade in the eighteenth and nineteenth centuries.[37]

It is true, of course, that Birmingham's overseas trade did not necessarily follow the national pattern in these years. Nevertheless, if Birmingham's trade in general was growing rapidly between 1760 and 1781 – a not unreasonable assumption in view of the increase in population and in house building, and taking into account contemporary comment – then it seems more likely that the increased demand was in the home market rather than overseas. More recently it has been asserted that there was a consumer boom in England in the eighteenth century, and that 'in the third quarter of the century, that boom reached revolutionary proportions'. Moreover, the same authority considers that the Birmingham toy trade was 'arguably *the* characteristic consumer industry of the commercial revolution'.[38] So it might be that the home market was the more important up to the 1780s, at least, with the foreign market increasing in significance thereafter. Certainly the national export figures in the boom of the 1780s suggest that Birmingham exported goods might be on the increase: exports of metalware grew from £1,622,000 in 1784–6 to £3,640,000 in 1794–6. Exports of ironware also increased between the same dates from £1,288,000 to £2,228,000.[39] In the absence of further information relating to Birmingham sales outlets at home and abroad, it would be unwise to speculate much further. It appears likely that Birmingham manufacturers were able to take advantage of the growth of consumer markets in England from early on in the eighteenth century, while at the same time being keenly aware of the possibilities in overseas markets even before 1750. In the 1780s they probably increased their foreign sales substantially, though whether they had become more important than home sales by 1812 really depends on how reliable the estimates made in that year by the Birmingham opponents of the Orders in Council might be thought to be. The safest conclusion would be that foreign trade was of great importance to Birmingham manufacturers throughout the eighteenth century, and that it is likely that its importance was increasing by the end of the century, thus becoming a vital element in the expansion of Birmingham industry.[40]

In this survey of the most prominent aspects of Birmingham's economic growth, it has been necessary to move with caution. Since even the most zealous of econometric historians have hardly been successful in solving the many problems of the causes of the Industrial Revolution, it would be foolhardy to claim to have identified the root causes of growth in Birmingham's economy in the second half of the eighteenth century. In fact, it is obvious that causes operating before 1750 continued to do so after that date, but in conjunction with powerful new forces such as the effect of the improved transport system and the lowered costs of Black Country iron. But things are not always what they seem: the results of puddling and rolling on primary iron prices in the Black Country did not take effect at the earliest till the 1790s, when Birmingham's economic growth experienced a distinct setback with the outbreak of war in 1793 (see chapter 4); and if the development of a banking system may be accounted a positive factor for growth, then it has already been pointed out that informal banking existed in the town long before the establishment of Taylor & Lloyd. As for the factors of production, a greater supply of capital was no doubt available after 1750, but industrial development even in the cotton industry was not capital-intensive in the eighteenth century, nor was it in the many small workshops of Birmingham. The supply of labour, of course, did improve with the rise in population nationally, and young children were essential to the functioning of many Birmingham work-processes, but immigration into town was no new thing after 1750, and in any case small mouths needed to be fed, with a consequent drain on family income and spending power. The more the historian attempts to draw up some sort of taxonomy of causes, the more the causes fray at the edges, lose their substance and become shadowy. Dr Johnson is supposed to have said of the man who claimed to have experienced the inexpressible, that he should not then try to express it. Similarly the historian sometimes feels reluctant to go on trying to weigh up the imponderable, whether qualitatively or in the more modern manner, quantitatively. The historial facts are there (or some of them), but the historical truth (to use an old-fashioned phrase) is not always readily apparent.[41]

It might be said that the problem is to explain industrial expansion in Birmingham without technological innovation; but it seems that if industry could respond so readily to growing demand at home and abroad, it was because of the basic fact that its existing technology could meet the demands for increased production without undue strain. One of the most important elements in Birmingham industry in the mid-eighteenth century was the division of labour, a kind of technological revolution which had taken place in Birmingham before 1750. This was a change of great consequence to the Midland trades as a whole, as Professor Court has rightly pointed out, and a significant development recently re-emphasized by Professor Wrigley.[42] Given this, together with the ready supply of labour, Birmingham industry could easily expand when demand increased, something which was impossible for the cotton industry without the invention of new machinery of a kind which increased productivity to a substantial degree. In one sense, Birmingham manufacturers had only to respond to national developments in the improvement of transport and in the better provision of banking facilities for their sales and profits to mount. This is not to discount the problems which faced the businessmen of the day, or the importance of the entrepreneurial skills necessary to overcome those problems. On the contrary, it serves to emphasize the significance of such skills at a time of developing markets at home and abroad. The times favoured the businessman who was willing to seize opportunities for expansion, and by the mid-eighteenth century Birmingham entrepreneurs had the experience and resources to play their full part in the national transformation of industry and commerce which was to come in the second half of the century.

Indeed ultimately it might be best to return to the human element, and to argue that the sheer drive and initiative of the Birmingham businessmen were as important as any other factor for change discussed in this chapter. Given a favourable economic climate, it was up to the Birmingham industrialist to exploit it to the full. All turned ultimately on the extent to which he took his chances as both the local and the national economy expanded. Moreover, this had to be done on the basis of existing modes of production and without the benefit of the technological breakthrough which characterized both the textile industry and the iron industry. The measure of his success is to be seen in the massive expansion in Birmingham industry which occurred in the second half of the eighteenth century. Thus, at the heart of the industrial growth of Birmingham lay the entrepreneurial skills of its manufacturers and traders whose fortunes will be examined in chapter 5.

3

Industrial Change

In chapter 1 an attempt was made to sketch the outlines of Birmingham manufacturing industry in the mid-eighteenth century, emphasizing its vigorous and prosperous state. In this chapter the aim is to show how industry expanded in the decades which followed, the story being taken as far as the 1840s. This is no easy task, partly because of the lack of quantitative information, and partly because the heterogeneous nature of Birmingham industry makes it difficult to impose any very precise form of order on what material is available. The simplest solution appears to be to trace the history of the most important industries in turn, and then to comment on matters arising, such as the most significant changes in industry as a whole, the importance of the larger industries relative to each other, changes in the size of the work unit, the employment of steam power and the use of the apprenticeship system.

It was stated earlier on that by the middle of the eighteenth century the gun trade in Birmingham had become highly specialized, and that the first available Birmingham directory, dated 1767, lists gun-makers and pistol-makers separately, together with the makers of different parts of guns such as barrel-makers and gun-lock makers.[1] In fact, the organization of the trade was extremely complex, and even the term 'gun-maker' can be misleading. Usually a gun-maker did not manufacture guns at all; he was an entrepreneur who marketed guns made up of parts which had first been fashioned by specialist workmen (the 'material men', working on sub-contract), and then assembled by other workmen (the 'fabricators', or 'setters-up').[2] By the mid-nineteenth century there were as many as sixty-three constituent parts to a gun, and the total number of processes on the

Enfield musket of the 1853 pattern was more than 600.[3] It follows that there was an extraordinary profusion of specialist trades within the gun trade. One recent authority gives a list of these trades for the second quarter of the nineteenth century, taken from the trade directories of the time.[4]

Material Men	*Setters-up*
Breech-pin forger	Gun- and pistol-maker
Gun-stock maker	Gun-barrel maker
Gun-worm maker	Gun-lock maker
Gun-loop maker	Gun-stocker
Barrel-forger	Gun-stock polisher
Barrel-welder	Gun-stock stainer and varnisher
Barrel-borer	Gun-breecher
Barrel-filer	Percussioner
Barrel-rifler	Gun-barrel ribber
Barrel-polisher	Gun-barrel browner
Gun-sight maker	Gun-screwer
Nipple-maker	Gun-inlayer
Ramrod-maker	Gun-engraver
Gun-lock forger and filer	Gun-finisher
Gun-lock and furniture forger and filer	
Gun-furniture polisher	
Pistol-filer	

By the 1860s this list had lengthened to thirty-two types of material-makers, spread over ten major categories, and sixteen types of setters-up.[5]

These specialist craftsmen worked in small workshops, employing hand tools without powered machinery except where gun-barrels were produced by rollers rather than under the hammer on the anvil. Gun-barrel makers were concentrated away from the Gun Quarter mostly in Aston, Deritend, Smethwick and West Bromwich; and lockmaking in the Black Country in Darlaston, Wednesbury, Willenhall, and Wolverhampton.[6] Apart from these two trades, all the remaining trades were carried out within a small area of half a dozen streets, thus facilitating the work of the gun-maker in organizing production of the finished weapon. Few women were employed, and those mostly in giving a final finish to the stocks; others worked at polishing and gun-boring, which was generally thought to be a dirty and laborious job. Many young boys were employed, however, carrying guns and gun parts to and from the workshops.[7]

Since the organization of the trade remained virtually unchanged during the whole period 1760–1840, the question obviously arises of why so complicated a system lasted so long. The simple answer is that it met quite adequately the needs of the time. Since the basic processes all required considerable manual skill, it was inevitable that the work should be carried out in workshops of the traditional type; except for barrel-making, there was no call for either steam or water power. It is true that the gun-maker could have supervised the various branches of manufacture more efficiently if they had all been assembled under one roof; but this presumably would have meant heavy commitments in buildings and labour. It was more convenient for him to call on skilled labour as required, bearing in mind the ebb and flow of demand. Orders would be heaviest in times of war, since the Government was reluctant at this time to stock-pile weapons in times of peace. When the war ended, the gun trade would slump badly. Thus, the loose and flexible organization of the industry suited the gun-maker admirably, and there was no incentive to adopt anything resembling a factory system, at least not before the 1850s.

In fact, there were only two technological developments in the period which are of importance. The first was the production of gun-barrels by rollers driven by water-powered or steam-powered machinery, an invention generally attributed to Henry Osborn, who patented his process in 1812 and again in 1817, though similar patents for the use of grooved rollers date from 1806.[8] The second advance was the invention of the percussion gun, that is, a gun in which the charge is fired by the ignition of a percussion cap instead of by the operation of a flint-lock. This led to the development of the modern, breech-loading gun, using a self-contained cartridge, which required a new kind of percussion lock. However, although the first patent for a detonating lock dates from 1807, it took many years before the percussion gun was widely adopted; the War Office did not decide finally to change to the new form of gun till about 1839.[9] These two inventions were of considerable importance to the gun trade, but brought no fundamental change in working techniques for the majority of gun-trade workers.

Against this background, the major changes in the location and nature of the industry may now be traced in the period 1760–1840. As already indicated, the gun trade was situated within a relatively small area of the town. At the beginning of the eighteenth century, it appears to have been located very largely in the Digbeth area, but by the mid-century the trend was towards a concentration in the neighbourhood of St Mary's. By 1829 some two-thirds of the trade was to be found in the district bounded by Slaney Street, Shadwell Street, Loveday Street, and Steelhouse Street.[10] As for the output of the industry, it did not change much in nature during the eighteenth century. It took the form of sporting guns, guns for the slave trade, and most important of all, guns for military purposes. Because of the frequent occurrence of war during the century and especially from 1793 onwards, with the outbreak of the Revolutionary War against the French, the gun trade expanded very noticeably. Government viewing rooms were opened in Bagot Street ('the Tower') in 1798, with a staff of sixty to seventy. A public proof house was erected by Act of Parliament in 1813. According to *Aris's Gazette*, dated 11 October 1813:

> The principal gunmakers of this town after very considerable pains and expenses having procured an Act of Parliament for the erection and establishing of a Proof House, proceeded on Wednesday last, October 6, to lay the first stone of the building, which is situated in Banbury Street near the Fazeley Canal, and will be of uncalculable benefit to the town and to the community. All the barrels of all guns manufactured in Birmingham must be of full Tower proof, by which persons may use such firearms with the greatest safety.

The number of guns made in Birmingham in the war period, 1804–15, for the Board of Ordnance was very large – 1,743,382 – which was more than double the numbers made elsewhere in England in the same period. The entire production of guns of all kinds for these twelve years has been estimated at nearly five million.[11] If components are taken into account (that is, barrels and gun-locks), the total of guns and components made for the Government rises to 7,660,229. It has been further estimated that when components for the East India Company are included, and also nearly 500,000 sporting guns, then the annual production figures for 1804–15 amount to 763,352, not counting slave guns.[12]

Impressive as these figures are, they would have a greater significance if output figures both before and after the French wars 1793–1815 were available. Sadly they are not, though undoubtedly production slumped badly after 1815, and no military arms at all were made for the Government for at least ten years after 1817. Subsequently trade recovered. The average annual production of barrels proved (excluding arms for the British Government) between 1855 and 1864 was 327,781, as compared with a similar period without a major war, 1816–26, when the annual average was 127,337.[13] Meanwhile, the number of firms, which was 125 in 1815, had risen to 455 in 1829, and to 578 in 1868. The 1851 census gives a figure of 2,867 engaged in the Birmingham gun trade as compared with a total of 7,731 for England and Wales. It has been claimed that by this time the Birmingham gun industry was the greatest source of arms in the world, and that a large proportion of the arms used in the Crimean War and the Kaffir War were made in Birmingham.[14]

In many ways the gun trade may be seen as the archetypal Birmingham industry of the time. In the first place, it was a metal-working industry, employing a wide range of skilled workmen in small workshops, using hand tools. Then again it exhibited a high degree of specialization, as is shown by the extent of the division of labour and the great variety of different skills. Further, there was considerable scope for the organizational abilities of the gun-maker, merchant or factor with a view to achieving production at a suitable level for the time. In all these respects it provides an excellent example of the way in which a small master economy adjusted to the demands of a growing and thriving national economy. No doubt it made an important contribution to Birmingham's prosperity, especially during the late eighteenth and early nineteenth century, and was still among the foremost of its industries in the mid-nineteenth century.

The brass industry was another metal industry which expanded rapidly in Birmingham in the eighteenth century, and exports of brass goods to the Continent, especially to France, were becoming important even in the early years of the century.[15] At first the industry was confined to the manufacture of articles in brass rather than the production of the metal itself, which was brought into Birmingham from Bristol and from Cheadle in Cheshire. Presumably at first it was thought less expensive to import brass sheeting or brass ingots from a distance than the raw materials themselves (copper and calamine). From 1740, however, brass works were established, the first being set up by a Mr Turner in Coleshill Street. Thereafter supplies of the metal were available in Birmingham itself, though substantial imports continued from Bristol and Cheadle. Up to the 1760s brass articles were commonly manufactured by a simple casting process, but in 1769 the production of articles by the stamp and die was begun, and locally rolled sheets were used for this.[16]

The reason why the brass industry should have developed at all in Birmingham at this time is probably because there were long-established skills in the working of metals in the area, and also because of the demand for brass in the Birmingham buckle, button and toy trades. In the second half of the eighteenth century the brass industry became more specialized as the demand increased for a widening range of brass goods. These included fittings for carriages and harness, cabinet brassfounding of all kinds (candlesticks, door handles, curtain rings, castors, furniture hinges, locks, keys, screws and bolts), fittings for steam engines and plumbing requisites. From 1770 or earlier, cockfounding became a special branch of the industry (in 1770 there were five cockfounders in Birmingham), and steam engines required not only brass cocks and taps, but brass fittings for whistles, gauges and other accessories. The manufacture of coffin furniture also became important. At the turn of the century the increasing use of gas lighting was beginning to bring a further demand for brass gas fittings.[17] By this time the industry was clearly developing fast. In 1770 there were thirty-eight brassfounders in Birmingham, by 1788 the number had risen to fifty-six, and in 1797 to seventy-one.[18]

As the industry expanded, the need for better local supplies of brass became more and more apparent, until in 1780 something like a crisis arose with an increase in the price of copper of £20 a ton, and as a result, an increase in the price of brass of £13 per ton. This meant greater profits for the Bristol and Cheadle suppliers, but the Birmingham brassfounders were forced to raise their prices by 7½ per cent. The result was that the Birmingham founders set up their own brass-making company in 1781 in order to free themselves from dependence on outside suppliers. By this time the canal system was making it far cheaper to transport raw materials. The new company, the Birmingham Metal Company, erected its works off Broad Street, next to the canal, on a site marked today by Brasshouse Passage. This was contrary to the advice of Matthew Boulton, its most prominent supporter, who favoured a site in Wales where he had important copper connections; he thereupon resigned from the Birmingham Metal Company. However, in spite of the opposition of the established brass suppliers, the new company appears to have prospered. It had a ready-made market in the form of its own Birmingham subscribers who had agreed to buy brass in proportion to the shares which they had purchased.[19] Some years after, the need to obtain their own supply of copper led in 1790 to the formation of the Birmingham Mining and Copper Company, which took shares in copper mines and set up smelting works in Swansea and Redruth. This proved so successful that another copper company – the Rose Copper Company – was floated with another smelting works in Swansea; subsequently a further company, the Crown Copper Company, was established with works in Neath.[20]

The significance of all this is clear enough; the brass industry in Birmingham had increased to such an extent that it was strong enough to break the monopolies in the supply of brass and copper to the town. Admittedly the new company for making brass was not able to supply entirely the needs of the local manufacturers, but it operated powerfully against the monopolies of the Bristol and Cheadle companies. Moreover, the industry was fortunate in supplying not only the needs of a growing consumer society as expressed in the demand for brass fittings in the home, but also the increasing demand from steam engine manufacturers and from sanitary engineers, especially when the sanitary reform movement gained momentum. Yet all this refers only to the home market. According to Hamilton, the foreign market was even more important, and Birmingham had the bulk of the trade in Europe in brass and copper goods. The highest point in the eighteenth century was reached in 1790–91, just before the outbreak of war against France.[21] Thereafter the trade suffered from the interruption of its European trade by the war until peace returned in 1815.

From then on the brass industry continued to expand, a notable additional product being the making of brass bedsteads in the 1830s. In 1838 the production of seamless brass tubes began, these being more suitable for boilers than brazed tubes. The same decade saw the development of a new method of making brass (the crucible method) instead of the older cementation process.[22] The 1830s were therefore a period of great advance for the brass industry. The number of manufacturers increased substantially, together with the number of works:[23]

	1800	1830	1865
Number of manufacturers	50	160	216
Number of works	50	280	421

Some of these establishments were of a considerable size. During the

French wars, for example, Thomas Messenger employed up to 250 workmen, though the number dropped to a hundred in 1812, a year of depression. In the same year James Ryland, maker of harness and saddlery, employed 150, and William Blakeway, lampmaker, employed sixty hands.[24] In 1833 a brass founder named Jenkins used steam power of 100 horse power, and employed about 250.[25] Naturally, where brass itself was manufactured and steam-powered rolling machinery was used, the size of the works tended to be large; but the vast majority of employers at the beginning of the century were small men employing only a few hands, and sometimes just members of their own family.[26] By 1840 the active expansion of the industry was just beginning to change this picture. Specialization was still growing, and there was a remarkable increase of numbers employed from 1,800 in 1831 to 3,400 in 1841. By 1851 nearly half the work-force was employed in cabinet brassfoundry and in making gas fittings and lamps; other brass-workers were engaged in plumbers' brassfoundry, engineers' brassfoundry, naval brass-foundry (a new alloy, Muntz's metal, had been invented earlier in the century for ships' sheathing), and general brassfoundry. In these circumstances even the smaller establishments tended to grow in average size. By 1866, the typical place of work was a workshop employing twenty or thirty hands, while the seventeen brass-houses averaged 115 each. One exceptional works, Wingfields, which employed just over a hundred in 1835, had grown to employ 700 or 800 in 1860. Nevertheless, even then there were many small firms of the traditional character in cabinet brassfoundry and cockfounding, where all that was required for efficient production was a lathe, a vice, and a few hand tools in a small workshop.[27]

It is evident that with no natural advantage save the availability of skilled labour, the brass industry flourished greatly both before and after the French Revolutionary and Napoleonic Wars. By the end of the period 1760–1840 the rate of acceleration was increasing. Already in 1800 Birmingham had become by far the greatest centre of the brass and copper trades (Wolverhampton being a poor second), and the brass industry was the most important industry in Birming-ham.[28] By the mid-nineteenth century it had maintained and strengthened this position.[29] It was the good fortune of workers in this industry to be engaged in producing articles in particular demand in an expanding industrial society, so that by 1840 Birmingham led the world in the manufacture of brass and goods made of brass. W. C. Aitkin summed up the importance of the industry by the 1860s in a striking passage:

> What Manchester is in cotton, Bradford in wool, and Sheffield in steel, Birmingham is in brass; its articles of cabinet and general brassfoundry are to be found in every part of the world; its gas fittings in every city and town into which gas has been introduced . . . on the railways of every country, and on every sea its locomotive and marine engine solid brass tubes generate the vapour which impels the locomotive over the iron road, and propels the steam boat over the ocean wave . . . its yellow metal bolts, nails, and sheathing hold together and protect from decay 'wooden walls' of our own and other countries' ships – its 'Manillas' [coins] once made in tons, are the circulating medium of the natives of the Gold Coast – and its rings and ornaments of brass, sent out in immense quantities, are the chief decorations of the *belles* on the banks of the distant Zambesi.[30]

The toy industry is another industry which increased in importance during the second half of the eighteenth century and the beginning of the nineteenth century, though there were changes in the relative importance of its various branches during this time. In chapter 1 the industry was defined simply as the manufacture of small articles in brass, iron and steel. More elaborate definitions, however, emphasize the significance of frequent changes in design at the dictates of fashion, holding this to be an essential characteristic of the industry – 'novelty sold the object' it has been said – and at the same time extending the definition to include heavy steel toys, even including edged hand tools, such as carpenter's tools.[31] The most extensive single branch of the toy industry in the mid-eighteenth century was the making of buttons, and it will be recalled that Birmingham's leading manufacturer at that time was a button-maker, John Taylor, and so was Matthew Boulton, in partnership with John Fothergill. Pin-making may also be considered part of the toy trade, together with the plating of silver on copper. Another offshoot of the toy trade which assumed great importance later on was the jewellery trade.

A survey of the history of the toy trade for the period 1760–1840 shows that the major changes which occurred were partly the result of changes in fashion and partly the consequence of technological improvements. The best-known example of the influence of fashion is the remarkably rapid decline of the buckle trade after an earlier period of great prosperity. In 1777 there were forty buckle-makers listed in Pearson & Rollason's *Birmingham Directory*. Ten years later the trade was in great distress owing to the adoption of the new fashion of shoe strings. In 1791 the manufacturers petitioned the Prince of Wales, and he and the Duke of York ordered their followers to wear buckles instead of shoe strings. A second petition was presented to the Duke and Duchess of York in the following year, but in spite of royal sympathy, the making of buckles had almost ceased by 1800.[32] Although the collapse of the trade must have caused considerable distress at the time, many buckle-makers transferred their skills to the brass trade or button trade.[33]

If the buckle trade suffered as a consequence of the vagaries of fashion, the button trade profited from the new preference for metal buttons and especially gilt (that is, plated) buttons from the 1760s onwards. Moreover, it became fashionable to wear larger and larger buttons, the more of them the better. As demand increased, production was improved with the invention in 1744 of Heaton's machine for making the shanks of buttons, and with the widespread use of the stamp in the late 1760s. By 1770 a wide variety of buttons was available, and according to *Sketchley's Directory* they included:

> gilt, plated, silvered, lacquered, and pinchbeck, the beautiful new manufacture platina, inlaid, glass, horn, ivory and pearl; metal buttons such as Bath, hard and soft, white etc. There is likewise made link buttons, in most of the above materials, as well as of paste, stones, etc.

The importance of plating is illustrated by the fact that both John Taylor and Matthew Boulton employed plated material on a large scale, and Boulton took the lead in having the Birmingham Assay Office set up in 1773. Up to this time it had been necessary to send plated goods to Chester or London for hallmarking, an obvious inconvenience and additional expense. Thereafter articles could be hallmarked in Birmingham at the office in Little Cannon Street, though it was not until 1824 that gold as well as silver could be assayed.[34] Plating was an important off-shoot of the toy trade, but never developed on a really large scale. It has been estimated that there were at the most about 800 hands in the trade, and of the ninety-six platers in *Chapman's Directory* (1799), many were engaged in making coach harness, spurs and buckles rather than in the toy trade proper.[35]

Edward Thomason also began the manufacture of plated wares about 1796, and another large firm, Waterhouse & Ryan, commenced business in the plated trade about 1808.[36] The plating industry continued as a valuable branch of the toy industry until 1840, when the older type of plating process fell into disuse as a result of the introduction of the Elkington electro-plating process.[37]

Meanwhile the button trade became very prosperous in the 1780s. Of the twenty-one grants of patents for improved buttons granted between 1770 and 1800, nineteen came from Birmingham; of these, ten were issued between 1785 and 1787.[38] The trade certainly benefited from the fashion for large buttons on long tailcoats, breeches buttoned at the knee and gaiters buttoned throughout their length. This fashion continued into the 1830s, so that this period has been termed the Augustan age of button-making in Birmingham.[39] The range of buttons made after the Napoleonic Wars was extended by the invention of the cloth-covered button with a flexible canvas shank (patented 1825), the fancy silk button (patented 1837 by William Elliott), and the linen button, patented in 1841 by John Aston.[40] By the 1840s the hey-day of the button trade was nearly over, though it was still an important sector of Birmingham industry. Metal and pearl buttons remained the staple branches of the trade, and the numbers employed in the making of buttons were still considerable. In 1841 they amounted to 2,888 – second only to those engaged in the brass industry as founders and moulders (3,056). By 1851 the numbers in the button trade had actually grown to 4,980, still very close to the brass trade, but they were to decline thereafter.[41]

Pin-making also expanded during the Industrial Revolution. It appears to have been started by Samuel Ryland in the middle of the eighteenth century, who transferred the business to his nephew, Thomas Phipson, in 1785. Thomas Phipson & Co. were the leading manufacturers in the first half of the nineteenth century, and their works were inspected (and commented upon unfavourably for their treatment of the children employed) in 1833 and 1843. For most of the period 1760–1840 pins were made by hand by a system of division of labour which became well-known; the work of fourteen different individuals went into the making of a single pin, and the employment of numerous women and children was a prominent feature of the industry. In 1824, however, a patent was taken out in this country by an American, Lemuel Wellman Wright, for a machine for making pins; but it was not until 1833 that the machine-made pin was actually placed on the market.[42] The first Birmingham patent for pin-making by machine (that is, other than by the use of the stamp or other hand tools) was issued in 1831 to Daniel Ledsam and William Jones. This patent was for two machines, one for heading and the other for pointing.[43] Nevertheless, it took a long time before pin-making became completely mechanized, and it was not until after 1840 that the use of machines of this sort became widespread in Birmingham.[44]

By 1840 the older part of the toy trade concerned with the making of iron or steel toys or trinkets had declined, having been absorbed by the jewellery trade,[45] which grew from comparative insignificance at the beginning of the nineteenth century to become one of the most prominent of Birmingham's industries at the mid-century.[46] In 1800 there were probably not more than a dozen workshops in the trade, employing about 400 workers. In the 1830s the trade expanded greatly, and continued to grow in the 1840s, becoming concentrated in the St Paul's district of the town. The trade produced a wide variety of goods, from small articles in gold or silver incorporating precious stones to articles of tableware and cheap imitations of expensive jewellery (the gilt toy trade). As with so many Birmingham industries, the industry was workshop-based, the numbers employed being from five to fifty; though it was said (and there is a parallel with the brassware trade) that all a workman needed to set up as a master was a bench, leather apron, two or three pounds' worth of tools (including a blow pipe), and for materials a few sovereigns and some ounces of copper and zinc.[47] In fact, the press and stamp were also indispensable for efficient production. By 1841 the printed census returns record the number of jewellers, goldsmiths, etc. as 1,398, increasing in 1851 to 2,494, together with a further 1,153 workers in gold and silver.

The three metal industries – guns, brass and toys (used in the widest sense to include buttons and jewellery) – were the most important industries in Birmingham during the classic period of the Industrial Revolution, but there were many smaller industries besides. Of these smaller industries, the manufacture of flint glass must be mentioned. The first known glasshouse was situated in Snow Hill in 1762, and at least two others were established before the end of the century, though the industry never attained the importance of the glass industry in Stourbridge. Nevertheless, by 1851 there were 1,117 workers engaged in Birmingham glass-making. Two other industries of some importance are papier-mâché manufacture, and japanning. The making of papier-mâché in Birmingham was pioneered by Henry Clay, who patented his method of producing paper board in 1772.[48] The result was the production of a variety of articles, including panels or roofs for coaches, bookcases, cabinets, tables and chairs, and tea trays. Such articles were often given decorative finishes, including that of japanning which was first made popular by the printer John Baskerville, who is said to have effected an entire revolution in the manufacture of japanned articles.[49] The minting of coins was also well-established in Birmingham at the beginning of the nineteenth century, though confined principally to Boulton and Edward Thomason. The former established his mint at Soho in 1786, supplying coins to a number of foreign countries, to the East India Company and, after 1797, to the British Government. Thomason, who has already been mentioned in connection with plating, became a very successful toy-maker, who also specialized in tradesmen's tokens and commemorative medallions.[50] Lastly, the manufacture of steel pens had begun in the 1830s, the principal makers being Josiah Mason (whose pens bore the name of the firm for which they were made, Perry & Co.), and Joseph Gillott; but it was not till the 1840s that metallic pens were made on a large scale, employing the press and die, as in the button trade.[51]

The sketch given so far of industrial developments in the period 1760–1840 is by no means comprehensive. It merely indicates the major developments in the main industries without seeking to include minor industries such as the making of umbrella frames, or screw-making, or nail-making by machines. Nevertheless, enough has been said to make it possible to survey industrial change as a whole, and to try to answer more general questions.

What were the most significant changes in the nature of Birmingham industry during the Industrial Revolution? The first is, of course, the enormous expansion of industry in Birmingham. The most noticeable change by 1800 was that whereas fifty years previously it was based very largely on articles made in iron and brass (or to a more limited extent, in steel), by the end of the century it had become more diversified so as to include a wider variety of iron and steel wares, together with the use of both non-ferrous and precious metals, glass, and papier-mâché. By that time it had also begun to manufacture Boulton & Watt steam engines (see chapter 5). By 1840 there was a further change of emphasis so that the two most important industries were non-ferrous trades – brass and jewellery. This was the result of the boom of the 1830s which expressed itself in part in an increasing demand for small finished articles, many of them of a luxury or semi-luxury kind. At the heart of Birmingham's industry throughout there was the skill in metal-working which by the mid-century made the town the biggest centre in the country for guns, brass-work (particularly the cabinet and lighting branches), jewellery (especially middle-class jewellery and cheap trinket ware), buttons, pins, screws, and bedsteads.[52] By the 1840s there were as many as ninety-seven different trades, far more than in other towns, according to contemporary opinion, and a great number of separate firms, as many as 2,100.[53]

The wide range of trades can be seen in the principal occupations in 1851 as set out in the census of that year:[54]

Blacksmiths	1,091	Iron manufacture	2,015
Brassfounders	4,914	Other workers and dealers in iron and steel	3,864
Bricklayers	1,694	Labourers	3,909
Button-makers	4,980	Painters, plumbers, glaziers	1,097
Carpenters, joiners	1,851	Messengers, porters	2,283
Cabinet-makers	1,027	Milliners	3,597
Cooks, housemaids, nurses	1,113	Shoemakers	3,153
Domestic servants (general)	8,359	Tailors	2,009
Glass manufacturers	1,117	Tool-makers	1,011
Goldsmiths, silversmiths	2,494	Washerwomen	1,965
Other workers in gold and silver	1,153	Workers in mixed metals	3,778
Gunsmiths	2,867		

These figures are not entirely reliable, and the classification of occupations is not always very helpful. Nevertheless, they give a broad, general picture of occupations in the mid-nineteenth century. The largest single occupation, of course, was that of domestic servant, as it was nationally; and domestic servants, together with the separate group of cooks, housemaids, and nurses constituted an occupation which was nearly twice as large as any other single occupation. As milliners, shoemakers, tailors and washerwomen were all sizeable occupations, they are a useful reminder that trades concerned with dress and apparel were an important part of the industrial structure. This said, it is apparent that the greatest emphasis in Birmingham industry still lay in the working of metals: the two largest occupations after domestic service were those of brassfounders and button-makers. Further, in addition to the major groups of gunsmiths, workers in gold and silver, and iron-workers, there were two large and somewhat ill-defined other groups of metal-workers: the 'other workers and dealers in iron and steel' (3,864), and the 'workers in mixed metals' (3,778); this last category presumably includes workers in different varieties of brass and in mixtures of copper, zinc and nickel. It is also a fair assumption that a proportion of the group of labourers would be engaged in the many branches of the metal industry. The census returns therefore provide overwhelming evidence of the continued significance of metal-working in Birmingham industry during the Industrial Revolution.

The question as to why Birmingham industry continued to grow after 1800 may now be asked. Reasons for the expansion of particular industries have been suggested earlier in this chapter, and, broadly speaking, it appears that the same factors which brought expansion in the second half of the eighteenth century continued to exert their influence after 1800 – that is, the demand for consumer goods, and the capacity of a community skilled in metal-working to meet that demand, given adequate supplies of raw material available locally. There is the further point, of course, that in addition to consumer demand as expressed in the market for buttons, jewellery, and guns, there was an increasing need for the products of plumbers', engineers', and naval brassfoundry as the national economy became more industrialized. Like industry elsewhere, Birmingham industry also profited by the development of the railways, though it was not until after 1840 that this began to have a significant effect. What cannot be argued is that expansion before 1840 was due to any major techno-logical breakthrough, or (more specifically) to the universal adoption of steam power.

The use of steam power has already been discussed in chapter 2, where it was argued that it could not conceivably have been a direct cause of industrial growth in Birmingham before 1800. Steam power was still relatively unimportant up to 1830, and even in the 1830s when there certainly seems to have been a noticeable increase in its use, the engines used were of low power and few in number. If the period 1760–1840 is taken as a whole, therefore, it is difficult to maintain that steam power was a major cause of industrial development. On the other hand, it could be argued that its wider use helped to sustain expansion in the 1830s just when industry in Birmingham was once more getting into its stride after the depression following the end of the Napoleonic Wars. Further, it has been argued that the significance of the wider use of steam power in Birmingham in the 1830s lies in the fact that it was used in the manufacture of the metal which was essential to so many local manufactories. Thus, in 1835 about 1,770 horse power was employed in working metals, as for example, in rolling copper and brass, drawing wire, and in iron forges and wrought iron mills. This provision of wrought iron, sheet metal, and wire by the superior force of steam had important repercussions in basic costs for all the industries using these semi-raw materials; so that even if the amount of steam power used was still relatively small, it had great significance for Birmingham industry as a whole.[55] This argument is persuasive, but scarcely modifies the conclusion that steam power was not an important cause of industrial growth in Birmingham during the classic period of the Industrial Revolution, 1760–1840.

The subject of steam power and of steam-driven machinery in large factories leads naturally to the question of how far the factory or large workshop was the norm in Birmingham industry by 1840. It is necessary to rely for information upon the limited evidence of the parliamentary reports of the first half of the century, together with such other contemporary descriptions of industry at the time which have survived. There is no doubt, of course, that very large establishments existed even in the mid-eighteenth century (see chapter 1), but they were highly exceptional. What has to be determined is how far the average size of the smaller factories or workshops had increased by the 1840s.

Early in the nineteenth century it is certainly clear that the majority of firms were still on a small scale. Thus, in 1799 it was said that in Birmingham 'there are very few that may be called large capitals. There are many manufactories in Birmingham which do not employ £100; some about £1,000, and speaking in general of the higher description of manufactures, about £6,000 or £7,000.'[56] A decade or so later, a further comment on the size of the smaller firms was made before a committee of the House of Commons: 'The important part of the population of Birmingham as a manufacturing town is composed of small manufacturers possessing from £300 or £400 to £2,000, £3,000 or £4,000 capital, employing 5 to 10, 20 or 30 hands.'[57] Those manufacturers who gave evidence in 1812 before this committee were clearly among the town's largest employers, but even they did not have very extensive establishments. Some of the brass manufacturers have already been mentioned earlier in this chapter: James Ryland, with 150 hands, Thomas Messenger, who employed 100, but in more prosperous times had employed 250, and Jenkins, who similarly had about 250 workers. In addition there were William Bannister, with a plating works of 120 hands, and Joseph Webster, whose wire works had 100 workmen. By 1833 the situation appears to have changed little; the largest manufacturers mentioned in the report of the Factory Enquiry Commission were Thomas Ledsam & Co., employing 318 workers in their button factory, Richard Phipson, the pin-maker, who employed about 250, and Jenkins the brassfounder, also with about 250. The report commented that a very large proportion of the work in Birmingham was 'paid for by the piece and given out to be executed at the houses of the work people'. Many thousands of children were employed, scattered in small numbers, in a great proportion of instances working in the houses of their parents.[58]

Ten years later emphasis was still being placed on the limited size of the average workplace. Grainger's report to the Children's Employment Commission (1842) stated that there were no factories at all similar to those in the North of England. Indeed, all over Birmingham there were workshops in which children and young persons were employed in numbers varying from three or four to fifty, sixty and a hundred.[59] Larger establishments were still to be found; the largest seem to have been in the button trade – Turner & Sons were said to employ 500 (though this might have included out-workers); Chatwin employed more than 200, and William Elliott, 253.[60] Radcliff's brass foundry had about 150 hands, and Rice Harris, the proprietor of the Islington Glass Works, claimed to employ about 540.[61] There were also some sizeable screw works: James James employed 360, and J. Hawkins & Co., 192. Boulton & Watt, makers of steam engines, had a modest establishment of 246 workers.[62] Visitors to Birmingham, in 1844 and 1856, made comments which together epitomize the most striking aspects of the town's industry. The first visitor remarked upon the size of the larger firms. Watt's works, it was said, employed about 400 workmen (a marked increase, it will be noticed, on the numbers in Grainger's report, dated the previous year). Turner & Co. had 'several hundred' workpeople in their great button manufactory, while Jennings & Bettridge, makers of papier-mâché, had about 200 hands, and Phipson & Co., 'some hundreds of children'.[63] The second visitor was impressed by the fact that nothing in Birmingham in 1856 was on a large scale, and observed that the development of large enterprises had not taken place as in the North, and that most master manufacturers employed only five or six workers.[64] Local sources in the 1850s also refer to the continued existence of great numbers of small masters: 'a singular and peculiar class in Birmingham'; though one article speaks critically of this class of garret-masters: 'an anomaly in the working world'.[65]

On the whole, it seems that over the period 1760–1840 the size of the industrial unit in heavy industry was usually relatively large, as might be expected where steam-powered rolling and grinding machinery had to be employed, but that in the small metal trades only the most successful manufacturers had 200 hands or more. Most employed far fewer, and in the metal trades the economies of large-scale production were far less attractive than in textiles or in the primary iron industry. Hence production on a small scale utilizing hand machines such as the press and stamp, with only a limited use of steam power, often from a shared steam engine, was still very common in 1840.[66] Even in the brass industry, where undoubtedly there were some large works, it has been argued that at the mid-century, the heavy section 'had hardly emerged'.[67] Of course, this is not to say that there was no growth at all in the average size of the industrial unit between 1760 and 1840; this would be an absurd suggestion. Obviously the more thrusting and successful small manufacturer would increase the size of his works, often in the way described by Samuel Timmins in 1866:

> Beginning as a small master, often working in his own house with his wife and children to help him, the Birmingham workman has become a master, his trade has extended, his buildings have increased. He has used his house as a workshop, has annexed another, has built upon the garden or the yard, and consequently a large number of the manufactories are most irregular in style.[68]

Nevertheless, it remains true that increased demand for Birmingham goods in the first half of the nineteenth century resulted not solely in the concentration of industry into bigger and bigger factories, but also in the multiplication of small workshops. Professor Allen considered that even as late as 1860 work premises might be divided up into the large factory, employing 150 persons and above; the small factory, with thirty or forty to 150 workers; the workshop, employing up to thirty or forty persons; and the workshop of the garret-master, a domestic workshop employing only his family, and an occasional journeyman or apprentice. Only in the first instance were the premises usually specially built. The small factory often consisted of a chain of converted dwelling houses, while the workshop and the garret workshop were similarly in domestic premises, and their proprietors were commonly dependent upon a factor for their raw materials and the marketing of their goods.[69] Thus the physical development of much of Birmingham industry took a markedly different form from both the textile industry in the North and the Black Country finished iron industry nearer to home.

Lastly, a few observations on the subject of industrial training and apprenticeship may be helpful. To judge from the increase in population between 1760 and 1840, the work-force in Birmingham must have grown by roughly eight times between these dates, so that there was a need to train great numbers of mostly immigrant workers. This training was achieved partly by the process of learning on the job, and partly by the more formal method of apprenticeship. In some trades little skill was needed, for example, in the operation of a stamp or press. In other trades, delicate and precise work was required, as in the jewellery trade and in gun-making, so that apprenticeship would seem to be essential. Given the fact that the Birmingham workman was often highly skilled, it might be expected that apprenticeship would be an important part of the industrial system. But the reality appears to be otherwise. According to Timmins, in the seventeenth and eighteenth centuries: 'No trades unions, no trade gilds, no companies existed, and every man was free to come and go, to found or to follow or to leave a trade just as he chose. The system of apprenticeship was only partly known.'[70]

It is certainly true that the absence of craft gilds in Birmingham meant that there were no established bodies to supervise the workings of the apprenticeship system. Then again, the wide opportunities for employment open to young persons and children from as early an age as seven or eight must have made an apprenticeship from fourteen to twenty-one at a reduced wage an unattractive proposition. Further, it was often held that as there were so many metal trades in the town, when one suffered trade depression, its workers could readily transfer into another, more prosperous trade. If this were so, any rigid system of apprenticeship would clearly be a hindrance.

For all these reasons, it seems that apprenticeship did not feature very widely in the Birmingham trades during the period 1760–1840, but the problem still remains of determining which trades did use apprenticeship, and to what extent. Few apprenticeship indentures have survived, and the modern Index of Apprenticeships which has been compiled is a very imperfect guide, as it is based on references in local collections rather than on collections of indentures.[71] In 1843 an observer of the Birmingham industrial scene commented that few were bound apprentice, and there even appears to have been a certain amount of hostility to apprentices among some manufacturers. One of several witnesses in the brass industry before the Children's Employment Commission said that he would not take in-door apprentices as they were too troublesome, and that many boys did not wish to become regular apprentices. Two other employers agreed with this verdict, and declared that many apprentices were petty thieves, being both troublesome and bad – and getting worse every year. Another gave his opinion that 'The system of apprenticeship is quite changed. No respectable manufacturer will trouble himself about them . . . many parents will not bind their children, because they hope they will gain a man's wages before the time of their serving expires.'[72]

Nevertheless, twenty years or so later, apprenticeship had by no means disappeared. It continued in the jewellery trade, in saddlery (where it was said, 'in most respectable manufactories, the applications for apprenticeships are far more numerous than can be satisfied by appointments') and in artistic trades such as that of stained glass.[73] Although it has been recently suggested that apprenticeship was virtually absent from the gun trade,[74] all the same, the Index of Apprenticeships records fourteen bound apprentices in the gun trade between 1840 and 1872. Since the Index is so incomplete, it may be that there were considerably more bound than this, and that apprenticeship in the trade was not entirely dead at this time. The same reasoning may be applied to the goldsmiths, to whom seven apprentices at least were bound between 1862 and 1869. Admittedly, an average of about one bound a year is very low, but it would be strange if more did not become apprentices in a trade with such a long tradition of apprenticeship elsewhere.

As the evidence is so fragmentary it would be unsafe to venture much further. Nevertheless, it may be that apprenticeship was more widespread than has been hitherto supposed. A good deal of it was of an informal kind, based on a mere verbal agreement between the workman and the apprentice, and did not run to a formal indenture specifying a term of seven years. One witness in 1843, a brassfounder, said he had only one apprentice, but that his men had many.[75] Apprenticeship certainly seems to have survived into the mid-nineteenth century in some occupations outside the metal trades, and there are forty-seven instances in the Birmingham Index of apprenticeship to cordwainers and shoemakers. Lastly, it is reasonable to assume that as an institution apprenticeship was stronger in the second half of the eighteenth century than it was by 1840 – in the earlier period advertisements are not uncommon in *Aris's Gazette*, both for apprentices in the toy trade and for runaway apprentices – but by the 1840s apprenticeship was of diminished importance, though by no means extinct.[76]

To sum up, it might be thought that the industrial history of Birmingham during the period of the Industrial Revolution is in one sense unremarkable, as it displays none of the technological virtuosity which characterizes the textile industry. Birmingham's claims to fame in the realm of technological innovation belong to the mid-eighteenth century or earlier, rather than to the later period, and even though it was the home of the Boulton & Watt steam engine in the 1770s, steam power did not transform Birmingham industry as a whole before 1840. Although by then large industrial establishments employing steam power were commonplace, the smaller workshop was still overwhelmingly predominant. Yet in another sense, Birmingham was truly remarkable, for it demonstrated in a striking fashion the vitality and potential of the industry of the so-called pre-industrial period, which was able to expand to a phenomenal degree as the basis of the national economy shifted from agriculture to industry. Thus, Birmingham industry grew larger and ever more complex, feeding first the oddly contrasting national demands for ornament and for weapons of war, and then later supplementing these with all the varieties of brassware required by an emerging industrial nation.

There is, however, one particular difficulty in attempting an overview of industrial change during this period. It is very easy to convey an impression of steady and sustained growth when, in fact, industrial expansion was neither uniform nor even. This will become evident when the changes in trade during the years of the Industrial Revolution are traced in the next chapter.

4

Changes in Trade and Services

Any discussion of the significance of the Industrial Revolution will tend inevitably to focus on the growth of industry rather than of trade, and particularly on developments in textiles, iron and coalmining, the staple industries of the time. This approach is understandable enough, given the nature of the subject, but it brings with it not only the danger of failing to take sufficiently into account the wide range of industries in non-textile towns such as Birmingham but in addition it too often ignores the importance of other aspects of the urban economy such as the trading and service sectors. If industry manufactures goods, it must have markets at home and abroad in which to sell them, together with appropriate marketing systems; without commerce, industry must perish. It is equally true that neither industry nor commerce can thrive without the service or tertiary sector of the economy – the provision of housing, clothing, furnishing, transport facilities, and the professional services of the lawyer, banker, accountant and physician. The purpose of this chapter is therefore to examine changes in the commercial and service sectors of the Birmingham economy in the period 1750 to 1840. For convenience, the chapter is divided into three sections: the first section covers the years up to 1793, when war began against France; the second deals with the years of war which lasted until 1815; while the last section surveys the period c. 1815–40.

There can be no doubt that trade expanded greatly in the years up to the beginning of the Revolutionary War in 1793. Enough has been said already about the extraordinary rise in population, the amount of building, and the improvement in coach and canal services, all of which provide evidence for the expansion of trade. Of course, at the same time, trade was subject to fluctuations arising from a number of causes, some due to variations in the state of the national economy, others due to purely local or regional factors, such as the state of the weather, bad harvests and bread riots.

Sometimes the state of trade in Birmingham reflected national conditions, sometimes it did not. For example, both nationally and in the Birmingham area the years immediately before the coming of war in 1793 were years of prosperity, whereas depression seems to have affected Birmingham trade in 1772, which was a year of some prosperity elsewhere.[1] More specific causes of depression affecting Birmingham trade include such incidents as the period of court mourning in January 1766,[2] which had repercussions for the button and toy trades, and the earthquake in Lisbon in 1755, Portugal being an important overseas market for Birmingham traders. Curiously enough, overseas wars before 1793 do not appear to have had any marked or sustained effects on the Birmingham export trade. Certainly the Seven Years War, 1756–63, seems not to have affected the town's foreign trade very greatly, though trade did come to a standstill just before war began against the American colonists in 1775, leading to a Birmingham petition to the House of Commons complaining of the continued stagnation of trade resulting from the dispute with the colonists. This petition gained support from a number of members of the House, including Edmund Burke.[3] Trade certainly picked up subsequently, and the end of the war in 1783 saw the formation of the Birmingham Commercial Committee.[4]

This committee is generally thought to have been the result of concern among Birmingham manufacturers at the proposal to permit the free export of brass,[5] but it may well be that the coming of peace also brought a mood of optimism and a general agreement that Birmingham employers might meet together regularly for their better advantage. A large committee of a hundred members was set up at a town meeting held at the Birmingham Hotel on 12 August 1783.[6] The committee met thereafter from time to time to discuss matters such as the proposed commercial treaty with Ireland in 1785 and the commercial treaty with France in 1786. The support of the committee for the French treaty led to a disagreement with the General Chamber of Manufacturers in London, to which it was affiliated. On another subject, anxiety over the dangers of Birmingham workers being enticed abroad by foreign rivals resulted in a reward of £50 being offered in 1785 for information leading to the conviction of any person committing this offence, while in 1786 the committee decided to make known its intention to exclude all strangers from its workshops. In 1790, however, the committee appears to have split up over a dispute concerning the importing into Birmingham of German sword blades, and there are no further records of its activities between 1790 and 1794, when a new commercial society was established.[7]

The significance of the work of the Commercial Committee is not easy to assess with any certainty, but at least it is clear that the leading manufacturers thought that the time was ripe for the setting up of such a body, not only to facilitate joint action in local matters, but also to make representations to the government. The committee appears to have been one of the earliest to have been formed in the country, the only other bodies of this kind existing at the time being those of Leeds, Halifax and Exeter. According to Wright, the Manchester Committee was not established until 1794, although this has been disputed.[8] On the other hand, during its short existence from 1783 to 1790 the Birmingham Committee does not seem to have achieved very much, and the spirit of independence which characterized Birmingham entrepreneurs may have told against any concerted action when matters of controversy arose. All could agree to keep strangers out of their workshops, but it was clearly a different matter when it was proposed to import German swords to be sold in competition with Birmingham-made blades. The town's traders and manufacturers disliked any interference with their trade from outside – witness the forming of the Birmingham Metal Company and the Mining and Copper Company, which was described in the last chapter – but they were also sensitive to any move on the part of one of their own number to take an unfair share of trade. Thus, in 1763 a meeting of manufacturers expressed fears that trade and production were in great danger of being monopolized unless the manufacturers acted to prevent this.[9] Proceedings of the new commercial society set up in 1794 have not survived, and it was not until 1813 that another body, the present Chamber of Commerce, was established on a permanent footing.

Meanwhile, the expansion of trade in the period 1750–93 was on a remarkable scale. This is reflected in the changes which took place in the trading and service sectors.[10] Some indication of these changes is given in the numerous trade directories which were published at this time. *Sketchley's Birmingham Directory* (3rd edition, 1767) helps to set the scene for the earlier part of the period:

Building
Masons and Bricklayers   20
Clothing
Hatters   9
Drapers   26
Milliners   10
Peruke-makers   54
Shoemakers   47
Tailors   64
Woodworking trades
Cabinet-makers   12
Carpenters   9
Joiners   26
Drink
Publicans   294
Maltsters   32
Booksellers   7
Foodstuffs
Bakers   50
Butchers   32
Grocers   50
Druggists   11
Printers   7
Attorneys   21
Factors and chapmen   20
Apothecaries and surgeons   20
Merchants   38
Miscellaneous
Excisemen   7
Gardeners   14
Professors of the polite arts
(mostly schoolmasters)   21

These figures cannot be more than approximate, but they do give some idea of the relative importance of the different trades. In fact, trades and occupations other than those in the metal industries are numerically as important as many of the metal trades themselves. For example, the number of drapers (26) is larger than the number of edge-tool makers, even though the directory considers Birmingham to be the first town in the country for edge-tools. Further, there were more shoemakers (47) and tailors (64) than there were gun- and pistol-makers (35) and brassfounders (32). Two decades or so later, *Pye's Directory* (1788) provides some interesting comparisons with *Sketchley's* figures:

	1767	*1788*
Professional services		
Surgeons	20	27
Attorneys	21	26
Food trades		
Butchers	32	67
Bakers	50	66
Grocers and druggists	61	70
Drapers and mercers	26	38
Merchants and factors	38	133

Again, it should be emphasized that these figures are only approximations, and that eighteenth-century trade directories have their known imperfections. In particular, apart from the question of the accuracy of the figures, categories of trades and occupations vary from one directory to another. An example of this is provided by *Sketchley's* figure for surgeons including apothecaries, while *Pye's* does not. Again, *Sketchley's* lists as two separate categories factors and chapmen (20) and merchants (38), while *Pye's* gives one figure for merchants and factors combined (133). Yet when allowance is made for difficulties of this kind, the upward trends are very clear. By the early 1790s, the *Universal British Directory* shows a further increase in bakers from 66 to 85, and of butchers from 67 to 86.

The absence of any kind of statistical data for the trading and services sector makes it impossible, of course, to compare it in quantitative terms with the manufacturing sector, and in any case the two sectors overlap in that some manufacturers sold direct to the public and not through factors. Nevertheless, a survey of Sun insurance policies taken out in Birmingham in the period 1777–86 emphasizes the importance of the trading and service sector.[11] Although the largest policies were issued to button and toy manufacturers – William Taylor (presumably the son of John Taylor), John Richards, and Claud Johnson jointly took out a policy for £7,000 in 1778, while in 1783 Taylor and Richards took out another policy for £6,200 – an analysis of the occupations of policy holders shows that although button-makers constituted a substantial body, the largest group among those holding policies of £1,000 or over were the mercers, drapers and haberdashers, who were obviously not industrialists at all. Moreover, a further breakdown of all policies shows that well over half of the holders were not engaged directly in industry, but were in the trading and services sectors. These non-manufacturing insurers included those in the building and furniture trades; the food trades (butchers, bakers, grocers, victuallers); the clothing and soft furnishing trades (shoemakers, breeches-makers, tailors, peruke-makers, hosiers, drapers, mercers and milliners); and the beer, wine and spirits trades (innkeepers and brewers). Policies were also taken out by booksellers, stationers and bookbinders; druggists and surgeons; and attorneys. Table I gives some indication of the range of policies issued.[12]

Sun Insurance Company Policies Issued to Birmingham Insurers 1777–86

	1777	1778	1779	1780	1781	1782	1783	1784	1785	1786	Totals
Policies issued	72	70	94	72	90	66	33	49	73	74	693
Policies											
(1) below £500	42	42	48	38	43	34	18	35	52	38	390
(2) £500–£999	18	13	26	24	30	23	8	10	16	20	188
(3) £1,000 and above	12	15	20	10	17	9	7	4	5	16	115
Trade and services policies											
(1) in range £500 and above	23	14	27	20	30	23	10	6	12	20	185
(2) over whole range	44	39	52	36	54	41	15	24	38	43	386

All this is a useful sign of the liveliness of the trading and service aspects of the Birmingham economy, even though the figures cannot be taken to be exact. Not all manufacturers, for instance, bothered to take out insurance policies on their property and machinery, whereas drapers with their large and inflammable stocks would have been foolish if they had not done so. Be this as it may, the contemporary evidence is overwhelming in its testimony to a greatly increasing volume of trade and services before the advent of the French wars. Among the most striking aspects of this must be the growth of population and the consequent demand for housing, which in turn required more bricklayers, slaters, carpenters, glaziers and labourers. These increasing numbers led to a greater provision of food suppliers such as butchers, bakers and tea dealers. The working classes still purchased most of their necessities from street markets, and these were expanding everywhere in the industrial towns. Indeed, the Birmingham Improvement Commissioners appear to have given more attention to the working of the principal markets than to matters of sanitation and scavenging. Middle-class requirements of clothing and furnishing fabrics are demonstrated by the increasing numbers of tailors, mercers and drapers in the trade directories, and also by the growth in the number of shops. The amounts levied in Birmingham each year for shop tax in the years 1786 to 1789 when this tax was applied were over twice the whole sum levied per year for the county of Cheshire.[13] By the beginning of the nineteenth century, the central shopping area was well established in New Street, High Street and the Bull Ring. There was only one house in High Street not occupied as a shop (that of Mr Taylor, the banker), and houses in this street had trebled in value because of their position. William Allin, a woollen draper, having had his rent raised from £30 p.a. to £120 p.a. in only a few years, decided to purchase the property for £3,000, but then had to pay out £1,000 in renovations, the building being so old and in such a bad condition that if it had not been used for trade it would not have been worth £500 – or so he claimed.[14]

As for the country trade, Birmingham manufacturers seem to have relied on several different ways of gaining customers for their products. One of the best known was the employment of factors or middlemen. The nature and function of factors were touched on in chapter 1, and the fact that their numbers increased from eighty-five in 1777 to 175 in 1815 is an indication of their importance to the growth of trade.[15] They were employed by both large and small firms, though the larger firms might also have their own representatives in London and deal direct with foreign customers. In the early 1780s, Boulton & Fothergill were trading directly with at least eleven firms in St Petersburg, and many more in Hamburg.[16] In the home market, however, a favoured means of selling at a distance was the use of travellers who worked regular circuits, either on horseback or by stage coach. If on horseback, their samples would be carried in saddle bags, together with catalogues and illustrations of their wares. Travel by coach was rather more comfortable if in seats in the inside, but it was more expensive. The stage coach was also used for the transport of goods or raw materials where speedy delivery was required, though here again, delivery by coach was much more expensive than by waggon: in 1832 Richard Westall, a Birmingham linen draper, paid 8s 4d per hundredweight for supplies by coach from London compared with 5s by waggon.[17] Travellers were important to a firm, for a good salesman could increase business, strengthen the firm's reputation and, if sufficiently trustworthy, collect debts and settle accounts. The loss of a reliable and skilful traveller could be a serious blow.[18] Many of the smaller firms, of course, were represented on the road by their own principals, though they might also employ travellers. Thus, Julius Harvey, a Birmingham button-maker employing between thirty and forty men, visited customers in London personally, while his partner and brother Joseph also travelled on the firm's Welsh, northern and Leicestershire journeys. In addition, Julius Harvey employed two travellers, Mr John Undrell, who was sent to Wolverhampton and Walsall in May 1789 in search of useful contacts with merchants and factors, and Mr Ainge, who undertook the Cheshire journey in the following month.[19] Travellers such as these were essential links in the chain connecting manufacturers with customers living at a distance from Birmingham.

Another method of reaching customers was by providing showrooms centrally in Birmingham, though presumably only the larger firms could afford to do this. Boulton maintained showrooms in London as well as at Soho, while Thomason had extensive display rooms attached to his factory premises in St Philip's Square. Smaller manufacturers might exhibit their wares in Charles Jones' 'Pantechnatheca' or General Repository of Art, built in New Street in 1823.[20] In all these ways the distributive network had attained some degree of sophistication and complexity before the coming of the railways brought great changes to the system in the late 1830s.

Finally in this section, something must be said about leisure and recreational activities, although this subject will be examined in detail in chapters 8 and 9. For the working classes, the numerous public houses were often a centre for the spending of leisure time, not only in drinking and conviviality, but also for the meetings of the numerous friendly societies, for the playing of skittles and quoits, and sometimes for dogfighting and cockfighting. There were three wakes a year, and two ancient fairs, which were occasions for much eating and drinking. For the middle classes there were the many clubs, the theatre, weekly assemblies, two lodges of freemasons, the libraries and, beginning in 1768, the triennial music festivals. All these activities together provided services for all ranks of society, and they expanded with the growth of population, providing an important adjunct to the growth of commerce in its various forms, either through factors or in the form of retailing in shops and markets.

It is evident that the trading and service sector of the Birmingham economy experienced boom conditions in the period from the mid-century to 1793, and the attention customarily paid to industrial expansion in these years should not be allowed to overshadow this fact. How far all this may be held to be a part of the consumer revolution which some historians claim to have taken place in the second half of the eighteenth century is a matter for conjecture. As noted in chapter 2, it has even been argued that the Birmingham toy trade was perhaps '*the* characteristic consumer industry of the commercial revolution'.[21] Whatever the truth of this, there is no doubt that the pin, button, toy and jewellery trades in particular grew fat on affluent middle-class demand, and that trading in both the home and foreign markets, coupled with the provision of services, contributed much to the prosperity of the Birmingham economy before 1793. Nor should it be forgotten that not only did Birmingham meet the needs of its own inhabitants, it was also of great importance as a regional centre to the surrounding manufacturing and agricultural districts.

The declaration of war against France in 1793 brought a remarkable change in the fortunes of Birmingham trade and industry. Although it was not expected that the French would withstand the advance of the Prussian and Austrian armies for very long, in fact they were soon driven out, and fighting continued in Europe until the Peace of Amiens was signed in 1802. Hostilities were resumed in 1803 and lasted until 1814, followed by a final period of fighting which was brought to an end at the Battle of Waterloo in 1815. Thus, the British nation had to undergo nearly twenty-two years of conflict and of much dislocation of both European and American trade, especially after 1807 when all British trade with the Continent was forbidden by the Orders in Council. In addition, the closing years of the war were made more difficult for traders by the war of 1812–13 against the United States. So long a period of fighting on both land and sea naturally had severe repercussions for the nation as a whole; the economy suffered from inflation, high taxation, and a heavy demand for manpower by the army and navy. To these consequences of the wars there must be added the effects of bad harvests and the soaring price of bread. Birmingham was subjected to all these adverse influences on trade, with very noticeable results.

Certainly the early months of the war in 1793 brought an immediate depression in Birmingham trade to which the diary of Julius Harvey, the button-maker referred to earlier in this chapter, bears eloquent witness.[22] As soon as fighting began, Harvey noted that Consols★ had dropped from ninety-seven to seventy-three or even lower, and predicted that the war would be ruinous to England: loans to the government would drain the nation of its circulating cash, 'the sinews of trade'; great quantities of labour would go into the army; business on the continent would vanish in the neighbourhood of the contending armies – who, asked Harvey in his diary, would attend the great Spring Fair at Frankfurt with such hordes of Prussian troops near at hand? By 30 April 1793, he had had to dismiss half his work-force, and could find no more than half-employment for those who remained. By May, as trade continued very dead, Harvey expressed fears as to what would happen to his workmen's families, and concluded that they would simply starve: 'In so short a space as a few months, from great prosperity we are plunged into general misery and wretchedness.' By this time his workmen were at work only four days a week, and his workshops had been shut on the first two days of the working week for some time past. There can be no doubt that the early months of war hit the button-making trade hard, though later there was some adjustment to the new conditions. In November 1795 Harvey repaid a loan to his brother Charles of £350 which he had borrowed in February 1792, so it is apparent that he was still in business. Presumably, of the other branches of industry in Birmingham the gun trade in particular must have benefited from the war, even if other sectors of industry were depressed for a time.[23]

However, trade had not recovered anything like its former prosperity by the end of the century. According to Nemnich's *Account of Birmingham* (1802), the most flourishing period of manufacturing in Birmingham before the war was between 1790 and 1792, and the quantity of goods made in 1799 was not above half what was made in 1791. The reasons for this, he claimed, were the war, the great

★Government securities.

fluctuations in the price of copper and, rather curiously, the dishonest methods of some button-makers who sold buttons as plated and gilt which were in fact only of white and yellow mixed metals and 'merely watered over with silver'.[24] It is unlikely that this dishonesty had much to do with depressed trade conditions, though it is possible that button-makers were driven to cut costs by the dullness of trade; but there is plenty of contemporary comment to testify to the slackness in trade at the turn of the century. Thus, trade was said to be very bad in November 1798, with no more than four days' work available a week. There was still distress in 1800, with bread riots occurring in September of that year. According to Langford, 1800 was 'a year of suffering', while the following year was equally one of scarcity, suffering and violence. When peace was signed in 1802, he remarks that the prosperity of the gun and sword trades gave but small satisfaction in view of the depression of the thousand and one industries on which the inhabitants of Birmingham depended.[25]

The second period of the wars against France seems to have brought little all-round improvement, judging from the representations made by Birmingham manufacturers in 1812 to the House of Commons committee investigating the petitions against the Orders in Council. It is true that their protests were probably well-orchestrated by Richard Spooner and Thomas Attwood, the bankers, so that allowance must be made for exaggeration. All the same, the witnesses referred frequently to the importance of the American markets then under threat by the Orders in Council, to the necessity of standing men off work, and to the reduction in the numbers employed. As noted in chapter 2, it was claimed that Birmingham's trade to America was roughly equal to its home trade in England, Ireland and Scotland, and that it was worth a million pounds a year or more.[26] This trade was gravely threatened by the restrictions imposed by the Orders in Council; for example, John Room, a japanner, usually employed forty workpeople but had reduced this number to fifteen, while Joseph Webster, a wire manufacturer who normally employed about 100 hands, had cut this number to seventy-five or eighty.[27]

No doubt there was an element of special pleading in all this, but Birmingham was only one of a number of towns to present a petition against the Orders in Council in 1812, and export figures from Britain appear to have fallen off markedly from 1810 to 1811 in several products. For example, iron and steel manufactures fell from £1.2m in 1810 to £861,723 in 1811, and brass and copper manufactures for the same years from £291,763 to £245,807. Even the exports of the booming textile trade received a severe check at this time – cotton exports in 1810 of £13.8m were reduced to only £7.5m in the next year, and woollens dropped from £5.2m to £3.7m.[28] As for exports to the United States, these declined dramatically from £7.8m in 1810 to £1.43m in 1811. Admittedly they recovered somewhat in 1812, the year war broke out with the States, only to sink to nil (officially, at least) in the statistics for 1813, and to only £7,000 in 1814 when the war ended.[29] It would appear, therefore, that Birmingham manufacturers had good reason to fear not only the threat to trade generally presented by the Orders in Council, but also the danger of war with America, which they knew might prove disastrous for this important section of their foreign trade. In fact, the actual consequences of the war with the United States were all accurately predicted in detail in their petition to the House of Commons.

In perspective, it certainly seems that the French wars constituted a severe setback to Birmingham trade, and to the service sector as well. Whatever adjustment took place in the early years of the war, trade conditions were still much affected by hostilities at the end of the eighteenth century, and again in 1812–14. One of the earliest comments on all this is to be found in the fourth edition of Hutton (1809), which refers to 'the ruinous war with France which has been the destruction of our commerce, caused 500 of our tradesmen to fail, stagnated currency, and thinned the inhabitants'.[30] Yates, whose work on Birmingham was published in 1830, says much the same, also including a reference to the notorious Priestley riots of 1791 which were sparked off by a dinner in celebration of the French Revolution:

> The rage for building, which produced so many additional homes, was miserably checked by the combined or consecutive effects of war, stagnation of trade, scarcity, and the high price of provisions. Numbers of workmen, thrown out of employ, entered the army or navy – their masters, the Gazette – and their wives and families the workhouse or the grave.[31]

Yates also draws attention to the apparent decline of population in the town, as shown by Hutton's figures in the 1809 edition, from 73,653 in 1791 to 69,384 in 1801 – a loss of 4,269. Unfortunately for Yates, Hutton did not correct his 1801 figure by referring to the national census figure of 73,670 for the combined parishes of St Martin and St

Philip, Aston and Edgbaston. This would make a much smaller loss of only seventeen, and even that is assuming that Hutton's 1791 figure is more or less correct. That there was a severe check to population growth seems very likely, but it is obviously unwise to rely on Hutton for illustrative figures here. It is probably better to compare the official census figures for Birmingham for the second part of the war, and these show an increase from the 73,670 of 1801 to 85,755 in 1811 – an improvement of 16 per cent. Yet even these figures represent a lower rate of increase than in other large industrial towns such as Manchester and Leeds, and are only just above the national increase in population of 15 per cent for the same period. It follows that even if Hutton's figures for the decade 1791 to 1801 exaggerate the loss of population, the increase for 1801–11 is very different from that of the boom years earlier on. Immigration into the town in the period 1801–11 must have been on only a limited scale, and this in itself supplies a fair indication of the dullness of trade at the time.

Why was Birmingham so hard hit by the French wars? It seems beyond doubt that the war period was indeed a time when the prosperity of the earlier years was lost. Later in the century it was sometimes said that the sheer number of trades in Birmingham made bad trade throughout the area almost impossible: if some trades were depressed, others would still be prosperous, and a workman was free to transfer from one trade to another.[32] Clearly, however, this did not apply during the French wars. Of course, there is the possibility that bad harvests were really the major cause of discontent during the wars, and were perhaps a greater cause of distress than fluctuations in trade. But although it is true that there were bad harvests and high bread prices in several years, notably in 1795, 1800 and 1801, these years of scarcity cannot be considered as the sole or even principal cause of distress during the twenty-two years of war; there are too many contemporary references to stagnation in trade for bad harvests to be the explanation for all the suffering. The fault must lie mainly in the disruption of trade, and especially the dislocation of foreign trade. Although earlier in this book doubt was thrown on claims that in 1759 five-sixths of Birmingham's manufactures went abroad, there is less reason to doubt the claims that in 1812 foreign trade was of equal importance to home trade. The proportion appears to be actually higher than the national proportion of industrial output which was exported in 1801, this being about 35 per cent, manufactures themselves constituting 88.1 per cent of total exports.[33] If exported manufactured goods had become so important to Birmingham, it is not surprising that employers were deeply concerned by the continued interruptions to trade in Europe and North America.

Whether in fact Birmingham manufacturers suffered more than manufacturers in other parts of the kingdom can only be guessed at, but it seems probable that they were harder hit than others, especially up to 1802. Phyllis Deane has characterized this period as being one of continued upsurge in British overseas trade, growth averaging 4.5 per cent in the period from 1791/5 to 1800/4, a period in which Britain's main commercial rivals were heavily disadvantaged by war conditions. There are few, if any, signs of this upsurge in Birmingham's export trade. However, Deane considers that the second half of the war saw a period of deceleration in which restrictions on trade were tightened, culminating in 1806–13 with the continental blockade and the closing from time to time of North American ports to British shipping. Growth in British overseas trade in this period was more than halved.[34] This certainly corresponds much more closely to the Birmingham experience.

It appears therefore that the French wars constituted an unhappy episode in the history of Birmingham trade, principally owing to the disruption of foreign markets. In addition, of course, all suffered from heavy taxation (both income tax and property tax were introduced in 1799), and from the bad harvests which brought higher bread prices and general unrest. The end of the wars in 1815 brought the promise of better things to come.

Unfortunately, the return of peacetime conditions saw the beginning of a period of economic confusion and disruption which lasted several years as overseas markets adjusted to the return of peacetime trading, while the home market had to absorb discharged soldiers and sailors who flooded the labour market: during the wars more than half a million were serving in the army and navy. Hutton's sixth edition (1835) makes this comment:

> Many thousands were thrown out of employment by the peace of 1814 who had previously been engaged in the manufacturing of the various military implements, for which so great a demand had been created by the long and ruinous war with France; together with the disbanded soldiers, so over-handed those trades in which employment remained, that an immediate decrease in the price of labour and an increase in the Poor Rates were the consequence.[35]

In addition, the agricultural interest in Parliament had secured the passing of the 1815 Corn Law, intended to protect agriculture by forbidding the import of foreign corn when the home price was less than 80s per quarter. The Birmingham Chamber of Commerce opposed the bill for keeping the price of bread artificially high, thereby requiring the paying of higher wages and increasing the price of every article made at home.[36] In May 1817 it was said that the depressed state of industry was such that many families had vacated their premises and were crowded together in small houses. Things were no better the following year, when trade was said to be in 'a degraded state'.[37] Commercial depression continued into 1819, while in 1820 petitions were presented by the Chamber of Commerce to both Houses of Parliament, claiming that the depression had 'lately increased to an alarming extent'.[38]

Thereafter matters improved somewhat, and trade generally recovered until 1825–6 with the result that, according to Hutton's editor, good and plentiful harvests brought money to the pocket of the mechanic, and moderated food prices, so that 'in 1823, 1824, and 1825 we find Birmingham as well as every part of the Empire in full and constant employment'; but this was not to last. He continues:

> But this shining picture for the mechanic, and hey-day for the publican, which the improvidence of the former always created for the latter; at times when plenty of money is to be obtained by labour, keeping up the good old custom of getting money like horses, and spending it like asses, was destined to be of short duration.[39]

In December 1825, trade in Birmingham began to decline again, as did the national economy. Of the six Birmingham banks in business at the end of the wars, Gibbins, Smith & Goode failed altogether (though creditors later received 19s 8d in the pound), while Galton, Galton & James survived the crisis but closed down some time later.[40] Trade was so depressed that in 1826 loans of £500 to £10,000 were made available by the Bank of England as 'temporary relief' to the town and neighbourhood of Birmingham. How far this offer was taken up is unknown, but the Chamber of Commerce undertook to establish a local Board of Commissioners to administer the loans. The Bank made its loans subject to a number of safeguards: loans were generally to be repayable over a period of four months at 5 per cent interest, and were to be secured by the deposit of yarns, manufactured goods, raw produce, non-perishable merchandise, or by personal security; all goods were to be placed in approved warehouses and insured. It might be thought that the Bank was over-cautious in its approach, but felt obliged to provide some help in view of the failure of banks not only in Birmingham but in other parts of the country. It seems likely that such stringent conditions resulted in few manufacturers applying for loans, but the very existence of the scheme (which was also extended to other large towns) shows the seriousness of the depression of the time.[41]

Trade improved to some extent after 1826, but complaints about the slackness of trade were still to be heard in 1827, while in 1829 Attwood was referring to 'the present distress', and in February 1830 declared: 'The ruinous depression of the trade of the town of Birmingham has been progressively increasing for the past four years, and has now arrived at an extent never before equalled.'[42] Trade does not seem to have improved very greatly until the mid-1830s, when at last in 1833 it was said to be very good, with the same opinion expressed again in 1836 when everything looked prosperous. In that year, two new banks were started – the Town & District Bank, and the Birmingham & Midland Bank, under the famous manager, Mr Geach.[43] Yet even then trade soon fell away again, and once more in 1837 it was said that there was much commercial distress. Langford refers to a memorial signed by more than 13,000 workmen regarding 'the want of confidence and suspension of business depriving the labouring classes of employment, and causing distress rapidly approaching to starvation'. The following year the distress was said to be terrible, and 190,000 quarts of soup and 30,000 loaves were distributed.[44]

Of course, the late 1830s and the early 1840s constitute a period of very considerable national depression, certainly among the worst depressions if not *the* worst of the whole nineteenth century. In Birmingham things were especially bad in 1842 and the first half of 1843; in January 1842 it was said that in the fancy steel toy trade, wages were reduced by a half. In the plating trade they dropped by 30 to 40 per cent, and in brassfoundry by half to two-thirds. There were similar reports of reductions from the lamp-makers, gun-makers, silver workers, sawyers, wood turners, tin-plate workers, screw-makers, hinge-makers and others. The pawnbrokers were running out of money to lend.[45] These conditions were not confined to Birmingham, and extreme distress was also experienced in the Black Country. A slow improvement began in the second half of 1843, and the remaining years of the decade proved much more buoyant, with the exception of a setback in 1848. Thereafter the 1850s were years of industrial recovery and prosperity in trade, with a striking national increase in foreign trade to which Birmingham's brass manufactures made a substantial contribution.[46]

Nevertheless, when the period from 1815 to the 1840s is surveyed, the tone of contemporary comment on trading conditions in Birmingham is quite different from that of the years before the French wars. As noted earlier, it may be that the extent of trade depression during the war years was exaggerated because of the contrast with the prosperity of the preceding ten years of peace; and it is possible that reports of poor trading conditions from 1815 are similarly exaggerated and fail to give a fair overall impression of the state of trade. All the same, the contrast is very marked. On the other hand, it may be foolish to expect any lengthy period of prosperity in Birmingham trade after 1815, given the state of the national economy in the immediate post-war years and subsequently. Birmingham could hardly hope to escape the results of general depression in these years. Nevertheless, the population continued to expand in Birmingham in the first four decades of the nineteenth century, and increased by about two and a half times, compared with the national increase in England and Wales of about two-thirds, though the increase varied significantly in Birmingham from decade to decade, being less in 1811–21 and in 1831–41 than in 1821–31. (The figures are: 1811–21, an increase of 23.5 per cent; 1821–31, 37.3 per cent; and 1831–41, 27.3 per cent.) To judge by this crude indicator of economic activity, the 1820s in Birmingham are best described as a period of recovery after the war, while the 1830s are a decade in which there is again a falling-off in prosperity, especially from 1837 onwards.

Before concluding this chapter, something should be said about the service trades during and after the wars. Obviously they expanded as industry, trade, and the process of urbanization all developed together, though at a slower pace than before the wars. In the second half of the 1830s, a revolution in transport began with the opening in 1837 of the Birmingham to Liverpool railway line, and of the Birmingham to London line in the following year, but the full effect of these advances on trade and industry was not to be seen until the next decade and the coming of the railway mania of 1845–6. Although coach services to London were hit as early as 1839, canal companies continued in business for some time, often reducing their charges considerably. For example, the charge for carrying a ton of hardware from Birmingham to London by canal dropped from £3 in 1836 to £2 in 1842.[47]

As for the contribution of service trades to the Birmingham economy by 1840, there is again the problem of how to make any quantitative estimate; but there are several useful indications of their growth. In banking, for instance, there was considerable activity in the ten years after the 1826 Banking Act, four new banks being started and remaining in business (including a branch of the Bank of England in 1827), and a further three opened but later closed down.[48] Reference to the 1851 Census shows that service trades were still very prominent. Of these, domestic servants formed by far the largest group, numbering 8,359 in all, while there were 3,597 milliners and 2,009 tailors. These numbers may be compared with industrial occupations such as button-makers (4,980), brassfounders (4,914), labourers (3,909) and gunsmiths (2,867). It is clear that services employed substantial groups of workers other than those in the metal trades. Although it is difficult to say what proportion of the total work-force was taken by service trades in the 1840s, an estimate based on the 1861 Census returns twenty years later is that some 40 per cent of the working population were so engaged, that is, nearly 61,000 out of about 150,000 workers. Moreover, the wholesale and retail trade occupied nearly 20,000 men and women, which was about a third of all those in the service trades and 13 per cent of the total work-force.[49] The national figure for trade, transport, public services and professions as a percentage of the total occupied population in Great Britain in 1861 has been estimated at 38 per cent,[50] so that it seems likely that Birmingham resembled other large towns in this respect by this time.

Certainly, retail shops had spread throughout the town. According to an 1842 report: 'The more important retail shops are situated in New Street, High Street, Bull Street, and the Bull Ring, but there is scarcely a street in the town which does not contain retail shops of various descriptions.'[51] The smaller shops included many of great importance to the working classes, such as the so-called huckster shops, selling provisions in small quantities at inflated prices, and small cook-shops, providing dinners for workmen. There were 717 huckster shops in 1834, and a great number more by 1842.[52]

In tracing the growth of trade and services in Birmingham during the period 1750–1840 there remains much that is suppositional. This is partly due to the lack of figures on which to base generalizations, and partly to what seems to be the understandable tendency of contemporary observers to lay emphasis on bad rather than on good or satisfactory trading conditions. Times of moderate prosperity appear to attract less comment than times of depression. However, the broad outlines of development of trade and services in Birmingham remain tolerably clear. On the whole, they flourished in the period 1750–93, a period which constituted the great epoch of economic growth in Birmingham's history, particularly the years just before the war. During the war period they undoubtedly suffered – there is too much contemporary evidence for it to be otherwise –[53] and by then it is probably true that an increasing proportion of Birmingham trade was in overseas markets, itself a reason for the difficulties experienced towards the end of the wars. In the years of peace which followed, trade expanded further, but periods of real trading prosperity were limited in duration: there were lean years in 1825–6, and again in the late 1820s and early 1830s, but especially in the early 1840s – the so-called 'Hungry Forties'. All these patches of depressed trade coincided with periods of national depression, and it was not until the years of expansion of the 1850s that Birmingham trade appears to have experienced prosperity on the scale of the boom years before 1793.

PART 3

The People 1760–1840

5

The Entrepreneurs

In recent years historians have emphasized the importance of entrepreneurship during the Industrial Revolution, and have tried to
analyse the functions of the typical entrepreneur. In general terms he
has been defined simply as any person who undertakes an enterprise
for profit; but more specifically, he has been seen essentially as an
organizer. As Mantoux put it, he had to organize the different aspects
of a business undertaking, and he 'fulfilled in one person the functions
of capitalist, financier, works manager, and salesman'. Further, he
might find himself having to take on new functions, such as the
provision of local currency, shops, housing and schools. In this way,
he became 'a new pattern of the complete businessman'.[1] Attempts
have also been made to trace the social origins of eighteenth-century
entrepreneurs, and to investigate the contributions made by dissenting groups and by the so-called Protestant work-ethic to entrepreneurial success.[2]

How far did the business leaders of Birmingham conform to the
heroic image depicted by Mantoux and others? Certainly the City of
Birmingham has always had a reputation for producing vigorous
businessmen, some of them becoming national political figures in the
early nineteenth century, such as Thomas Attwood, the banker, and
later in the century the Chamberlain family. It will not be disputed
that the industrial and commercial successes of Birmingham during
the Industrial Revolution owed much to the initiative and drive of its
leading industrialists, factors, retailers and bankers; while in addition
there was a host of smaller entrepreneurs in the service trades and
industries, including all those providing professional services such as
lawyers, accountants and architects. Hutton's views as to the lively

and energetic atmosphere in Birmingham on his first visit in 1741 were quoted in chapter 1, and he believed strongly in the motivation supplied by profit-making: 'It is easy to give instances of people whose distinguishing characteristic was idleness, but when they breathed the air of Birmingham, diligence became the permanent feature. The view of profit, like the view of corn to the hungry horse, excites to action.'[3]

Certainly in Birmingham the middle years of the eighteenth century saw the emergence of a number of notable industrialists who acquired national renown. The biggest manufacturer at this time was John Taylor, with a works in the Dale End area producing principally gilt buttons and enamelled snuff boxes. Little is known of his origins (Professor Court has referred to him as 'the shadowy Taylor'), although Hutton says he was of humble birth. But there can be no doubt of the respect in which he was held. Boulton in 1767 called him 'our great manufacturer', while Hutton, writing six years or so after Taylor's death in 1775, lavished praise upon him:

> . . . the late John Taylor, Esq., who possessed the singular powers of perceiving things as they really were . . . him we may justly deem the Shakespear or Newton of his day. He rose from minute beginnings to shine in the commercial hemisphere, as they did in the poetical and philosophical. . . . To his uncommon genius we owe the gilt button, the japanned and gilt snuff boxes, and the numerous race of enamels.[4]

The comparison may seem a shade comical today, but in 1825 Drake also emphasized Taylor's shrewd eye for profit: 'No source of profitable speculation connected with ornamental manufacture seemed to escape his attention. He appeared to possess an inexhaustible invention, combined with the rare faculty of an almost intuitive perception of the final acceptableness of any novelty which struck his active mind.'[5]

Contemporary opinion therefore spoke highly of him, and visitors to Birmingham were taken to see his works as a matter of course. As already mentioned in chapter 1, he employed about 500 workers, and the reports of visitors always dwelt on the extreme division of labour which he displayed in the manufacture of buttons. It was said that his orders for buttons alone were worth £800 a week, and his best workmen painting snuff boxes could earn up to £3 10s weekly.[6] It is not surprising that a man with such a reputation for seizing business opportunities should have become interested in banking, and as we have seen in chapter 1, he joined with Sampson Lloyd II in founding Birmingham's first bank in 1765, Taylor & Lloyd.

Although Taylor was clearly the leader of the industrial community in Birmingham in his time, little else is known about him save that he died a very wealthy man.[7] It may fairly be claimed that he was an outstandingly successful entrepreneur, though as far as we know he did not provide amenities for his workers as did some of the more complete businessmen, the textile mill owners of the North; but then, he was not founding new industrial communities, as was the case with some of the rural cotton mill manufacturers in Lancashire. The roots of his success seem to lie partly in the division of labour and the use of an efficient hand technology, and partly in his eye for business, generally acknowledged to have been superb. Lack of information regarding his family background makes it difficult to say whether he is really an example of rags to riches, and today most historians are increasingly wary of the myth of the self-made man.[8] Nevertheless, if we are to believe Hutton, he had no social advantages in his birth, and presumably his capital came mostly from accumulated profits. Since he does not appear to have been a member of any of Birmingham's dissenting communities, it may be assumed that it was simply his native wit and intelligence which allowed him to forge ahead, rather than religious convictions or membership of a religious group.[9]

If John Taylor is a shadowy figure, the reverse may be said of Matthew Boulton, who is extremely well known through his association with James Watt and the fortunate preservation of their business archives. Chapter 1 has already given some incidental account of Boulton's earlier career before his partnership with Watt was formed in 1775, and his business life up to that time may first be briefly summarized.[10] Boulton was born in more comfortable circumstances than Taylor, going to school in Deritend and entering his father's toy business in Livery Street in 1743 at the age of seventeen. From this one would judge that there was no immediate necessity for him to start work at an early age, and that his life at this time was not attended by any hardship. In 1759 he inherited his father's business, and in 1762 the firm was extended when he entered into partnership with John Fothergill, each putting £5,000 into the new company. Shortly after this, Boulton drew up plans for a new and larger manufactory at Soho, some two miles from the city centre, where water from the Hockley brook could provide the water power unobtainable in Livery Street. These new works were planned to cost £2,000; by the time they were finished, the cost had risen to £10,000 – a somewhat extraordinary increase above the original estimate. Once completed, the Boulton & Fothergill Soho works immediately became an even greater tourist attraction than Taylor's famous works. Boulton claimed that he had created the largest manufactory in the world. *Swinney's Birmingham Directory* for 1775 described the new factory in a well-known passage:

> The building consists of four squares, with workshops, ware-houses, etc., for 1,000 workmen, who in a great variety of branches, excel in their several departments. . . . The number of ingenious mechanical contrivances they avail themselves of, by the means of water mills, much facilitate their work, and saves a great portion of time and labour.

In this earlier part of his career, Boulton acquired great fame as a leading and highly successful entrepreneur, rivalled only perhaps by Josiah Wedgwood. He shone especially as a publicist, promoter and salesman, making frequent visits to London and maintaining contacts with the royal family, the nobility and British ambassadors abroad. For clients on this distinguished level, he sought to gain a name as a maker of articles of artistic merit, often borrowing models from both the royal family and the aristocracy. Annual sales of his products were held in London at Christie's, and advertisements were placed in the London newspapers. Always interested in the sale of new products, he regularly bought new books of prints and engravings through his London bookseller, and he set up his own drawing school at Soho, introducing silver plating and ormolu work into the workshops. Yet at the same time he did not neglect the sale of goods of humbler quality, being well aware of the returns that could come from 'great quantities with small profits', as he put it. Not all of his ventures were successful, of course – the Eginton picture-copying process was dropped in 1780 – but as an active and vigorous salesman Boulton must rank high among the entrepreneurs of the Industrial Revolution.

However, in other directions Boulton's record is not quite so unsullied.[11] In addition to being a sales promoter, he had necessarily to be a capitalist and financier (to borrow Mantoux's phraseology), and also a works manager, for it was agreed between him and Fothergill that the running of the works should be his particular responsibility. As Fothergill put it, in the course of a somewhat heated exchange of views in May 1773: 'You undertook the entire management of the factory, it was your desire, it was your delight.' It is true that as a capitalist Boulton always seemed able to raise large sums of money. Both his first and second wives were co-heiresses, and each brought to the marriage (and to the firm) a fortune of £14,000. In 1767 he mortgaged his wife's property for £4,000, and in the mid-1770s he sold landed property to Lord Donegall for £15,000. Many other loans to help the firm were raised from time to time, both locally and in London, and even in Amsterdam. All in all, at least £60,000 was borrowed, loans often being short-term and secured by bills of exchange. However, the need for these frequent borrowings was brought about by the simple fact that in spite of the glittering façade provided by Boulton's activities, the firm of Boulton & Fothergill was often near to bankruptcy, and was encumbered throughout its life by the heavy running debt (£20,000 in 1773) known to the partners as the Bill Account. Things were so bad in 1778 that only a loan of £23,000 secured on the engine business saved the firm from financial ruin.

Thus, in the first half of his career Boulton often sailed perilously close to the wind as a financier. In his other role as works manager, he also ran into difficulties. This is hardly surprising, considering that by his own admission he spent up to half his time in London and elsewhere away from Birmingham. A crisis developed in 1773, when first Fothergill accused Boulton of mismanagement, referring pointedly to 'a want of proper economy and management at Soho', and (even more directly) to 'bad management at Soho'; then John Scale, who managed the works when Boulton was away, drew up a list of alleged weaknesses in the running of the factory. According to Scale, some £10,000 had been lost in the previous five years, due principally to a faulty system of pricing, and to paying so many workmen by the day rather than by the piece (that is, by results). The year 1773 was undoubtedly a bad year for the firm, although in the following years some moderate profits appear to have been made before Boulton dissolved the partnership at the end of 1781, but Boulton's failure to supervise the work closely enough seems evident in 1773 at least. It was not that he lacked ability as a manager, but that he failed to give sufficient time to it.

This less successful side to Boulton's earlier career has been overshadowed by the success which was achieved with the steam engine following the partnership with Watt begun in 1775. After the renewal of Watt's patent in that year for a further twenty-five years, the new firm enjoyed increasing sales of the new engine, though it was left to the purchasers themselves to assemble the engines; Boulton & Watt acted merely as consulting engineers, supplying plans and specialized parts from Soho, and usually requiring the employment of John Wilkinson, the Shropshire ironmaster, to supply the cylinder, which was bored to new standards of accuracy under Wilkinson's patent of 1774. In return for their services, Boulton & Watt asked for a third share of the savings in fuel resulting from the use of the new engine – an odd arrangement, which was changed in 1786 to a charge of £5 per horse power per annum.[12] By the end of the century, ample profits were being made, much of them being based initially on the erection of engines for pumping purposes in the Cornish tin mines, while the steam engines themselves were by this time manufactured by Boulton & Watt in the new foundry built at Soho and opened in 1796. Meanwhile, Boulton had become more and more interested in the minting of coins, at first supplying them to foreign governments and to the East India Company, and then to the British Government from 1797 onwards. Boulton died in 1809, leaving £150,000 – not an enormous sum, but then according to Watt he had always been more interested in fame than fortune, and fame he certainly achieved, especially through the marketing of the steam engine.[13]

Boulton was undoubtedly the most famous Birmingham entrepreneur of his day – so how may his career be summed up? His reputation as a brilliant salesman and publicist remains undiminished, and rightly so; and among his many attributes was the good mechanical sense which allowed him to see the potential in Watt's engine which could make for world-wide sales.[14] To an outstanding extent he did fulfil in one person all the classic functions of the entrepreneur of the Industrial Revolution – he was capitalist, financier, works manager, merchant and salesman. At the same time, he continued the paternalistic traditions of an earlier age: the Soho works contained accommodation for workmen (rent being deducted from wages), Christmas presents were given to all employees in 1799, and an insurance society was set up with payments to workmen or relatives in the event of sickness or death.[15] The weakness seems to have been in his earlier business years, with his constant resort to loans to keep Boulton & Fothergill going, and with his own shortcomings at times as works manager. His financial problems during the period before the marketing of the steam engine have led one historian to remark that it was only good fortune and a lucky gamble on the steam engine which saved him, rather than sound judgement; but this seems too severe a verdict. It might equally well be argued that it was his acute business acumen which allowed him to see the possibilities in Watt's invention. Indeed, it is worth reflecting that our assessment of Boulton's career is based on a far more detailed knowledge of his business transactions than is available for any of the other Birmingham entrepreneurs. If we knew more of the possible financial vicissitudes of John Taylor's earlier career, for instance, our final appraisal of him as an industrial tycoon might be marginally less favourable. When the two men are compared, it is hard to say who was the greater entrepreneur, particularly as Boulton was presented with opportunities, with the arrival of Watt in 1775, which were denied Taylor. It is enough to say that the two men are justly famed as the industrial leaders of the Birmingham of their day.[16]

As for the remaining early pioneers, among the best known is John Baskerville, who was born at Wolverley, near Kidderminster, and who seems at one time to have been footman to a clergyman in King's Norton, and in the 1720s to have been a writing master, opening a school in the Bull Ring.[17] Thus, his origins were modest, though clearly he had some education, and according to Hutton he was heir to a paternal estate of £60 per annum.[18] By 1740 he had turned to japanning, setting up a workshop in Moor Street, and in the words of the Birmingham historian Hawkes Smith, he brought about 'an entire revolution in japanning'. By 1745 he had prospered sufficiently to buy an estate of eight acres off Broad Street and Easy Row, later turning to the printing and typography for which he is famous. His first book was an edition of Virgil's *Aeneid* in 1757, and from 1758 to 1768 he was printer to the University of Cambridge, his greatest achievement being the production of the Cambridge Bible in 1763. The high quality of his paper, ink and binding, and the clarity of the type he designed have made his name outstanding in the history of typography, but of course he was not really a typical Birmingham entrepreneur. According to Hutton, he made little out of printing –'he possessed the least, but none of it squeezed from the press'. In fact, he left only a small estate when he died in 1775. Although so well known in one respect, clearly he does not rank in economic terms with either Taylor or Boulton. He appears to have had little obvious initial advantages save his native talent, and he was not connected with any religious group. Indeed, he seems to have been a person of marked individuality. Hutton says of him:

> If he exhibited a peevish temper, we may consider, good nature and intense thinking are not always found together. . . . His aversion to christianity would not suffer him to lie among christians; he therefore erected a mausoleum in his own grounds for his remains, and died without issue, in 1775, at the age of 69.[19]

Another successful industrialist of the earlier period is Henry Clay, though again little is known of his career in detail. He was apprenticed to Baskerville during the latter's earlier career as a japanner, and in 1772 took out a patent for the manufacture of a superior form of papier-mâché, from which a variety of goods was made – snuff boxes, buttons, tea trays, panels for coaches, even tables and chairs. According to Dent, he amassed a princely fortune, becoming High Sheriff of Warwickshire in 1790. Not much else is known about him, though all accounts emphasize that he made great profits, and that he resembled Boulton in having an eye to royal patronage, at one time presenting a sedan chair made of papier-mâché to Queen Caroline.[20]

There are other names which must figure in any shortlist of the early entrepreneurs of the Industrial Revolution period in Birmingham.[21] In 1738 John Wyatt, together with Lewis Paul, patented a machine for spinning with rollers. It had little success at the time, but was later adapted by Arkwright, who made a fortune from it. John Wyatt spent some time as a debtor in the Fleet Prison, although later on he was employed by Boulton. Another well-known name is that of Samuel Garbett, already mentioned in chapter 1 as a partner of John Roebuck. In addition to the Birmingham plant for the making of commercial sulphuric acid, a similar plant was set up at Prestonpans in 1749. Garbett seems to have begun adult life in Birmingham as a humble brass worker, having no education beyond writing and accounts. In 1760 he and Roebuck established the famous Carron Ironworks in Scotland, and by 1770 he was involved in four or five businesses in all. Like John Wyatt, Garbett became insolvent in 1772, ascribing his failure largely to 'external monetary influences', though it appears to have been caused by the incompetence of his son-in-law and partner. His misfortune did not affect his friendship with Boulton, or prevent him from playing a prominent part among Birmingham's business-men; in 1783 he became the first chairman of the Commercial Committee, and for twenty-eight years he was a Guardian of the Birmingham Assay Office. For many years he was regarded as the obvious leader in the town's affairs. James Keir was a rather more successful manufacturer of chemicals, setting up a works in Tipton making alkalis, soap, and white and red lead. He also managed the Soho works for a time, and had a financial interest in Watt's copying machine, a very successful piece of office equipment and an early example of business reprographics. At the same time Keir engaged actively in scientific research, and became a Fellow of the Royal Society. Lastly, the name of William Murdock, Boulton & Watt's manager in Cornwall, must be mentioned. Although not strictly speaking an independent entrepreneur, he played an important part in developing the steam engine, inventing the slide valve, and contributing to the invention by Watt of the sun and planet gear. He also designed one of the earliest steam locomotives, and was the first to use coal gas for lighting purposes, gas being used to light the Soho works by 1803. In addition, he employed compressed air in various ways, including the operation of machinery and of lifts. His own house had a door-bell worked by compressed air, together with hot-air central heating and, of course, gas lighting.

So much for the leading figures in the Birmingham economy in the early days of the Industrial Revolution; something must now be said of the great mass of smaller businessmen whose names are relatively unknown, although they played a vital part in the thriving economy of the time. The problem here is sheer lack of information beyond the oft-repeated belief that there were large numbers of small manufacturers in Birmingham. For example, it has already been pointed out in chapter 3 that in 1812 the important sector of Birmingham as a manufacturing town was composed of small manufacturers possessing from perhaps £300 or £400 up to £2,000, £3,000 or £4,000 capital, and employing from five to ten, twenty or thirty hands.[22] No doubt these figures should not be taken too literally, but the evidence provided by the Sun Insurance policies already discussed in earlier chapters certainly confirms the existence of many small industrialists and other entrepreneurs of modest means. This is well illustrated by the fact that in 1765, of the seventy-six policies issued to Birmingham insurers, forty-four (that is, over half) were for amounts of less than £500; thirty-three were for £300 or less, fifteen of these for £200, and four for only £100. As for the other sample period, 1777–86, over half the policies again were for amounts of under £500 (390 out of 693).[23] Thus, while previous references to these policies have been to the size and nature of the larger policies, and to their relevance to the trading and service sectors, in the present context it is illuminating to look at the other end of the scale, and to note how numerous the smaller policy holders were. For the earlier period, at least, they provide ample confirmation of the conventional view that at this stage Birmingham's economy was based on a multitude of small manufacturers and traders.[24]

What of the later entrepreneurs after 1800? It seems that Boulton had always envisaged the establishment of a foundry for the manufacture of steam engines; and a quarrel with Wilkinson, together with the approaching expiry of the patent on the engine in the mid-1790s, made it advisable to take action. When the Soho foundry was opened in 1796 it was under the supervision of Boulton's son, Matthew Robinson Boulton, and James Watt Jnr. From then on it was possible to construct engines at Soho rather than have them assembled on the site of the customer by his workmen, so that whereas the fathers had been consulting engineers, the sons actually organized the building of the machines in their own works. The result was the creation of the first engineering factory, with the workers mostly on piecework rather than sub-contract. Its efficiency was such that the organization of production, and the costing and pricing techniques employed, would still have been regarded as modern a hundred years later. If the fathers were responsible for the marketing of the Watt engine (and the supply of some essential parts), the sons must be credited with its highly efficient manufacture from 1796 onwards.[25]

About this time the name of Edward Thomason was becoming increasingly prominent in the button and toy trades. His father had been a buckle manufacturer in a very comfortable way of business, with a house in St Philip's Square, the workshops and warehouses being situated behind.[26] The father was a strong supporter of the Church of England and a leading figure in the business community, becoming High Bailiff of the town before retiring at sixty-two, so that his son took over the firm in 1793. Edward had been apprenticed to Boulton, and in many ways followed his example. According to *Edward Thomason's Memoirs*, he concentrated on gilt and plated buttons, later extending his range of goods to include gilt and gold jewellery, works in bronze, statuary, and silver and gold plate. A speciality of the firm was the manufacture of coins and medallions. For example, in 1812 two million penny tokens were struck for the British forces in Spain, while after the war, in 1820 forty-eight illustrations of the Elgin marbles were produced. Ten years later Thomason struck sixty medals on scriptural subjects which were sent to the sovereigns of Europe – all this highly reminiscent of Boulton's publicity methods. Thomason also became vice-consul in Birmingham for eight foreign governments. In 1818 he followed his father in becoming High Bailiff, and he was knighted in 1832, retiring in 1844 to Warwick where he died in 1849.

Three other names stand out among Birmingham industrialists in the first half of the nineteenth century. Joseph Gillott was born in Sheffield in 1799, reputedly of poor parents who apprenticed him to the cutlery trade.[27] Coming to Birmingham in search of work, he soon began to manufacture steel pens in a garret workshop in Broad Street, adapting a press for the purpose. From there he moved premises twice, finally building his own extensive factory in Graham Street – the first Birmingham building in the modern factory style, according to one authority, who also estimates that at the time of Gillott's death in 1873, his factory was producing nearly nine million pens per week.[28] He appears to have been a considerate employer, and apart from his fame as a manufacturer he had a reputation as a patron of the arts, and was a personal friend of Turner.

The second notable name is that of Josiah Mason, who similarly came from a humble background, being the son of a Kidderminster weaver.[29] After a variety of jobs Mason came to Birmingham, at first working for his uncle and then entering into partnership with one Harrison, a manufacturer of split rings. After a while Mason purchased Harrison's share of the business, and in 1829 began making steel nibs for the London pen manufacturer, Perry. The manufacture of these steel nibs became very successful, though they were always marketed under Perry's name. Mason was later knighted, and he became the founder of Mason College, which at the end of the century received a charter as the University of Birmingham.

Lastly, the name of George Frederick Muntz must be included, though he is perhaps better known in the political history of Birmingham than in its economic history.[30] His father was a merchant in Amsterdam, and on his death in 1811 George took control of the offices in Great Charles Street and the rolling mills in Water Street. The invention of Muntz's metal, an alloy which was much cheaper than copper for the sheathing of ships' bottoms, made him a very wealthy man, the business bringing him 'a colossal fortune' according to a later account,[31] so that he could devote himself to politics.

To turn again to the smaller manufacturers in the latter part of the period under review, there is not a great deal to add to what has been said before except to repeat that contemporary opinion was unanimous that there were still very large numbers of small firms in Birmingham about 1840. The reasons for this are simple enough. In the metal trades the capital requirements for setting up a business were small – reference has already been made to the fact that in the jewellery trade all that a workman needed to set up on his own was a bench, an apron, his tools, and a few sovereigns and some ounces of copper and zinc for materials.[32] Again, small workshops could easily be rented, and steam power could be shared, if required. Second-hand machinery, such as stamps and presses, could also be bought cheaply, especially in times of depression. As a result, there was a marked degree of mobility between the ranks of the skilled workmen and the numerous small masters. Indeed, it was even suggested in 1812 that when trade was depressed, an unemployed workman might choose to set up his own firm as an alternative to going to the Poor Law authorities for relief. A similar claim was made in 1833 that some workmen might be obliged to set up on their own because of the retirement or failure of their employers, or because they had been dismissed, whereupon they might find themselves worse off than before, and obliged to give up.[33] Whatever the truth of this, it is clear that setting up independently was a very common phenomenon in Birmingham, and many of the myriads of smaller manufacturers must have come from the ranks of the skilled working men. It is less likely, for obvious reasons, that the unskilled labouring classes would have supplied many entrepreneurs in the metal trades.

The ease of transition from artisan to small master is sometimes put forward as one reason for the existence of relatively good labour relations in Birmingham, it being argued that the employer who had worked at the same bench as his workmen was much more aware of his men's needs and attitudes than the proprietor of a large factory. Labour relations will be examined again in later chapters, but it is convenient to remark here on the survival of paternalistic attitudes in Birmingham throughout the later eighteenth century and the first half of the nineteenth century. This is not to suggest that relations between employers and workpeople were always amicable, of course, but it is true that many employers took the view that some degree of consideration for their hands was not only right and proper in itself, but was also justified as a means of maintaining a good level of production. A number of employers expressed views of this sort before the Children's Employment Commission in 1842. Thus, it was reported of Mr William Elliott, a button manufacturer employing about 500 workers: 'Has paid considerable attention to the habits and conditions of mechanics. Has found that consideration and attention to the welfare and happiness of the workpeople has produced the best results. Decidedly thinks that the people are quite conscious of such attention, and grateful for it.'[34] Another employer, Mr John Bourne, the proprietor of a cabinet brassfoundry, made the same point: 'Has found, in the thirty years since he has been in business, that by conciliatory conduct and kind treatment, the men become attached to their employer. Many of them have worked here from 15 to 30 years; several have their children now employed.'[35]

Annual dinners, trips and treats, feasts on the coming of age of the employer's eldest son, celebrations on the completion of apprenticeship, were therefore common. By the 1840s the gipsy party had become very popular – a works outing organized by the firm to a local beauty spot. Among the first of these parties was an excursion organized by Joseph Gillott, the pen-maker, in 1845. Naturally, it is possible to regard all such expressions of goodwill merely as a form of social control, a way of keeping the workers docile and contented, but this would be to ignore the strength of traditional paternalism inherited from earlier times, and reinforced by the 1840s by evangelical beliefs which were strong among the employers. These beliefs, with their emphasis on good conduct at work – for example, the prohibition of drinking, smoking or swearing on the premises – might have been oppressive to the average workman, but they were clearly preferable to the harshness and brutality displayed by some employers. Even though some allowance must be made for a possible degree of hypocrisy and sanctimoniousness among the employers giving evidence before the Children's Employment Commission in 1842, a number of them went beyond pious statements of good intentions by positive action such as the establishment of sick clubs, contributions to church building, and teaching in Sunday school. Mr James Gardiner, foreman to Mr Elliott, the button-maker, over a period of nineteen years, said in evidence that the workpeople benefited greatly from the sick club, which in the previous year had paid out £83 16s to sick members, and on the last day of the year had paid a dividend of 6½d in the shilling to the contributors; one advantage of this was that it provided a fund sufficient to keep the workpeople going over Christmas during stocktaking, when the works were closed.[36] Further, it has been suggested that by the middle of the century, the old-style paternalism was changing into a new form of paternalism which emphasized the moral equality of master and man, whereas previously there had been a far greater assumption that the workman was morally inferior.[37] Whether the growth of evangelical belief really had this effect or not is hard to say, but it seems clear enough that some of the larger Birmingham entrepreneurs of the period 1760–1840 maintained paternalistic attitudes to a marked degree. There is less evidence of paternalism among the smaller employers who enjoyed fewer resources, but even here, annual trips and jaunts were still very common.

If co-operation between employers and the work-force was considered desirable, so was united action among the employers themselves. Many examples of this can be seen throughout the period. From time to time employers would come together to announce changes in wages or prices, e.g. in 1759 the gun-lock makers agreed to lower wages, while in 1780 the brassfounders put up the price of their goods by 7½ per cent.[38] More formal co-operation is seen in the setting up of the Birmingham Metal Company in 1781 by the brass-makers, and the Birmingham Mining and Copper Company in 1790, as noted in chapter 3. Close relations were maintained with the House of Commons, with representatives of the manufacturers appearing before Committees of the House in 1759, again in 1799, and especially in 1812, when strong represent-ations were made against the Orders in Council – with some success, in that the Orders were afterwards modified by the Government. Nor were the manufacturers slow in promoting legislation in their own interest, as in the passing of the Assay Act, 1773, setting up assay offices for silver goods in both Birmingham and Sheffield, and in the passing of the Public Proof House Act, 1813. They were also active in another direction with the appointment of the Commercial Committee in 1783, originally established to oppose a Bill permit-ting the export of brass, and already discussed in the previous chapter. It was noted there that the Committee became associated with the national General Chamber of Manufacturers; in 1785 it approached the Government over Pitt's Irish trade proposals, and it did so again in 1786 over the Eden Treaty with France. The chairman, Samuel Garbett, was assisted by an executive committee of twelve members. In 1813 it merged with the Birmingham Chamber of Commerce which was founded in that year.[39]

As might be expected, Birmingham entrepreneurs also participated fully in the government of the town.[40] Since it lacked a charter, the system of local government in Birmingham was rudimentary in the extreme until the 1760s. Up to then, the sole form of government was the ancient manorial court, with high and low bailiffs, high and low ale tasters, leather searchers, constables and headboroughs (assistant constables). The powers of all these officials were falling into disuse by the mid-eighteenth century. The rapid growth of the town made the creation of some other form of authority increasingly urgent, so that in 1769 the first Improvement Act (the Lamp Act) appointed fifty commissioners with powers to keep the streets clear and clean, to remove obstructions, and to widen the streets and light them. Among the first commissioners were a number of famous names – Dr Small, Baskerville, Galton, Taylor and Sampson Lloyd. The second Act, 1773, appointed twenty-nine new commissioners, including Hutton, and there were further acts conferring additional powers in 1801, 1812 and 1828. The commissioners continued to exercise their powers right up to 1850, though by that time the town had gained its first two MPs following the passing of the 1832 Reform Act (Attwood the banker, and Joshua Scholefield the manufacturer). Later in 1838 advantage was taken of the powers available under the Municipal Corporation Act, 1835, and the town at last obtained a charter and became incorporated. This participation in local government was not entirely altruistic in nature: the commissioners took the view that it was essential to keep the traffic flowing and have the main thoroughfares well-lit in the interests of trade and industry. By the 1801 Act, for example, the Bull Ring was cleared, and the general market moved there from the High Street in 1806. Again, the 1828 Act gave power to remove 300 houses in thirty-four streets in order to improve communications. Thus, although from the 1812 Act onwards the commissioners were in effect the town's first public health authorities, in practice they were more concerned to improve trading and industrial conditions than to begin the public health reforms which were to become increasingly necessary as the town continued to expand.[41]

At this point we may attempt to sum up the characteristics of the leading entrepreneurs of Birmingham during the Industrial Revolution. It seems tolerably clear that their social origins give little support to earlier beliefs that the Industrial Revolution was brought about largely through the efforts of self-made men. It has been estimated recently that only about 10 per cent of industrialists of the time came from the working classes, and most of these were from the skilled working classes.[42] In Birmingham, relatively few of the leaders had working-class origins – Taylor might perhaps fall into this category, and possibly Clay and Garbett, but Baskerville with his inheritance from his father is only marginally classified as working class, while Fothergill, Boulton, Roebuck and Keir obviously were not. In the early nineteenth century, Matthew Robinson Boulton, James Watt Jnr and Edward Thomason all had a good start in life, though Gillott and Mason came from more humble backgrounds. Thus, only a minority of the leaders may be considered working class in origin, and the majority may be categorized as middle class or lower middle class. For these men, social mobility appears to have operated for the most part within the broad conventional classes rather than from one class to another.[43] However, it may be otherwise when one shifts attention from the leaders to the multitude of small masters in Birmingham who came from the lower ranks and whose social position rests uneasily on the borderline between the working classes and the middle classes – a kind of middling class whose existence shows up the inadequacy of the customary three-tier class model of society.[44]

Closely associated with the question of social origins is the problem of the provision of capital. It is worth stating again that very little starting capital was required in the metal trades, and thereafter additional capital from outside the business appears to have been readily available in the form of loans from family, business associates or banks – that is, if Boulton's activities are anything to go by. In practice the small amount of capital required in most trades meant that shortage of capital seems rarely to have been a problem; as the business grew, profits would have been ploughed back to aid further expansion. Having classified the wealth of Birmingham's principal inhabitants as it stood on 10 December 1783, Hutton goes on to remark: 'Out of the 209, 103 began the world with nothing but their own prudence. 35 more had fortunes added to their prudence, but too small to be brought into account; and 71 persons were favoured with a larger, which, in many instances is much improved.'[45] Boulton himself said before a committee of the House of Commons in 1799 that all the great manufacturers he had ever known had begun the world with very little capital.[46] Presumably he would have regarded himself as a great manufacturer, though he had the advantage of inheriting his father's business, and so in his turn, did his son. Here it would appear that if so little starting capital was needed, it is surprising that not more of the leaders in industry were from the working class. However, allowance must be made for the fact that Hutton's figures were guesswork, albeit shrewd guesswork. As he put it, not altogether convincingly:

> Some may ask, 'How came you to know what property the inhabitants are possessed of; they never told you?' I answer, the man long accustomed to shoot with a gun, cannot be a bad shooter; he will sometimes hit the mark, seldom be far from it. The man who has guessed for thirty years, cannot be a bad guesser.[47]

His logic is open to question, to say the least. Again, Boulton did not specify how little is 'very little capital'. One can only conclude that it was fashionable to argue that all that was required to rise in the world was hard work and determination, and that the idea was not without foundation in Birmingham, but that the advantage still lay with those who had a comfortable amount of capital to start with, and existing trade and family connections.

If the leading entrepreneurs were mostly lower middle class in origin, it follows that most of them were men of some education – Boulton was well-read, and so was Fothergill, while Keir was a graduate of Edinburgh University. Watt was an inventor rather than an entrepreneur, but he was a skilled instrument-maker, and his inventive genuis was such that he was elected to the Fellowship of the Royal Society. The extent of the intellectual interests of these men is seen in the regular meetings of the famous Lunar Society, founded in 1766.[48] Members of this society met monthly on the day of the full moon (to expedite the return journey home at night), and after dining together in the afternoon, would read and discuss papers on a variety of topics, often scientific in nature. With a membership of about a dozen, over half the members were Fellows of the Royal Society. Those attending included Boulton, Watt, Murdock, Keir, Baskerville, Samuel Galton (the gun-maker), Dr Erasmus Darwin, Dr William Small (another Edinburgh graduate), and the most eminent thinker of them all, Dr Joseph Priestley, the scientist and Unitarian minister of the New Meeting Church. It is clear that the most famous of the Birmingham industrialists in the second half of the eighteenth century were no uncouth mechanicals, but men of some culture and vision. Of the lesser manufacturers, not enough is known to generalize about their educational and cultural backgrounds, but the existence of a surprising amount of middle-class cultural activity in the town (see chapter 8) indicates that the middle ranks at least of the industrialists were not without some elements of refinement and cultural attainments.

There is one other comment to be made about Birmingham entrepreneurs. Dissenters were to be found among them – Lloyd the banker and Samuel Galton the gun-maker come to mind as well-known Quakers, while the pin-makers Ryland and Phipson were Unitarians – but there is nothing to show that Dissenters formed a significantly large proportion of Birmingham industrialists and businessmen. In 1851 almost half the church-goers were Anglican (a markedly higher proportion than in Leeds or Manchester), and the proportion of Non-conformists in the population of the town as a whole was not noticeably higher than in other large towns.[49] Further, it cannot always be assumed that because a manufacturer was a member of a Dissenting community, he would always be on cordial terms with his co-religionists who would be helpful to him in business. Samuel Galton's activities as a gun-maker drew criticism from his fellow Quakers, and at one time he was barred from attending Meeting. On the other hand, a good proportion of the membership of the two leading Old Dissent congregations at the New Meeting (Presbyterian, later Unitarian) and Bull Street (Quaker) were engaged in either medium-scale or small-scale industrial enterprise. For 1751–5 the numbers so engaged at the New Meeting were 37 per cent of the whole membership, for 1781–5, 42 per cent, and for 1811–15, 46 per cent. The figures for the Bull Street Quakers were: 1751–5, 47 per cent; 1781–5, 56 per cent; and 1811–15, 41 per cent. This is only to confirm the general impression that these Old Dissent communities were actively engaged in industry, though the figures for the Cannon Street Baptists are less impressive – for 1781–5, 11 per cent, and for 1811–15, 18 per cent.[50] There is no indication that Calvinism was a particular driving force for business success, and in fact it is not unlikely that if details were available of the proportion of Anglican and Methodist worshippers who were engaged in industry they would not be very different from the figures already given for Old Dissent. Indeed, evangelicanism influenced both Anglicans and Nonconformists in the 1840s,[51] and this factor alone might have increased the earnestness with which industrial success was pursued. As we have seen, it certainly seems to have contributed to the pious paternalism of some employers at this time. All in all, it would be unwise to attribute too much of the zeal of Birmingham entrepreneurs in the period 1760–1840 to religious conviction. It played its part, but was hardly a prime driving force. Hutton's 'view of Profit' probably supplied the stronger motivation here.[52]

All the same, Birmingham's pioneer entrepreneurs of the Industrial Revolution were very far from the modern image of the entrepreneur as a mere financier or manipulator of stocks and shares whose main interest is simply profit. The modern world of takeover bids and asset-stripping lay a long way ahead in the future. Most of the leading Birmingham men discussed in this chapter were at least technically competent, some were actually inventors, while many of them, such as Taylor, Boulton, Clay, Baskerville and Thomason, were innovators. They took pride in their products and had the keenest of eyes for market possibilities – Boulton and Thomason were outstanding in this respect in the attention they paid to contacts in the highest circles of society, both in this country and abroad. Finally, their active involvement in both their own enterprises and in the general business life of the community provides a fascinating glimpse of energetic entrepreneurship in an age of expanding opportunities before the coming of more easily obtainable limited liability, and the development of the larger industrial unit on a far greater scale after 1850. Up to that time, at least, the Birmingham entrepreneur still exhibited many of the characteristics of the eighteenth-century merchant and businessman, especially his lively enterprise and eye for profit, but still tempered in many ways with a concern for those whom he employed.

6

Working Conditions

In an earlier, brief discussion of working conditions in Birmingham in the mid-eighteenth century (see chapter 1), it was emphasized that flexibility of hours was the accepted pattern at that time. Since payment was usually by results, the workman could vary his daily labour to suit himself. Monday was often a day of rest, with longer hours being worked towards the end of the week. No doubt the weekly total of hours worked still left only limited time for leisure, and the need to earn a living wage must have imposed severe limitations on the apparent freedom of choice of hours. All the same, the traditional Monday off, the keeping of customary holidays and the rise and fall of demand in the market all made for a working week which must have varied considerably throughout the year.

With the coming of the factory system in England towards the end of the eighteenth century, a new work discipline began to evolve in the textile industry which placed emphasis on regular attendance at work, strict attention to time-keeping and uniform hours of labour from one week to the next. Workmen were encouraged to keep set hours by bonus schemes and other inducements, and were liable to dismissal or fines for breaches of factory rules.[1] The need to impose a new, time-orientated work discipline on raw recruits from the countryside led to great efforts to condition their attitude to work. In a (by now) well-known passage, E. P. Thompson maintains that 'by the division of labour; the supervision of labour; fines; bells and clocks; money incentives; preachings and schoolings; the suppression of fairs and sport – new labour habits were formed, and a new time discipline was imposed.'[2] Thompson stresses not only the strict regulation of working practices, but also the inculcation of a new work-ethic and a cutting down of leisure activities in the interest of fostering new attitudes to work.

All this applies particularly to work in the textile factory, and it is true that the growth of the brass industry in Birmingham led to the establishment of large foundries where working routines were inevitably different from working conditions in garret workshops. However, as was seen in chapter 3, the typical place of work in Birmingham during the Industrial Revolution was still a workshop, not a factory, and the use of steam power was still on a minor scale up to the 1830s (see chapter 2). The question therefore arises, how far were factory routines adopted in Birmingham workshops? Did working hours increase? Were holidays reduced in number? Even if steam power was not extensively used, it is still possible that even in the smaller workshops a greater regularity of work might have developed in conformity with a national trend in this direction. In theory, the use of a more sophisticated hand technology could lead to changes in work routines, or again, a more aggressive attitude on the part of employers might lead to a weakening of traditional work practices and to an intensification of work discipline. All these are possibilities, though it is perhaps the wider use of steam-driven machinery which has the most serious implications for the survival of eighteenth-century practices and for their replacement by the factory system.

Just how far factory discipline was adopted in the larger workplaces in Birmingham is impossible to determine with any certainty. Admittedly the principle of the division of labour was applied in the biggest button factories where the making of buttons was broken down into many different and separate operations (see chapter 1). It was in these workplaces that large numbers of women and children were employed; by analogy with the textile mills, it is here that the severest work discipline might be expected. Yet there is little in the reports of the Factory Enquiry Commission (1833) to suggest that working conditions in the larger establishments were unduly harsh. In fact, there was said to be no works in Birmingham where children were collected to work together in large numbers, a very large proportion of the work being paid for by the piece and given out to be carried out in the homes of work people. The one exception cited was the pin factory of Richard Phipson, where 130 children were employed, a greater number than the commissioners had heard of elsewhere in Birmingham. Here there was some conflict of opinion regarding punishment of the children, one ex-employee of the firm saying that the children were punished 'not severely, but by a cane, and sometimes from a fool's cap', while the owner claimed strongly that corporal punishment by the overlookers was not permitted and that he would not suffer it. The report itself merely comments on the fact that 'the premises are somewhat confined, and the children seem to us to be too much crowded together'.[3] The next largest group of children, at Thomas Ledsam & Sons, numbered eighty-seven out of a total work-force of 318. Smaller numbers of children were to be found in other larger firms, for example, a Mr Jenkins, a brassfounder, employed about 250 hands, of whom about thirty were children under fourteen, none being under nine years of age.[4]

Ten years later in a longer and more detailed report by the Children's Employment Commission, it was affirmed that there were no large and crowded factories in Birmingham such as abounded in the cotton districts.[5] Only two firms – those of Phipson and of Palmer & Holt – were criticized for ill-treating children, but these were 'strikingly opposed to the general good usage of children in Birmingham'.[6] However, many of the children were in a deplorable condition, and seemed not to have had enough to eat, perhaps because of the severe depression in trade of the time.[7] It still appears that with the exceptions already noted, the work discipline in the larger workplaces in Birmingham in the 1830s and 1840s was not as harsh as in the textile mills of the time which gave rise to the Factory Acts of 1833, 1844 and 1847. Probably there was little basic difference between the working conditions of children at this time and those of children helping to operate stamps in the mid-eighteenth century.

Nor is there any evidence to show that the hours worked by either children or adults had lengthened drastically since the mid-eighteenth century. In 1833 John Blews, a small manufacturer of locks and iron candlesticks, gave evidence that there was 'a general rule in Birmingham laid down that we work but 10 hours: it is a regular understanding when we go into a manufactory not to work more than 10 hours'.[8] In the larger establishments the working day was usually one of twelve hours less two hours for meals. There were many variations of this. For example, the manager of Thomas Ledsam & Sons, John Sexty, stated that their hours were 8 a.m. to 7 p.m. in winter, with 1¾ hours off, and in summer 7 a.m. to 7 p.m. with 2¾ hours off. Phipson's hours were 8 a.m. to 7 p.m., less 1½ hours for meals. On the basis of evidence of this kind, the commissioners of the

1833 enquiry concluded that the working hours of children in Birmingham did not exceed ten, though they had heard that children sometimes worked longer in the homes of their parents.[9]

By 1843 there was again little change. It was said that the average age of children for starting work was either nine or ten, and the hours of work were generally the same. According to the commissioner, R. D. Grainger, these hours

> are generally moderate in Birmingham, the common hours being 12, out of which 2 are usually deducted for meals, so the actual time of labour is 10 hours: this may be considered the rule. In some manufactories 13 hours are the regular time . . . on the whole, it may be stated that the hours of labour are probably shorter and less fatiguing than in any other large manufacturing town in the kingdom.[10]

Although this seems a fair general statement on the basis of the oral evidence given before the commission, it must be said that the condition of the women and children in particular workshops was strongly criticized. Grainger thought that the work undertaken by women was sometimes too heavy for them:

> I saw, in some manufactories, women employed in most laborious work, such as stamping buttons and brass nails and notching the heads of screws: these are certainly unfit occupations for women. In screw manufactories the females constitute from 80 to 90 per cent of the whole number employed.[11]

There are repeated references to the ill-effects within the home of so many women being employed, often in place of the labour of men. The strongest remarks to this effect were contained in a long written statement by a witness, Mr Joseph Corbett, a mechanic, whose mother had eleven children, but who still continued at work:

> As the family increased, so anything like comfort disappeared altogether. Poor thing, the power to make home cheerful and comfortable was never given to her . . . not one moment's happiness did I ever see under my father's roof. All this dismal state of things I can distinctly trace to the entire and perfect absence of all training and instruction to my mother.[12]

Certainly there was much prejudice against the married woman with a family continuing at work, even though the practice does not appear to have been very widespread in other districts.[13]

As for Grainger's statement that the average age of starting work for children was either nine or ten, there are plenty of exceptions to this in the oral evidence of witnesses and at least one direct statement to the contrary in Theophilus Richards' Report on Apprenticeship, where it is said that 'great numbers' began work at seven or eight.[14] If this is so, then it certainly limits the time which could be given to full-time schooling. Apprenticeship commonly began at fourteen, and has already been discussed in chapter 3. There is nothing to show that apprentices were more ill-used than other non-apprenticed children, unlike their counterparts in the early cotton mills. Again, although as we have seen, Grainger claimed that children in Birmingham were generally well-used with respect to being beaten, and that the children in Phipson's and in Palmer & Holt's were an exception to this, in fact, witnesses in several cases testified to the employment of women with a stick to beat children when they became sleepy and slowed down in the evening. This was a practice well-known and deplored in the textile factories.

How far children were treated really cruelly in some of the workshops is difficult to ascertain. The overlooker at Phipson's, Elizabeth Dace, who had occupied that position for sixteen years, was reported as saying that

> If the work is not done properly, she gives the child a 'tap' with the cane on the back; has never struck a child over the head or face. If the work is getting slack, the cane, held in the hand, is as good to keep them on as if used. Has seen Mr Field strike the children with the cane, but not so as to hurt them so as to make wounds.[15]

Evidently the taps administered by Elizabeth Dace were substantial enough, for the porter at the works gave evidence that he 'Often hears the children crying; has once or twice heard 2 or 3 at a time. Thinks there is more crying out at night than in the daytime. Has never known a child laid up from being beat.'[16]

The worst working conditions for children all round seemed to have been at Palmer & Holt's, Lancaster Street. There was only one small fireplace with a small fire in it, so that the children complained greatly of being cold, the one privy for the forty or fifty children was in a most disgraceful state ('loaded with excrement in all directions'), the master kept the time by an hour-glass ('evidentially a most objectionable plan, and liable to abuse'), while there had been much cruel treatment of the children in the past. The methods of former supervisors were vividly described by Sarah Clarke, aged twenty-one, according to Grainger, 'a very kind-hearted young woman and deserves great credit for her humanity':

> A former overlooker of this manufactory, Satchwell by name, has taken witness, then a child, by the hair and beat her with his fists on the head. This man did not use a cane but a strap; has seen him fetch blood 'by using weapons' such as a file or anything which came near him. Has herself many times been beaten till the blood came. Satchwell is a very violent man.[17]

Another witness, Elizabeth Wooldridge:

> Has herself been severely beaten by Satchwell, so that the blood ran down her back. On one occasion, when he was beating her over the head, a long pin shank was driven into the skin so deeply that the pincers were used to extract it. Thinks that Bramer, another master here, was worse than Satchwell; he was a very savage person.[18]

This was confirmed by a young man, Edward Boden, who had become a police constable, who said of Bramer that 'He was very much given to passion, and was in the habit of beating the children over the head and shoulders, not caring where he struck with the cane.' Boden's wife Mary said that she had seen Bramer strike a child with the handle of a hammer, and in his passion had seen him hit children on the head. Both Bramer and Satchwell cut children's heads badly enough as to make them bleed.[19]

Certainly children were to be found almost everywhere in the workshops: in the horn button trade, one man required as many as three boys, while in metal button-making, stampers needed boys to arrange the buttons into *rouleaux* for stamping (called 'cobbing'). In brass-casting each adult required a boy, and in gun-making boys were employed as a means of communication between makers of different parts. The worst job of all for children appears to have been pin-heading (as at both Phipson's and Palmer & Holt's), where only children of the very poorest were employed. Pin-makers were regarded as the most wretched part of the population, no decent mechanic (it was said) allowing his children to go to this work. Mr Phipson himself described pin-heading as 'the refuge for the destitute'. According to Grainger: 'In the whole of my enquiries, I have met with no class more urgently requiring legislative protection than the unhappy pin-headers.'[20]

One other general comment must be made on working hours: that the evidence available may not always be very trustworthy, given the fact that much of it comes from employers and middle-class observers, who might have thought it wise to understate the hours actually worked. Nevertheless, there seems no reason to suppose that deliberately false or misleading information was given either in 1833 or in 1843, or that the commissioners were deceived by it. A twelve-hour day was considered normal at this time in the Black Country, and there is a good deal of evidence given by working-class eye-witnesses to support this in the 1840s.

To turn to practical considerations: it could be argued, of course, that although there was general agreement as to the normal length of the working day in the 1840s, in practice the employer could adjust hours as he thought fit because recalcitrant workmen could be disciplined under the Master and Servant Acts. Under these acts any workman failing to complete his work satisfactorily could be prosecuted and sent to prison, being in breach of his contract of employment. Thus, Julius Harvey, the button-maker, when given (as he put it) 'a good deal of trouble' by one of his workmen, Thomas Winwood, took out a warrant and had him 'lodged in the dungeon' overnight before being brought before the magistrate. Ultimately Winwood had to pay four guineas legal costs, which Harvey hoped would teach him a lesson.[21] Thus it was not merely that the employer had the right to hire or fire employees, but he could also threaten them with fine or imprisonment. On the other hand, the more benevolent employer would not wish to antagonize his work-force by taking too severe action. This was not merely one aspect of the traditional paternalism discussed in the last chapter, but also a practical matter of retaining good and reliable workmen. Boulton provides a good illustration of this. On being advised in 1768 by a well-meaning correspondent to reduce his financial commitments and to do less business, he retorted: 'I cannot say to the workmen, go your ways and come again twelve months hence', and went on to point out that he had been 'to no small trouble to collect such a set of work people'. Sensible employers knew they could not afford to play fast and loose with skilled workmen.[22]

Moreover, any manufacturer who wished to maintain good relations with his workmen would be aware of the existence of workshop practices and traditions which it would be foolish to challenge without good cause. Workers kept their own workshop discipline, not only on the bench itself, but also in such ritual practices as footales, when an apprentice finished his time, or the punishing of scabs. An employer would be ill-advised to try to change long-standing work practices without first consulting his men.[23] For their part, workmen had a number of means of opposing unacceptable changes proposed by their employer. The first, presumably applied only when personal relations had become very strained, would be intimidation of the employer by threats of physical violence to his person or property. For example, a threat printed in the *Birmingham Journal*, edited by R. K. Douglas, a strong supporter of the Birmingham Political Union, ran as follows:

> I believe you are going to turn your men out next Saturday but we will murder you. We have a plan to work upon that can blow your bloody branes out and it shall be done there is twenty of us united together and we shall catch you on the bonce. I thought I would let you know because you will know what it is for.
>
> One of the Witfield men.[24]

The second and more important method of opposing change in the workshop was by calling the men out on strike. Striking was not in itself illegal but forming a combination or union was illegal between 1799 and 1824, and even after 1824 men forming a union and going on strike might be prosecuted either under the Master and Servant Acts, already mentioned, or under the law of conspiracy. In spite of this, combinations or trade clubs were frequently formed, sometimes under the guise of friendly societies aiming to insure workers against sickness or unemployment. Although Birmingham had a reputation for good labour relations, in the first half of the nineteenth century strikes might be of considerable length, for example, seventy platers struck for three months in 1826, the Brass Cockfounders Society for fifteen weeks in 1840 and the Edge Tools Friendly Society for ten weeks, also in 1840.[25]

As for the frequency with which strikes occurred, it is impossible to obtain precise figures for the first half of the nineteenth century, let alone the period 1760–1840 as a whole, but in the period after the Napoleonic Wars they tended to occur more frequently in times of prosperity than in times of depression (which is usually the case). Thus, there were at least ten strikes in the years 1824–6, eighteen in

1833–5, and thirty-one in the years of recovery, 1845–8. These numbers do not seem unduly large, and some increase in numbers might be anticipated as the work-force continued to grow in size during the first half of the century. There might also have been some increase in militancy as a consequence of Chartist activity. At all events, the total of strikes for the fifty years 1800–50 is at least 103, and for individuals prosecuted in the course of trade disputes, 135.[26] These figures are minimum figures – not all strikes were reported in the press – but as they stand, they appear remarkably small; an average of two strikes a year (or even half a dozen from the 1820s onwards) in an industrial town of nearly a quarter of a million inhabitants by 1851 scarcely indicates a labour sector torn apart by continual disputes. It therefore seems that although Birmingham workers certainly had recourse to strikes during the first half of the nineteenth century (and this in itself indicates the existence of trade union activity),[27] they do not appear very significant over the period as a whole, and Birmingham's reputation for good labour relations remains largely unaffected up until 1850.

To what extent had the irregular hours of the eighteenth century been replaced by 1840 by a more uniform six-day week? For those who worked in the bigger establishments it seems likely that Monday was much more of a working day than it had been before, though not invariably so. In the smaller workshops, St Monday was still observed, long after 1840. By the 1860s there was increasing criticism of this survival of a traditional day of leisure. It was said that an enormous amount of time was lost not only by want of punctuality in coming to work in the morning and beginning again after meals, but also by St Monday: 'a licence which is often extended to part of Tuesday also'. A visiting commissioner of the Children's Employment Commission (1862), Mr J. E. White, commented that 'individual efforts are, as a rule, powerless to abolish this wasteful and injurious habit'.[28] St Monday might still be observed in the 1860s even in the larger works. Mr White said that one employer in 1864 had only about forty or fifty workers in on a Monday out of a total work-force of 300 to 400, and on Mondays few works were fully or even very partially employed. In one large foundry the casters were getting to work for the first time in the week towards midday on Tuesday. The employers complained greatly of this.[29]

Even when allowance is made for possible prejudice against the keeping of St Monday on the part of the commissioners and of those witnesses who were employers (and hence a tendency to exaggerate its prevalence), it is clear that Monday was still a holiday for many Birmingham workers up to the mid-century and even beyond.[30] It could be, of course, that other holidays had been cut down by the 1840s, so that there were fewer interruptions in the year's routine. Even if this were so, the larger firms closed for a week or fortnight at Christmas to take stock, just as they had in Boulton's time, and one or two days were also given at Easter and at Whitsuntide. The same time off was often allowed at some of the fairs or wakes.[31] In the 1860s Mr White thought the actual holidays were ample, whether allowed or not. In addition to St Monday, there were local fêtes and the annual works outings to Malvern or elsewhere. In many factories Saturday was a half-day, though in several factories this was made good by extra work performed earlier in the week.[32]

One other aspect of working conditions requires some comment: the actual working environment. Although it appears that Birmingham manufacturing processes were not particularly unhealthy (the exceptions were the manufacture of white lead, dry grinding of needles, dust in brass-making and button-making, and lacquering of metals), the workshops themselves were strongly criticized in 1842. They were generally too small, damp, badly glazed and poorly ventilated. Some of the more modern workshops were satisfactory, but many workshops were in garrets immediately under the roofing slates at the top of poorly constructed buildings, being too hot in summer and very cold in winter.[33] Grainger summed up the situation as follows:

> In general the buildings are very old, and many of them are in a dilapidated, ruinous, and even dangerous condition. Nothing is more common than to find many of the windows broken . . . great and just complaint is made upon this point by those employed. The shops are often dark and narrow; many of them, especially those used for stamping, are from 4 to 7 feet below the level of the ground; these latter, which are cold and damp, are justly complained of by the workers. From defective construction, all these old shops are liable to become 'suffocatingly hot in summer (and also at night when the gas is lighted) and very cold in winter'.[34]

In addition, the great majority of workshops were never whitewashed, and efficient ventilation was 'a thing unknown in these places' – a matter of some importance, as many shops were inconveniently crowded. Privies were usually situated outside the workshop in the yard which made for difficulties in bad weather but at least kept the smell outside the main premises. They were often in a foul condition, and the lack of separate accommodation for females was frequently criticized by witnesses. The use of privies in common was thought to be improper and to encourage immoral behaviour, presumably because of the absence of separate compartments. Accidents at the workplace were not uncommon, the principal categories of injuries being sprains and contusions, wounds, fractures, burns and scalds. Injuries to fingers, as might be expected, were commonplace, given the widespread use of stamps and presses, though the loss of fingers did not necessarily stop a worker from continuing in his employment. The most severe and fatal accidents were due to unguarded straps, bands and wheels, especially where women's hair or loose clothing was taken up by a machine.[35]

In attempting to sum up the working environment in Birmingham in the 1840s, there are problems in making comparisons both with working conditions elsewhere and with working conditions in the town in the previous century. As regards the first, in spite of his criticisms of the older workshops, Grainger thought that on the whole they might be considered 'less unwholesome' than the large factories in Lancashire; and the work processes were not in themselves dangerous to health, with the exceptions already noted. Nevertheless, Grainger commented on the poor physical condition of the population which he thought was due to badly-ventilated workshops rather than to the work in itself (an interesting illustration of the early Victorians' obsession with the benefits of fresh air).[36] Though the larger establishments were sometimes praised for their spaciousness and good ventilation, it was the smaller workplaces which were condemned, probably with some justification. The stench in some of the smaller works must have been remarkable: Grainger found Mr Wallis's mill particularly unpleasant (he seems to have fallen out with Mr Wallis):

Altogether I never saw a shop in more filthy or wretched condition. The mechanics are most rude, coarse, and ill-behaved. . . . The people in the neighbourhood complain of these works as a nuisance. Mr Wallis objected to my examining the children in his counting house because he stated 'it would make the place stink so, that his customers could not stay in it'.[37]

Whether conditions in the previous century had been any better it is hard to say. Presumably some premises then would have been newly built and rather less ancient, but others would have gone back to the seventeenth century and have been as objectionable as those criticized by Grainger. On balance, it seems unlikely that there would have been much difference between conditions in 1760 and in 1840, given the fact that the productive methods remained largely the same. The smallest businesses in both years were most commonly to be found in the cheapest premises, and that means in the oldest and most decrepit buildings. The larger workplaces in 1840 tended to be more recently built, of course, yet even here the work practices and the working environment had not necessarily changed. For example, at Mr John Bourne's cabinet brassfoundry, where thirty-two boys and one girl were employed, there was no machinery, all the work being done by hand.[38]

To return to the major issue: how far did Birmingham workmen become accustomed to a new work discipline during the period 1760–1840? It seems possible that those who worked in the largest establishments would become attuned to a more regular work routine than that practised in the smaller workplaces, even if they were still using hand tools and not utilizing steam power. The vast majority, however, still worked in small workshops in the 1840s, and clung to traditional work practices, taking Monday off, and having time off at Christmas, Whitsuntide and for local wakes. This was also common at that time in the Black Country.[39] In fact, the earlier habit of taking things easy at the beginning of the week and working very long hours at the end, seems to have continued even beyond the mid-nineteenth century. One historian has even suggested that in both the domestic workshops and the majority of factories the workers often tried to concentrate the week's work into the last three days of the week. Only when the work-force consisted of unskilled or female workers could the employer suppress 'this voluntary absenteeism'.[40]

All this is not to imply that no change at all took place in working conditions in Birmingham in the period 1760–1840. Discipline was probably stricter in the larger workplaces, and these grew more numerous towards the end of the period. It is equally obvious that work routines *may* have become more regular within the traditional framework of St Monday and customary holidays.[41] One recent suggestion is that by the 1830s the small master was so ground down by competition with the larger manufacturers and by the discounts imposed by factors that he was obliged to adopt factory methods of discipline. In this way (it is argued) he became the mirror image of the large-scale manufacturer.[42] If this is true, then notwithstanding the continuance of St Monday, a kind of factory discipline developed in the small workshop at the expense of the older, flexible eighteenth-century routines. This is an interesting theory, but there is very little if any contemporary evidence to bear direct witness to such a drastic change in workshop practices, and it seems more likely that the older disciplines prevailed as long as their level of productivity remained satisfactory. It must not be forgotten that these older disciplines themselves required sustained hard work over many hours, and were by no means a more relaxed or a more civilized and leisured approach to the business of earning a living before the coming of the factory system; but in Birmingham, of course, they were often based on a relatively sophisticated hand technology and not on steam-driven machinery. The major influence on work patterns in Birmingham during the Industrial Revolution may well have been not the demand for a speeded-up factory-type production, but rather the varying amount of work available; this in turn depended on local trade conditions, so that in boom conditions long hours would be worked every week, while in times of depression only a few days work a week might be offered by the employer.

In fact, the effect of slack trading conditions on the working day was well-known in the early nineteenth century, and great distress could result from fluctuations in employment, so much so that a Select Committee on the matter was set up in 1830, a year of considerable depression.[43] According to the evidence given before this committee, when less work was given out by employers, skilled workmen could usually fall back on some friendly society fund to tide them over (see chapter 9). Unskilled workmen, however, could not afford to contribute to funds of this kind, so employers customarily gave out as much work as before, but at a lower rate per piece, so that the workmen were forced to work longer hours to try to make up the difference. Hence the very long hours worked by some trades – the nailers are a well-known example – in times of depression. Recognition of problems of this kind led the Select Committee on Manufacturers' Employment to propose the setting-up of employment fund societies, with all workmen being obliged to pay regularly into a fund so that they could be helped over periods of slack trade; but it was not until the early twentieth century that the National Insurance

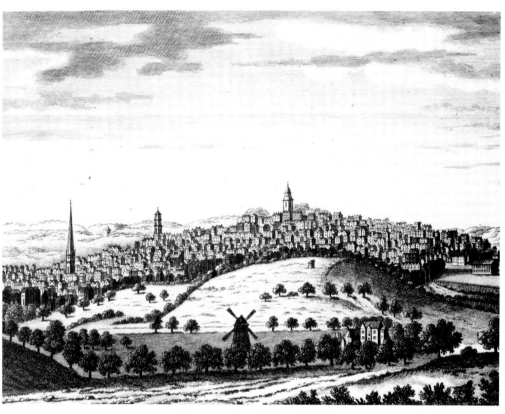

East View of Birmingham, 1779

The Bull Ring, Birmingham, 1812

Christchurch, Birmingham, *c.* 1830

Birmingham Town Hall, 1834

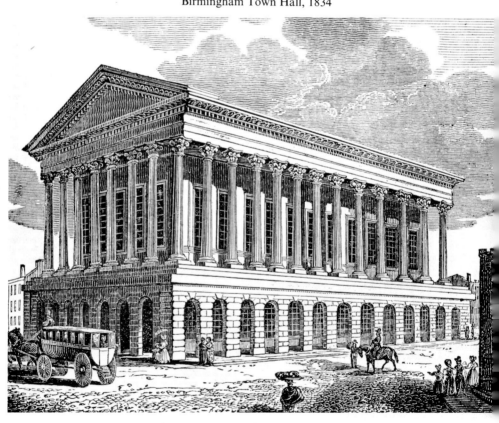

Memorial to Boulton, Watt and Murdoch, Broad Street, Birmingham

View of Aston Flint Glass Works and canal, Birmingham

ELEVATION AND PLANS OF HOUSES, IN GREAT RUSSELL STREET BIRMINGHAM.

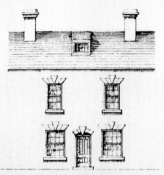

ELEVATION OF ONE HOUSE.

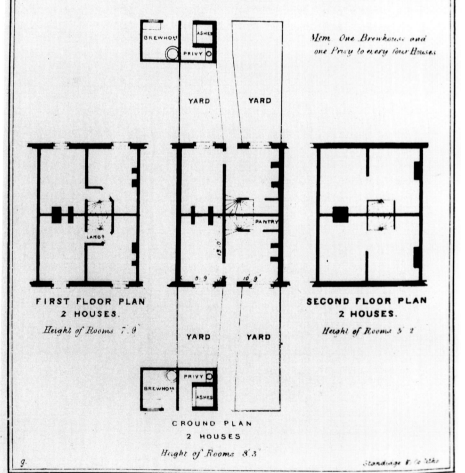

Mem. One Brewhouse and one Privy to every four Houses

YARD   YARD

BREWHOUSE   ASHES   PRIVY

PANTRY

LANDG

YARD   YARD

BREWHOUSE   PRIVY   ASHES

**FIRST FLOOR PLAN
2 HOUSES.**

Height of Rooms 7.9"

**SECOND FLOOR PLAN
2 HOUSES.**

Height of Rooms 5.2"

**GROUND PLAN
2 HOUSES**

Height of Rooms 8.3"

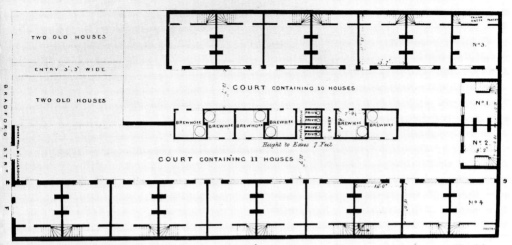

GROUND PLAN OF TWO NEW COURTS OF HOUSES IN BRADFORD STREET.
BIRMINGHAM.

TWO OLD HOUSES

ENTRY 3'.3" WIDE

TWO OLD HOUSES

COURT CONTAINING 10 HOUSES

N° 3

N° 1

BREWH'SE BREWH'SE BREWH'SE BREWH'SE PRIVY PRIVY PRIVY PRIVY ASHES BREWH'SE BREWH'SE

Height to Eaves 7 Feet

COURT CONTAINING 11 HOUSES

N° 2

N° 4

Houses N°ˢ 1 & 2 are two stories, & are without cellars. Rental 2/- per week. Houses N°ˢ 3 & 4 are let for 3/- per week. The whole of the other new houses, which, as well as the houses 3 & 4, are three stories in height, and have all cellars, are let for 3/6 per week.

HEIGHTS
Ground Floor Rooms 7' 8"
First Floor Dᵒ 8' 0"
Second Floor Dᵒ 7' 2"

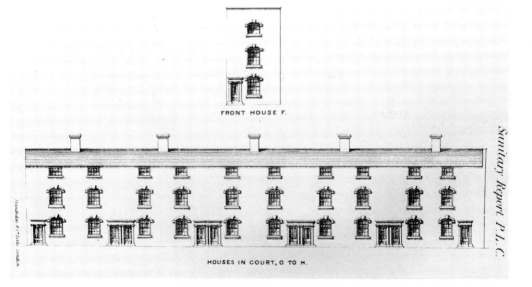

ELEVATIONS OF HOUSES, IN BRADFORD STREET BIRMINGHAM.

FRONT HOUSE F.

HOUSES IN COURT, G TO H.

Plans from Chadwick's Report on sanitary conditions (1842)

New Street, Birmingham, 1838

High Street market, Birmingham, early nineteenth century

William Hutton 1723–1815

Thomas Attwood 1783–1856

Pen–grinding room, Hicks, Wells & Co, Birmingham, 1851

The Gun Proof-House, Birmingham, 1851

Boulton & Watt's Soho Works, late eighteenth century

Act (1911) began to put this recommendation into effect. It seems undeniable that slackness of trade from time to time was a real problem, and its variations and consequences have already been traced in chapter 4.

In Birmingham many workmen were in fact highly skilled, so that it was possible for them to fall back on friendly society funds in times of underemployment or unemployment; but whether skilled or unskilled, hard times meant a change in work routines, and the alternation of good and bad times probably had a far greater effect on the working day or week than any attempt by employers to impose a new and rigorous work discipline. Thus, variations in demand, combined with the known preference of Birmingham workmen for working longer hours towards the end of the week, set severe limits on the employers' freedom to regulate hours, even assuming that they thought this desirable. It seems likely that employers were more interested in how much was produced at the end of the week than in the actual hours worked. The conclusion must be that although some change may have occurred in the direction of greater uniformity of work habits, it would be a mistake to assume that this resembled to any marked degree the much more rigid work discipline of the textile factory. However hard the working week might appear to twentieth-century observers, it exhibited a remarkable flexibility in Birmingham in the first half of the nineteenth century as compared with the working week in factories elsewhere.

Indeed, it must be said that industrial working conditions in Birmingham during the classic years of the Industrial Revolution from 1760 to 1840 exhibit few of the abrupt discontinuities of working life in the textile industries resulting from the transition from domestic to factory production. For a minority – for example, in the larger foundries – the work place became larger and more akin to a textile mill, even though little or no steam power was utilized. In his factory, G. F. Muntz had his men at work on Mondays as well as all day Saturday.[44] Yet even in the larger works, routines would naturally vary to meet the requirements of different productive methods: in both the largest glassworks, for instance, those of Bacchus & Sons, and of Rice Harris (the Islington Glass Works), the hours were the traditional six hours on, six hours off, of the flint-glass industry. Children working in the larger pin factories seem to be a special case, and even in the mid-eighteenth century, were already subject to the routines produced by an elaborate division of labour, and something very like mass production. But for the majority working in the button, toy, jewellery and gun trades, the place of work remained a small, dirty and inconvenient workshop, incorporating hand-operated machines in 1840 just as it had done in 1760. Another prominent group of workers, of course, were those in the trading and service sectors.[45] Little is known of their conditions of work, save that hours could be longer in the aggregate than in industry, especially in domestic service and in retailing (in the second half of the nineteenth century shop assistants worked the longest hours).

Finally then, the picture of working conditions in Birmingham over the period 1760–1840 is one of great variety. There was no massive change over to factory production, though examples of the division of labour are to be found plentifully as early as the mid-eighteenth century, and for the majority the small workshop remained the most typical place of work up until 1840. Patterns of work stayed relatively unchanged, St Monday continued to flourish, there was no noticeable change in the length of the working day or in work discipline, but change was on the way, with the continued spread of steam power and, in the second half of the nineteenth century, the gas engine.[46] Little overtime was worked, except in exceptional circumstances, as when business was particularly brisk; night work (it was said) was scarcely known in the town,[47] though this was necessary, of course, in the flint-glass glasshouses, with their six hours on, six hours off routines. The one aspect of Birmingham working conditions which invites a comparison with conditions in the textile factories is the widespread employment of women and children. In itself, there was nothing new in this, appalling though it may seem to twentieth-century observers. The assistance of children on hand machines was vital to their use, and no doubt the children had to work very hard at boring and monotonous tasks, having no protection under the Factory Acts of the time. It might be thought that Grainger passed over the treatment of children rather too lightly in his report. However, this kind of child labour was traditional enough, and at least its form and pace were not dictated for most Birmingham children by the requirements of steam-operated machinery which made such unrelenting demands on its operators in the textile mills of the North.

It was not until the 1860s that legislation began to affect working conditions in both Birmingham and the Black Country. In 1867 the Workshops Act defined a workshop for the first time, and applied existing factory legislation to the smaller workplaces. The Act did not make such a great difference to children's working hours as might be supposed, partly because of faulty initial enforcement through a system of locally appointed inspectors, and partly because most Birmingham employers who gave evidence before the Children's Employment Commission (1842), considered that stopping employment under the age of nine would be beneficial, and limiting hours of work in the thirteen to eighteen age range to ten would make little difference to existing practices; only a small minority of employers thought that restricting the hours of nine to thirteen-year-olds to eight hours would cause them difficulty. In the same year of the first Workshops Act, another Factory Act extended the definition of 'factory' to include other large workplaces such as iron works, foundries, and glasshouses. As the Education Acts of 1870, 1876, and 1880 made school attendance compulsory for children between the ages of five and thirteen (with exemptions from ten onwards), working hours and conditions for both children and women (whose hours were limited to ten a day) in Birmingham during the classic period of the Industrial Revolution were at last permanently regulated.

7

Living Conditions

It is a well-known fact that living conditions were very bad in industrial towns in the first half of the nineteenth century. Yet they were often as bad in a qualitative sense a century or so earlier in both towns and villages. The difference between the two periods is one of scale: the concentration of insanitary horrors was far greater in the expanding industrial towns of the nineteenth century than anything seen before. Everywhere the sheer pressure of immigration into the towns placed great strains on the housing stock. Lodging houses multiplied, older middle-class houses were divided up into tenements, attics and cellars were used as living quarters, and row upon row of new and sometimes jerry-built housing were rapidly constructed. The pressure was worst where immigration was heavy and continuous and where new building land was not readily available; or where the town was not naturally well-drained, or the water supply was inadequate.

It was fortunate that in all these respects Birmingham was better placed than many other industrial towns. To take immigration into the town first: this appears to have been considerable before 1750, and as substantial before 1801 as it was afterwards up to 1840.[1]

Year	Population
1720	11,400
1750	23,688
1778	42,250
1785	52,250
1801	73,670
1811	85,755
1821	106,722

1831	146,986
1841	182,922

It is the eighteenth-century figures which are of particular interest here. Birmingham's population appears to have more than doubled in the thirty years before 1750. As noted in chapter 1, it has even been suggested that in the first half of the eighteenth century, the town's population at least trebled and possibly quadrupled, the true figure for 1700 being between 5,000 and 7,000 instead of about 15,000 as is often assumed.[2] It then nearly doubled again between 1750 and 1778. Over the half-century 1750–1801, it increased by more than three times, well ahead of the estimated national increase of about 50 per cent. In the first forty years of the nineteenth century, Birmingham's population went up again by about two and a half times. Thus, there seems to have been a faster rate of expansion before 1801 than in the decades immediately following, and certainly Birmingham's growth was not as fast after 1801 as in other large towns.

As for the availability of building land before 1800, the construction of new housing seems to have been made possible in the central areas by a series of local private Acts. Thus the Colmore Estate Act (1746) opened up an area along the northern flank of the ridge between Easy Hill and Snow Hill, while an Act in 1766 made land available in the Bradford Street area, near Deritend; the next act in 1773 was for St Martin's glebe land, covering twenty-three acres at Five Ways.[3] According to the map-makers of the time, overcrowding increased. The average number of persons per house in 1750 was 5.8 (Bradford's map), and 5.9 in 1778 (Hanson's map).[4] It is not surprising that visitors to the town noticed the continual activity in the building of new streets. B. Faujas de St Fond estimated that during the war with the American colonists (1776–83) at least 300 houses were built annually, and that after peace was concluded this rate doubled. Whole streets were being erected, and a complete street might be constructed in less than two months.[5] Hutton was similarly impressed by the extent of house-building in the second half of the century. He estimated that 'From 1741 to the year 1781, Birmingham seems to have acquired the amazing augmentation of 71 streets, 4,172 houses, and 25,032 inhabitants. Thus, her internal property is covered with new erected buildings, tier within tier.'[6] He went on to suggest: 'Perhaps *more* are erected here, in a given time, than in any place in the whole island, London excepted.'[7]

In the 1780s there was no overall control of the methods employed by the builders. Hutton thought that as a result there arose 'evils without a cure: such as narrowness, which scarcely admits light, cleanliness, pleasure, health, or use'.[8] From the later 1780s rather more control seems to have been exercised in some areas, at least, over the quality of the work. For example, on some plots leased in 1790, the builders were required to keep to the specifications for the dimensions of interior timbers, and there were to be stone cornices and stone windowsills.[9] Further, there seems to have been no major problems of drainage at this time because of the town's situation on a hill; and the supply of good quality drinking water remained adequate.

With the coming of the wars against France from 1793 onwards, business activity eased quite markedly (see chapter 4) and building continued at a reduced pace. As Yates put it, 'The rage for building, which produced so many additional houses, was miserably checked.'[10] After the wars the main areas of building were to the north and north-west of the town. New housing was erected in the area of Warstone Lane, Great Hampton Street, and New John Street West. By the 1830s this area was becoming more closely packed, and by 1838 there was little undeveloped land in the eastern half of the parish. Nevertheless, small allotment gardens still ringed the central area of houses and factories on the west, north and east in the 1830s.[11]

The vast majority of the houses erected over the period 1760–1840 were for working people, of course, but a small proportion of them were for middle-class industrialists and professional men. In the eighteenth century, the traditional practice of the employer living near his place of work seems to have been followed by many of the manufacturers of the time; Boulton provides a good example, living next to the Soho works in Soho House, where he entertained distinguished guests and also boarded apprentices. Baskerville too lived centrally, and even in the 1820s Joseph Gillott lived at first in Newhall Street, close to his workshops. However, by this time the Newhall area in the vicinity of St Philip's had gone down socially. The large houses had degenerated into slum tenements, and workshops had been built in the gardens.[12] It is not surprising that by 1842 comparatively few of the wealthier inhabitants were to be found living in town, though most parts still had a few better houses, inhabited by master manufacturers or managers.[13] Many of the middle-class employers, including Gillott, had moved to Birmingham's purpose-built suburb for the middle classes, Edgbaston.[14]

Here the Calthorpes had begun a systematic development of the parish for building purposes, the first building lease being granted in 1786. By 1796, nine similar leases had been issued, and after the housing slump of the Napoleonic Wars period was over, more leases were granted from 1810 onwards, with a marked increase from the early 1840s. By 1825, changes in the parish were very noticeable. A visitor who returned to the district after an absence of twenty-five years exclaimed: 'How changed the scenery! Many of the fields which at that time were fine pastures of arable land are now covered with dwellings of elegant villas'.[15]

The emphasis was certainly on 'elegant villas'. Working-class housing, speculative building, industry and trade were all to be excluded, and rigorous control was exercised over all building undertaken. Plans were carefully examined by the ground landlords, and alterations were often insisted on. The houses built in Edgbaston were of a quality unrivalled in Birmingham, and the large gardens and the many trees made Edgbaston the archetypal leafy suburb of the mid-nineteenth century. It was by far the healthiest part of Birmingham, not only because of the low density of housing and population, the absence of industry, and the excellent standard of building, but also because its inhabitants were indubitably the best-fed, washed and clothed. In 1838 Edgbaston had the lowest incidence of deaths from measles, scarlet fever and typhoid, the lowest percentage of back-to-backs and the highest frequency of water-closets.[16] The story is somewhat different for the working classes living in other areas, for whom no housing at all, not even for the labour aristocracy, was provided on the Calthorpe estate before 1850.[17]

In such a large town as Birmingham, it is impossible to trace in detail the building of new housing for the working classes, but in general terms it may be said that as industrial expansion increased, so the demand for working-class accommodation grew near the place of work. In the mid-eighteenth century there were still plenty of middle-class houses in the central area with gardens or large yards and stables in the rear.[18] Here there was space available for the building of working-class dwellings, grouped in the courts which were to become widely prevalent in Birmingham as the most characteristic form of working-class housing. More land for building was also to be found on the outskirts of the town, for example, in the Deritend area. Hence additional building was erected either in the middle of the town by infilling of gardens, orchards, and other land not yet built upon, or in new streets on the periphery. Fortunately for the town, there were no commons on the outskirts which inhibited building. Nor does there ever seem to have been a real shortage of building land at the centre, at least of a kind which might have caused substantial overcrowding.

The results of the building developments during the period 1760–1840 may be surveyed in the public health reports of the 1840s.[19] The 1840 Report of the Select Committee considered that Birmingham was in a rather better state than some other industrial towns. The committee summed up their conclusions by stating that

> The great town of Birmingham . . . appears to form rather a favourable contrast, in several particulars, with the state of other large towns . . . the general custom of each family living in a separate dwelling is conducive to comfort and cleanliness, and the good site of the town, and the dry and absorbive nature of the soil, are very great natural advantages.[20]

These advantages are dwelt upon in detail in the report. There were no cellar dwellings in the town, unlike Liverpool or Manchester, and the water supply was very good. Generally speaking, the streets and drainage were 'very superior to those in Manchester and other towns in Lancashire'. All the leading streets had underground drainage, though there were some open sewers in Bordesley and Deritend, areas inhabited by the working class.[21] The principal witness, Dr Joseph Hodgson, considered that fever was comparatively rare in Birmingham; it was a very healthy town. He had seen 'the abodes of the poor' in Liverpool, Manchester and London, and he thought the poor in Birmingham were much better off. Admittedly there were some close courts in the old part without free access of air, but not many in the modern parts. There were many back-to-back houses, too, but this type of house was not always inferior to other types of houses. His strongest criticism was directed at the lodging houses, which he thought were great sources of disease.[22] On the whole, Hodgson touched only lightly on the state of some of the older courts, and it was left to Thomas Cubitt, the London builder, to give his opinion that there were many close courts in Birmingham 'which appear to be in a very bad state'.[23]

The favourable aspects of this report were confirmed by Chadwick's Report two years later. In summary form, the principal streets were well-drained, there was a good supply of water, there were no cellar habitations, fever was not prevalent, and some allotment gardens remained. As for back-to-back houses, they were very common, but again the point was made that they were not necessarily bad, provided the rooms were large and lofty and had chimneys, and that the doors and windows were of a good size; diseases were just as prevalent in houses of different construction.[24] Indeed, the 1842 Committee of Physicians and Surgeons remarked rather quaintly that even if the back-to-backs could be separated by a few yards, the resulting back yards or passages would only be used for pigs, rabbits or poultry, and made the receptacles for rubbish and filth.[25] On the other hand, the report laid greater emphasis on the bad state of the older courts, which were narrow, filthy, ill-ventilated, and badly drained. The privies in these old courts were in a very bad state. It was the common practice to empty the ash pits and privies at night into the street, and the contents would then be carted away the next morning, 'though some filth always remains'. It was also pointed out that although the water supply was generally ample, and there were pumps in nearly every court, the water was actually very bad in some of the courts near the River Rea, in Cheapside, Mill Street and Floodgate Street.[26] The strongest condemnation was again reserved for the lodging houses.[27]

Chadwick's Report is different from the other reports of the 1840s in that some indication is given of the actual plans and elevations of selected houses. The plans of an old court off Bromsgrove Street show that the entry into the court was extremely narrow – only 2 ft 11 ins, the court itself being only 4 ft 9 ins across. The houses themselves were either two- or three-storied, the three-storied facing onto the street. Houses with two floors had a ground floor room measuring 11 ft 9 ins × 12 ft, and two first-floor rooms measuring 9 ft 4½ ins × 11 ft 9 ins, and 7 ft 0 ins × 11 ft 9 ins. The height of the rooms was 7 ft 11 ins on the ground floor, 8 ft 0 ins on the first and 8 ft 2 ins when there was a third floor. Outside in the yard were privies and a shared brewhouse. The rent for a two-floored house was 3s per week, and for a three-floored house 4s 6d.[28]

A short distance away, Bradford Street (parallel and to the south of Digbeth High Street), provides an example of two new courts, one of ten and the other of eleven houses. Entry to the courts was by passageways measuring 3 ft 3 ins – an improvement on the entries in Bromsgrove Street – while the distance across each court to the line of brewhouses and privies separating the two courts was either 12 ft 7 ins or 11 ft 7 ins. Most of these houses were on three floors, with cellars, each room on each floor being 12 ft 0 ins × 13 ft 7 ins in one court, and 12 ft 0 ins × 14 ft 0 ins in the other. Room heights were, ground floor 7 ft 8 ins; first floor 8 ft 0 ins; and second floor 7 ft 2 ins. Rents of these houses were mostly 3s 6d per week. Clearly these houses were larger than those in the courts off Bromsgrove Street, and the courts were much more spacious.

Chadwick's Report also gives an example of back-to-back houses in Great Russell Street.[29] The houses here were three stories high with two rooms on the ground floor, 10 ft 9 ins × 13 ft 0 ins, and 8 ft 9 ins × 13 ft 0 ins; the larger of these rooms contained a pantry and the stairs. Upstairs there were two further rooms on the first floor, and an additional room on the second floor. The height of the first floor rooms was 7 ft 9 ins, but that of the top floor room only 5 ft 2 ins. Outside in front of each house was a yard with one brewhouse and one privy for each four houses.

Another type of house illustrated in this report was the so-called three-quarters house. Houses of this kind were built in twos, with a central tunnel entrance and front doors opening to left and right off this passageway. Each house had a ground floor parlour at the front (13 ft 0 ins × 12 ft 0 ins) and a kitchen of the same dimensions at the rear. Above were two bedrooms on the first floor, and two on the second. At the back there was a brewhouse and a privy for each house. Houses of this type in Tennant Street, near Broad Street, were rented at £18 per annum (7s a week), and appear to be of a superior kind. At the other extreme are court houses rented at only 2s 6d a week in Ann Street (off Livery Street), and in the Pershore Road. The first had only two rooms, one up and one down (ground floor 12 ft 3 ins × 12 ft 0 ins), and the second house, three one-room floors (ground floor 14 ft 4 ins × 11 ft 8 ins).

The First Report of the Commissioners of Inquiry into the State of Large Towns and Populous Districts (1844) adds little to the information provided by the earlier reports, but does lay greater stress on the bad condition of the older courts, where the entrance was too narrow for refuse carts to enter. This meant that barrows or baskets had to be used. A survey of 202 older courts between Summer Row and Snow Hill revealed that 139 were in a bad state of repair. Only nineteen were held to be excellent with respect to level, drainage, and repair.[30]

Five years after this report, a petition was presented by more than a tenth of the ratepayers asking for the terms of the Public Health Act

(1848) to be applied to the town. The result was a report by Sir Robert Rawlinson to the General Board of Health on sanitary conditions in Birmingham. Once more the advantages of the town were remarked upon, but at the same time the bad state of the older courts was again emphasized; there were about 2,000 close courts undrained, and many were unpaved, and the privies politely termed 'a frequent source of nuisance'. A survey of 285 courts in both the old and newer parts of the town gave the following results:

	Good	Bad	Imperfect	None
Drainage	134	74	77	–
Level	134	49	99	–
Repair	159	43	78	–
Water Supply	177	80	–	20

In the majority of cases, there was one privy to every four houses.[31]

However, some of the new houses in the suburbs with rents at 5s per week were said to be better designed. The Report contains plans of cottages in Bridge Street West with cellar, two ground floor rooms, two bedrooms above, a washhouse or brewhouse, a privy and a pump. Gardens are shown in the plans, back and front. According to Rawlinson, these cottages had 'a clean, neat, and cheerful appearance when new'; but they lacked a full supply of pure water, for the cesspool next to the privy could not fail to percolate into the well. There was also a lack of proper drainage. This applied to new housing on the outskirts, whether working-class or middle-class: 'The new streets on the outskirts are in a most neglected state for want of power to drain and pave them, and many of the best houses drain into the public road.'[32]

How is this mass of new working-class housing erected before 1840 to be assessed? The reports make it clear that housing conditions were better than in many other large industrial towns. The 1844 Report, for example, claims that Birmingham was 'perhaps one of the most healthy of our large towns', and gives mortality per cent for the three years 1840, 1841 and 1842:[33]

	Mortality Rate (%)
Bath	2.6
Birmingham	2.7
Bristol	3.1
Dudley	2.6

Hull	3.0
Liverpool	3.5
Manchester	3.2
Wolverhampton	2.8

Chadwick's Report also claimed that there was no part of the borough where fever was constantly present, or any part of the town more prone to it than others. In fact, typhus was very rare in Birmingham, and there were only twenty-four cases of cholera during the national outbreak in 1840, in spite of the virulence of the disease only ten miles or so away in Bilston, near Wolverhampton. On the other hand, infant mortality was high: it was greatest in Manchester, then in Leeds, Liverpool, then Birmingham. This was thought to be due most likely to want of proper nutriment and care, the mothers being employed in the workshops.[34]

As for the general condition of the industrial workers in Birmingham, they appeared to be less healthy than agricultural labourers, as might be expected, though this was blamed on their working conditions rather than on the home environment. Two witnesses in Chadwick's Report, both concerned with recruitment into the marines, testified on this point. The first, Mr E. T. Cox, a surgeon, was reported as follows:

> Has examined the results of the marines for 30 years, during 10 years he examined all the recruits enlisted in Birmingham. Has great experience of the physical state of the men who have been employed in manufacturers and agriculture. Those of the latter class are much stronger and more hale in most respects than those of the former. They are generally taller. The mechanics are shorter, more puny, and altogether inferior in their physical powers. Many of the men presented for examination are distorted in the spine and chest, which witness attributes to the confined position in which they work. Knows that many mechanics are rejected because they are below the standard of height, which in the marines is 5′ 6½″.[35]

The second witness, Sergeant Buchan, agreed that many men were not tall enough to be accepted: 'The general height of the men in this town is from 5′ 4″, to 5′ 5″. They are generally shorter than in any town he has known. Many of them are rejected for narrow chest, and for want of stamina.'[36]

This raises questions, of course, as to how far those volunteering for the marines constituted a fair sample of the male working population as a whole, but in fact the general state of health of the industrial workers depended on a combination of several factors, and in particular on conditions at work, conditions in the home, and nutritional standards. The worst health hazard at home would presumably be the state of the privy, together with the quality of the water supply (the commissioners for Chadwick's Report remark in passing that there was nothing relating to working-class furniture or bedding which could be thought detrimental to health, except that bedding was often scanty, 'consisting only of a small quantity of flock or feathers, the place of which would be better or more cheaply supplied by a liberal quantity of oat-chaff or straw').[37]

As for nutrition, it is obviously difficult to generalize. The 1842 commissioners believed that when trade was good, the work people would always buy the best joints and most delicate meats, inferior kinds of joint often being left to the employers to buy (it would be interesting to know how true this last statement really was). In fact, many working men had their main meal, the midday dinner, away from home in a cook shop, where they could buy a plate of meat for 3d and potatoes and bread for another penny. The meat was usually roasted, rather than boiled, though inferior joints might be mixed with vegetables in a stew, and sold in this form. Cook shops also sold soup at 1d per pint, and the older, less well-paid man might make do at midday with soup and bread. There were ninety-five cook shops in Birmingham in 1842, while cooked meat was also available for dinner in many public houses. At home, the wife and children dined on bacon and potatoes, though the more careful housewife might provide a meat stew with potatoes and onions. If the man of the house came home to dinner, he would expect meat in the form of steak or chops, and on a Sunday a good joint of meat was usual.[38] Obviously enough, all this depended on a good and steady wage. Things would be very different if the principal wage-earner was only a labourer, or he was out of work.

To return to the houses themselves: whether the type of building erected in the last decades of the eighteenth century was inferior to housing which went up before 1750 is impossible to say, though it would appear that the court dwelling houses built in the 1820s and 1830s were slightly more spacious both in room size and the size of entries and courts than those built earlier. So the design of building appears to have improved modestly in the early nineteenth century as compared with the late eighteenth century. But there was a noticeable variation in the amount and quality of accommodation offered from one part of the town to the other. The skilled and better-paid workman might pay as much as 7s a week for a three-quarter house in Tennant Street, while a labourer would pay only 2s 6d a week for a court house in Ann Street. The worst accommodation was in the older courts and in the lodging houses.

Of course, workmen needed to live reasonably close to their work, so that those who worked in the same industry tended to live near to each other. This seemed to apply in Birmingham (and in parts of the Black Country) whether the occupation was based on a domestic workshop or a larger work unit. In the gun trade, there was a strong concentration of workshops and of housing occupied by workers in the trade in the area of St Mary's, while jewellery workers were concentrated on the Newhall estate and the adjacent Vyse estate. However, the button trade was more dependent on the labour of women and children than other trades, so that the housing of these workers was more dispersed, dependent on the occupation of the male householder, and was often to be found in the gun and jewellery quarters. Since the brass foundries were also widely dispersed, there was a scattered residential pattern of brass-workers, too.[39]

As for the actual size of rooms, they seem similar to those in working-class housing elsewhere, though three-storied housing was an advantage not always found in other towns. The superior houses in Tennant Street had as much as 936 square feet in floor space, and even the back-to-back houses in Great Russell Street had 759 square feet, including attic space. Two-storied houses in the new courts off Bradford Street had rather less room, about 504 square feet. By way of comparison, the mass of back-to-back houses built in Leeds between 1815 and 1830 had a floor area of 450 square feet.[40] In Coventry, weavers' houses built in the 1830s had about 530 square feet of room space. In the 1850s both weavers' and journeymen watchmakers' houses contained about 730 square feet.[41] In Stourbridge in the Black Country the size of workers' houses varied from the smallest and meanest with only 250 to 350 square feet to the largest houses at 600 to 700 square feet.[42]

Birmingham does not fare badly in these comparisons, but of more importance than the actual room sizes was the amount of overcrowding, the quality of construction and the provision of amenities such as an adequate water supply. Although there may well have been some overcrowding in the 1780s – it was said that there were greater changes in the appearance of the town in this decade because of building than in the preceding forty years[43] – nevertheless the reports are unanimous that cellars were not lived in, and that each family had separate accommodation. Thus, overcrowding was not a long-term problem. Water supply was certainly better than elsewhere, though not in all parts; but there are few references in the reports to the need to buy water from carts which is so common a feature in the description of other industrial towns at this time.[44]

The quality of building is difficult to ascertain. As we saw earlier, Hutton referred to the lack of overall control of the methods employed by builders, and mentioned evils such as narrowness – perhaps a reference to the narrow entrances of some of the older courts; and it is a reasonable assumption that some of the houses put up so speedily to meet a rising demand were of indifferent quality. Some houses were undoubtedly jerry-built. Rawlinson mentions houses with external walls only 4½ ins thick, and with joists 'too slender and far apart'. Tenants could easily be found for such houses when they were new, but they soon deteriorated, and the tenants would move on as the new street, without drains, pavements, or public light, gradually declined. In this way, according to Rawlinson, 'district after district' was vitiated – a sweeping statement, though doubtless not without some truth. Such cottages cost about £60 to build, and their rents were not cheap – 4s a week, exclusive of ground rent.[45] On the other hand, some good quality building was erected. About ninety houses built after 1752 on land belonging to the Lench Charity Trust were described in the 1920s as mostly still standing 'in a good state of repair and occupied by respectable tenants, and likely to stand for another thirty or forty years'.[46] As for building-club houses, one would expect that they would be somewhat superior to merely speculative building, but they came under criticism in the famous articles on social conditions in the *Morning Chronicle* in 1850–1. It was there alleged that in Birmingham the clubs erected 'small and mean houses and cottages, built without any pretensions to beauty, and very often of the flimsiest materials', but at the same time it was admitted that their quality still exceeded that of speculative building in Lancashire.[47]

Naturally, much would depend on the extent to which landlords kept the property in good repair, and as most of them appear to have been small-scale entrepreneurs, it is not likely that they would be very

willing to spend additional money in this way. In the eighteenth
century, the building costs of small houses varied from £40 to £60,
while most building-club houses of this time were rather larger,
costing between £80 and £150.[48] Ownership of the smaller houses
seems to have been spread over a spectrum of occupations, including
the working classes themselves, who bought their homes through the
building clubs. We have already seen in chapter 1 that in 1765 two
bricklayers (probably small-scale jobbing builders) took out Sun
insurance policies on the houses they owned: Henry Gough insured
four houses for £220, and another four houses for £170, while James
Day insured eleven houses and a schoolhouse, the values of these
buildings ranging from £65 to £15. In the same year, John Roper, a
ringmaker, took out a policy for £400, covering a house for £80
(probably his own), another house for £60, a range of shops for £60,
three houses for £60, another three houses for £60, two houses for £40,
two houses for £30, and one house for £10.[49] Clearly these houses were
all small working-class properties. Many of the other holders of Sun
policies issued in the same year were small masters in the toy, button,
buckle, gun and woodwork trades, insuring small working-class
houses. As long as there were no regulations requiring them to keep
their properties in repair, it is doubtful whether they felt much
obligation to do so, as long as they could still find tenants.

The main problem, in fact, was not so much lack of maintenance,
but one which Birmingham shared with other towns, both large and
small: the problem of inadequate earth privies which were over-used
and rarely emptied regularly. When in addition to this, some courts
also lacked all forms of drainage, it is obvious that the older courts in
particular were highly insanitary. Nevertheless, living conditions in
early nineteenth-century Birmingham must be seen in perspective.
For most immigrants into the town from the countryside, the spaciousness of the housing might well be an improvement on their country
cottages, and earth privies with their offensive sights and smells were
familiar enough to them. Even where water closets were installed in
middle-class streets in Birmingham, they were still characterized by
objectionable smells. Thus, in the Hagley Road there were no drains,
and the water closets discharged their contents into open ditches on
each side of the road. In the words of Mr R. T. Cadbury, chairman of
the Improvement Commissioners: 'In the Hagley Road the gutters are
receptacles of drains and filth till they become in the most putrid state,
reeking with the contents of water closets in the finest neighbourhood

of Birmingham.'[50] Another witness confirmed this, remarking that: 'There is a drain from a water closet passes under my house out into the road in front, the effluvium from which at times is beyond measure painful.'[51]

There were also cesspits on many premises in this road. Workmen engaged for £2 to empty one cesspit here in 1849 found the smell so bad that they demanded an additional £1, then a further £1 and a pint of brandy for every hour.[52] Again, even where some houses possessed water closets as in Deritend, the situation might be just as unpleasant. Joseph Hodgson, then Medical Sanitary Inspector for the Corporation of Birmingham, described his visit: 'I would advise you to call at a butcher's shop near Deritend, and when you are sitting in the butcher's parlour it might happen to you as it did to me, that someone used a water closet of a neighbouring house, and the water and everything was discharged, so to speak, smack in our faces.'[53]

Thus, both middle-class and working-class families might suffer from inadequate sanitation, though of course the middle classes had the advantage of much more spacious accommodation, often in detached villas. For the working classes, all turned on the occupation of the householder: as already pointed out, the tenant who was a skilled workman and in regular employment could afford a higher rent and enjoy better housing than the unskilled labourer.[54] It was the labourer in intermittent employment who was to be found in the worst housing in the old courts of the town, full of insanitary horrors. However, the limited degree of overcrowding in the early nineteenth century made for less pressure on both the system of privies and the water supply. Hence Birmingham's relatively good health record at the time. It is hardly necessary to say that Birmingham's working classes lived in housing of a kind quite unacceptable by today's standards. Nevertheless, its quality does not seem to have deteriorated to any marked extent during the period of industrial expansion, and it might even have improved in the 1830s and 1840s; and it was certainly superior to working-class housing in some other great towns such as Manchester and Liverpool. Once more a clear distinction must be drawn between conditions in the textile towns in the North, and conditions in a town where industrial expansion began well before 1760, and took a very different course.

In drawing together the main strands of this chapter, it is manifest that much of our information regarding living conditions comes from the reports of the 1840s. How far were these reports biased by middle-class preconceptions and attitudes towards the working classes? Every now and again the modern reader is likely to be struck by the insensitive nature of some of the comments, for example, the view that oat-chaff or straw would be better or more cheaply supplied than flock or feather for bedding. However, opinions of this kind do not necessarily imply the distortion or omission of unpalatable facts, and on the whole the reports tell the same story, and there are few obvious signs of biased reporting. The 1840 Report seems to have paid insufficient attention to the state of the older courts, but this fault was corrected in subsequent reports. The fullest of the Birmingham surveys is contained in Chadwick's Report, and is unique in being prepared by a Committee of Physicians and Surgeons rather than by an individual, though whether this makes it more or less trustworthy is hard to say. Its plans and elevations of Birmingham houses are very helpful, but we cannot tell how far they constitute a representative sample of working-class housing. A check on the authenticity of the reports of the 1840s is provided to some extent by the previously mentioned articles in the *Morning Chronicle* (so-called 'letters', but really specially commissioned reports by named and reputable authors), and these confirm the general picture presented by the reports. All things taken together, it seems reasonable to suppose that the reports provide a fair survey of public health and especially housing conditions, and that deficiencies and shortcomings were not concealed. Certainly there is no shirking the description of extremely squalid conditions either here or in the reports of other towns and districts.

The general impression to be gained of the housing situation in Birmingham by the 1840s is that it was somewhat better than in other large industrial towns. This was due to a number of factors: the natural drainage of the town; the availability of land for building; a relatively good supply of water; and a slackening of the pressure of population growth in the first half of the nineteenth century. Overcrowding was a feature of the 1770s and 1780s, but did not occur again subsequently, nor were cellars used at any time as living quarters. A further consideration is that the amount of skilled employment available in Birmingham meant that higher rents could be afforded by a larger proportion of the working population than elsewhere.[55] Certainly more spacious accommodation was available for the skilled worker at rents as high as 7s per week (as in Tennant Street), while at the other end of the scale were court houses rented at only 2s 6d a week.[56] A considerable variety of housing was thus available for the working classes.

The darker side of the housing picture is provided by the older courts, dating back to the eighteenth century. These undoubtedly contained some of the worst and most insanitary houses, but again the point must be made that the state of the privies rather than the buildings themselves presented the greatest health hazard. It is tempting to regard the back-to-back housing as a further objectionable aspect of Birmingham housing, bearing in mind that it has been estimated that they accommodated two-thirds of the town's population by the mid-nineteenth century.[57] However, it will be recalled that they were not considered by the 1842 Committee of Physicians and Surgeons to be especially unhealthy, and they could contain as many as five rooms with a floor space of 759 square feet. There were still 43,000 of these houses in 1914, though by then many of the older, closed courts had been opened up by the demolition of one side of the court, thus permitting a greater influx of air.

Lastly, a word about nutritional standards: all that can be said here is bound to be merely impressionistic, and it may well be that middle-class observers took it too much for granted that working-class people recklessly spent their money on expensive cuts of meat when they should have been more provident and been content with humbler fare of a kind more suited to their station in life. Nevertheless, the impression remains that skilled workers did spend freely on meals when in full employment,[58] and indeed the extent of their leisure activities (see chapter 9) gives some indication of their having money to spend in prosperous times. Certainly living standards taken as a whole appear to have been rather higher than in other industrial centres, but times of prolonged depression could bring short commons and near starvation to even the skilled working classes.

Thus industrial urbanization appears to have brought no traumatic changes for the industrial community already in existence in Birmingham in the mid-eighteenth century. For newcomers from the countryside who provided so much of the great increase in population, there may well have been a degree of culture shock, but it must be remembered that housing conditions were qualitatively as bad, if not worse, in rural areas.[59] The lure of higher wages, possibly roomier accommodation, better opportunities for leisure activities and simply a sense of something going on,[60] must have made town life an attractive proposition to many, in spite of the universal dirt, the noise and atmospheric pollution. Whatever the drawbacks of town life, there were not many who chose to return to the life of the agricultural labourer.

8

The Culture of an Industrial Society: (1) the Middle Classes

Since Birmingham in the eighteenth century was a new town of a kind peculiar to the dawning of the industrial age, its middle-class inhabitants might be expected to lack the characteristics which were to be found in other, older towns. They had no aristocratic families to set them a social example. There was no resident, leisured class of the kind which might be found in York, Bath or Worcester. No one lived in Birmingham simply for the pleasure of it – it was too noisy, dirty and smoky. As the snobbish Mrs Elton remarks in Jane Austen's *Emma* (1815): 'They came from Birmingham, which is not a place to promise much, you know, Mr Weston. One has no great hopes from Birmingham. I always say there is something direful in the sound.'

In fact, the middle-class elite appears to have been quite small, only fifty or so of the inhabitants having houses in the country in the 1780s, and only thirty-six keeping private carriages. Nearly fifty years later, an estimate of fortunes in 1828 gave only fifteen with over £100,000, twenty-six with £50,000, and 300 or so with £5,000.[1] Only about this time was the town acquiring buildings commensurate with its size and industrial importance: the new Town Hall; new Corn Exchange; and an improved New Street, with its new church, Christchurch, at the top; the rebuilt grammar school, raised pavements, gas lighting, and new shops.[2] It would be pardonable to suppose that the culture of the Birmingham middle classes was harshly materialistic, with a strong emphasis on profit-making and self-advancement; and Hutton himself does little to modify this view with his discussion of Grenville's observations that commerce tends to corrupt the morals of a people.[3] Yet all this would be to misrepresent entirely the outlook of enlightened entrepreneurs such as Boulton and Thomason, and to

impute a philistinism to the Birmingham middle classes which is quite
at odds with their intellectual interests and leisure pursuits. The
purpose of this chapter is to examine the various influences which
helped to form their outlook and condition their activities.

As for the famed commercial spirit of Birmingham, little needs to
be added to what has already been said about the leading entrepreneurs
of the place. Hutton was struck by the air of purposeful activity in the
town when he first visited it, and from time to time Boulton refers in
his correspondence to 'this commercial nation'. Julius Harvey, the
button-maker, wrote in his diary of 'the necessity of one's being bold
and properly forward, not timid, bashful, or backward to do
business. . . . Nothing of that kind will do in London.'[4] Commerce
was the driving force behind the economic expansion of the second
half of the eighteenth century, and Birmingham was pre-eminent
among the new commercial and manufacturing towns. Consequently
its middle classes could scarcely avoid having selling and profit-
making in their blood; Pitt spoke for them in the Seven Years War
when he declared that 'When trade is at stake, you must defend it, or
perish.' But this rage for making and selling was tempered by a
number of factors. As we have seen in chapter 6, working conditions
were determined less by a ruthless, non-stop determination on the
part of the employer to exact the maximum from his workers than by
a combination of factors, such as variations in trade, traditional work
practices, and a rough and ready paternalism which varied from
employer to employer. Towards the end of the eighteenth century,
there developed a further refining element in the middle-class outlook
– the revival of religious thinking and the spread of evangelicalism.

How strong an influence religious belief became in the day-to-day
life of the Birmingham middle classes in the early nineteenth century is
impossible to determine, of course, except in the most general of
terms, but there can be no doubt of its significance for many men and
women. Reference has already been made to the strength of Dissent in
the town (see chapter 5), and it is well-known that some of its leading
men were Dissenters – men such as Ryland, Phipson, Lloyd, Priestley
and Hutton himself, who emphasized the variety of religious belief in
Birmingham. One reason for this, Hutton suggested, was that the
town was 'unfettered with charteral laws', and as the principles of
toleration were well understood, it was no wonder that there were
various modes of worship: 'The wonder consists in finding such
agreement in such variety. We have fourteen places for religious

exercise, six of the establishment, three dissenting meeting houses, a quaker's, baptist's, methodist's, roman catholic's, and jewish. Two of these only are churches, of which elsewhere.'[5] The two Anglican parish churches were St Martin's and St Philip's, and in addition there were several Anglican chapels which appear to be the sole response of the Church of England to the growth of population in the town in the second half of the eighteenth century.[6] The greatest religious activity was to be found among the Dissenters, and particularly among the Methodists. Wesley visited Birmingham nearly forty times, and commented on the growth of support in the town. The last decade of the eighteenth century witnessed the Priestley riots in 1791, when 'king and church' rioters were inflamed by a public dinner held to celebrate the fall of the Bastille, and attacked and burned the homes of leading Dissenters, especially those of the Unitarians: Priestley, Ryland, Taylor and Hutton. However, the riots were provoked as much by political as by religious fears, and the homes of Unitarians were attacked because of their criticisms of the British Government and support for French ideas of liberty rather than because of their doctrinal beliefs. Certainly the riots provide little indication of the strength of traditional religious feeling in the town at the time.[7]

Indeed, there is not much at the turn of the century on which to base an assessment of the extent of religious activity among the Birmingham middle classes, except that it is clear that Dissent continued to be influential; it is significant too that by tradition the Low bailiff, who held the greater power, was always a Dissenter. Thus, the ruling elite was divided into two groups, the leading Anglicans, and the leading Dissenters. Among the latter and the highest in the social scale, were the Unitarians and the Quakers, while rather lower in social esteem came the Baptists, Independents (Congregationalists) and Methodists. No doubt the consciousness of being different and apart helped to preserve the corporate identity of sectarian religion up to 1800 and beyond, but among the Anglicans there was little effective leadership at either St Philip's or St Martin's during the first decades of the nineteenth century. The rectors of both churches were virtual absentees: the rector of St Philip's divided his time between lecture-ships in London and livings in the country, so that only occasionally was he to be found in Birmingham before his death in 1844. The rector of St Martin's lived at his other rectory in Solihull until he died in 1829. In these circumstances it cannot be expected that Anglican activity would be very high.[8]

This is not to imply, of course, that the Dissenters were necessarily more devout or that they did more to put their beliefs into practice. For some, Christianity undoubtedly determined their way of life in a very real sense; for others, belief and practice were sometimes far apart. Samuel Galton the gun-maker was criticized by the Quaker monthly meeting in 1795 for making and selling instruments of war. At this point he retired, handing over the business to his son, who was still excluded from the Quaker business meetings in the following year.[9] Julius Harvey seems to have been prone to much moralizing, self-abasement before God and fear of death and judgement; but at the same time his diary contains few examples of Christian charity. It may be that he preferred to do good by stealth and failed to record his good deeds, but he refused to lend half a guinea to his neighbour, Mr Whitehouse, the schoolmaster. He disliked Quakers: 'Quakers are Quakers all the world over – self-interest with them is characteristic', and he turned his maid-servant out of doors as soon as he discovered that she was pregnant. He would have turned her out on the previous day but for the heavy snow and his friends advising against it 'lest anyone should impute it as a piece of cruelty'.[10] George Holyoake records in his reminiscences that his Dissenting employer, William Hawkes, at the Eagle Foundry in the 1820s was extremely harsh to his workmen, though he does say that another member of the firm, Mr Samuel Smith, a Unitarian, was 'a placid gentleman', who had a kindly word for the men, and would sometimes make them small advances when wages were low; while William Hawkes's brother, Timothy, became a fanatical Methodist when he was about the age of thirty, and 'so far from making him morose, it seemed rather to increase his kindly nature'. He used to go and comfort an injured workman and pray with him, and make him small gifts.[11]

By the end of the eighteenth century, the growth of population had far outstripped the provision of places in church and chapel, but it was not until 1813 when Christchurch was consecrated that more accommodation became available for Anglican worshippers. Four more large churches were built in the 1820s by the Parliamentary Church Commissioners, and there were another six new or extended churches in the 1830s. In 1838 it was claimed that there were still seats for less than a seventh of the population, and it was proposed to build another ten churches in five years; in practice, only five churches were built in the next decade. By 1851, the number of churches in the town and Edgbaston had more than trebled, but had still failed to keep up with the growth of population. The religious census of that year showed that accommodation existed for only 13.3 per cent of the town's inhabitants; this was a good deal less than the compiler of the census, Horace Mann, thought necessary to provide seats for the 58 per cent he considered were available to go to church or chapel at any one time. Further, only 36 per cent of those who could have gone to church or chapel actually attended on census Sunday – a not unduly low figure for such a large manufacturing town, but below the national average of roughly 50 per cent, and below Wolverhampton (53 per cent), and much below the non-industrial city of Worcester (66 per cent). Moreover, in spite of the strength of Dissent in the town, the Anglican percentage of total attendance was 47 per cent as compared with the figure for Dissenters of 45.9 per cent. This is higher than in other towns of comparable size, and considerably higher than in Leeds or Manchester. [12]

No doubt the bulk of the 36 per cent who attended divine worship were middle class, though there is no way in which this can be confirmed statistically without further research into the social composition of individual congregations. As will be seen in the next chapter, there were considerable difficulties facing working-class men and women who wished to attend church or chapel, such as the existence of pew rents for over half the seats available in 1851, the need for respectable clothes, and perhaps most important of all, the consciousness that both church and chapel were essentially middle-class institutions. The result was that working-class worshippers could not fail to be aware that they were in the presence not only of the Almighty but also of their social superiors in the rented pews. The other aspects of this was that for the middle classes, attendance was a social obligation which could not be ignored or taken lightly. For these reasons it may be supposed that religious observance was an important part of middle-class culture in Birmingham as it was throughout the country in the mid-nineteenth century.

Without any indications of a statistical nature of church or chapel attendance in the previous century, it is difficult to generalize usefully about the changing importance of religion in Birmingham over the whole period 1760–1840. Nevertheless, it is a fair assumption that its influence among the middle classes increased towards the end of the eighteenth century with the spread nationally of evangelicalism. This movement, with its emphasis on the preaching of the gospel and on salvation by faith in atonement had an effect both on the Anglican

Church and on Nonconformity. In Birmingham, Thomas Moseley became rector of St Martin's in 1829, and instituted a number of reforms, not the least being his taking up permanent residence in the town, while at Carr's Lane, John Angel James became minister in 1804, and was soon acknowledged as the most influential Evangelical among the Dissenters. The Evangelicals believed strongly in the employment of visitors and missioners, and continued and expanded the existing provision of help to the poor by the churches in times of distress. This had been well-established in the mid-eighteenth century, when the churches and chapels distributed half of the tickets for food, clothing and fuel which were organized by the town relief committee.[13] By the mid-nineteenth century, Evangelicalism had taken a firm hold among Birmingham clergy, and inevitably influenced the thinking of many of the town's middle-class inhabitants. One contemporary even claimed that it was Evangelicalism which had saved Birmingham from the 'horrors' of Chartism and disorder in the late 1830s and 1840s,[14] but this may well be to exaggerate its influence beyond the ranks of the middle classes.

All in all, it was Dissent which held the centre of the stage in Birmingham in the eighteenth and early nineteenth centuries, and the Dissenting beliefs of some of its most prominent manufacturers need little further emphasis. For families brought up in this tradition, religious observance was an important element in their lives and their beliefs must have played a significant part in their daily life. For Anglicans, the earlier part of the period was one of laxity in the Church generally, but the influence of Evangelicalism brought about great changes in Birmingham from the 1830s onwards, so that by the 1840s the Anglican Church had become much more active and better organized; and it must not be overlooked that, as pointed out earlier, the number of Anglican church attendances in 1851 was actually higher than the number of Dissenting attendances. The importance of Dissent among the Birmingham middle classes must not be allowed to overshadow the importance of a revived and reformed Church of England by the middle of the nineteenth century.

How far did this earnestness in outlook extend to the provision of social amenities in the growing town? A sketch of the work of the town commissioners in chapter 5 has already given some idea of the participation of the middle classes in the government of the town, and the impression gained is that the major aim of the commissioners was to clear the streets of obstructions and to light them in order to facilitate trade, rather than to make life more agreeable for the town's inhabitants. This is understandable enough, given that all improvements had to be paid for through the rates, collected for the most part from the middle classes. It appears that service as a commissioner was not popular, and meetings were often adjourned because of the limited attendance. [15] It is evident that civic pride took some time to develop in Birmingham which lagged behind other towns up to the 1830s even in the provision of a town hall. It seems remarkable that a town hall was not built and opened for use until 1834, it being necessary previously to hold town meetings in Beardsworth's Repository, the largest room available. [16]

Nevertheless, it would be wrong to suppose that on the whole the middle classes were indifferent to the need for local institutions before 1800. Perhaps the best-known example of a local amenity was the building of the general hospital. The movement for its establishment was led by Dr John Ash, a local practitioner, and building began in 1766. It is true that the completion of the building was delayed by lack of funds, but finances were eventually provided by the beginning of the famous triennial musical festivals. The hospital contained about a hundred beds, being completed in 1779. New wings were added in 1790[17] and thirty additional beds were endowed by Samuel Galton. Other medical institutions, all set up by middle-class initiative, included the Dispensary (founded in 1792 in Temple Row), and then between 1817 and 1823, the Institute for Bodily Deformity, the Eye Infirmary, a second Dispensary, and the Fever Hospital. [18] Clearly the growth of population necessitated the setting-up of institutions of this sort, while as early as the 1780s it became necessary for the local Poor Law system to be reorganized, this being achieved by the establishing of a Board of Guardians under a private Act in 1783. However, plans for a new workhouse fell through, and there was to be no new building for the poor until 1850 (see chapter 9 for further details of the Poor Law system).

It could be argued, of course, that both the general hospital and the reformed Poor Law system were forced on the Birmingham middle classes rather than the result of any great benevolence on their part. The hospital was made necessary by the increasing numbers of newcomers who lacked a settlement in the town, and who as a result were debarred from applying to the workhouse infirmary for help. The new Poor Law administration was similarly the consequence of the need for an improved organization to deal with the ever-increasing numbers of immigrants who sought assistance when times were bad. In the same way, middle-class support for working-class education in the form of Sunday schools and church day schools (see chapter 9) was based, in part at least, on the need to discipline the new working masses of an expanding industrial town. As for middle-class educational requirements, they were met very largely by the King Edward VI Grammar School, where the curriculum was heavily classical until 1837 when a new commercial department was set up in the rebuilt school in New Street. Earlier proposals were made to Parliament to build a new classical school on the outskirts, but they were met by considerable opposition, not only by middle-class radicals but also by the skilled working classes; there were petitions against the plans from 7,000 artisans, from the Birmingham Co-operative Society, and even from the Board of Guardians. Subsequently the sons of manufacturers appear to have been almost equally divided between the classical section and the commercial section. A new proprietary school, the Edgbaston Proprietary School, was also set up in 1837 by Dissenting businessmen, since in spite of the reforms of 1837 the Edward VI Foundation remained an Anglican school. The Edgbaston Proprietary served as the successor to the progressive Hazelwood School in Hagley Road which had moved to London.[19] Thus, middle-class educational needs were rather better served after 1837, and indeed the 1830s saw the middle classes taking vigorous action to further their interests both nationally in the field of parliamentary reform and locally in seeking municipal incorporation.

Both these developments are of a political nature, and fall outside the intended scope of this book, but they demonstrate the increasing need felt by middle-class leaders to assert and protect their interests both at Westminster and in the town itself. So far as parliamentary representation is concerned, the Birmingham Political Union (BPU) played a prominent part in the agitation which accompanied the passing of the 1832 Reform Act.[20] The Union was established in 1830 as a political union of the middle and working classes following on the failure in the House of Commons in the same year of a move to transfer the parliamentary seats of the rotton borough of East Retford to the town of Birmingham. The aim of the Union was not merely to secure representation for the town, but to gain widespread electoral reform, such as the vote for all male taxpayers and the payment of and abolition of property qualifications for MPs. Indeed, its programme included five of the six points of the People's Charter of 1838. Yet in spite of its democratic nature, the main aim of its principal founder, Thomas Attwood, was to achieve currency reform through a reformed House of Commons, his belief being that no such reform would be possible in the old, corrupt House and that currency reform was essential to cure the economic ills of the country.[21] How far his beliefs were shared by the curious mixture of middle-class Ultra Tories and Radicals who dominated the council of the BPU is hard to say; but certainly the cause of political reform proved immensely popular in Birmingham and monster meetings were held on Newhall Hill in support of the Union during the struggle for the Reform Bill. However, Attwood insisted at all times on strictly legal action and the whole movement was remarkably peaceful. When the Lords rejected the Reform Bill in October 1831, Attwood and his supporters drew up the following address:

> Friends and Fellow Countrymen! The Bill of Reform is rejected by the House of Lords! Patience! Patience!! Patience!!! Our beloved King is firm – his patriot ministers are firm – the House of Commons is firm – the whole nation is firm. What then have the people to fear? Nothing – unless their own violence should rashly lead to anarchy, and place difficulties in the way of the King and his Ministers. Therefore there must be no violence. The people are too strong to require violence. By peace – by law – by order – everyone must rally round the throne of the King.[22]

A warning by the Union in May 1832, that the populace might have to arm themselves in self-defence should disorders break out, was not repeated and was never implemented.

The strength of the BPU was such that similar unions were set up in many other towns and even villages, and when the Reform Act was finally passed there were enormous rejoicings in Birmingham. It certainly seemed that a middle-class organization enjoying much working-class support had scored a major triumph. It appeared that great local demonstrations had proved as effective as the lobbying of the House of Commons practised by Boulton and others in an earlier age. Attwood himself had no doubt that the passing of the Reform Bill owed much to Birmingham. In his own words: 'I cannot but express the great delight I feel in Birmingham having been mainly instrumental in the accomplishment of this glorious consummation.'[23] Yet this may be to suppose too much. There is really very little evidence to show that the actions of either the king, or of his ministers, or of the House of Lords were significantly influenced by events in Birmingham. Understandably, Attwood may have deceived himself in this respect.[24] Further, the new House of Commons proved as indifferent to currency reform as the old. Attwood and Scholefield were the first MPs elected to represent Birmingham, and Attwood's speeches on currency matters were greeted with ridicule, and his basic aim, the repeal of the Banking Act (1819), was not to be achieved in his lifetime.

The passing of the great Reform Act did not signal the end of the BPU. After closing down in 1834, it was revived in 1837 as trade depression deepened, and again set forth a programme of political reform, this time including universal male suffrage, together with the repeal of the Corn Laws, and of the 1834 Poor Law Amendment Act. For two years its council sought to work in association on the one hand with the London Working Men's Association (the parent body of the Chartist movement), and on the other hand with the leader of northern Chartism, Feargus O'Connor; but in spite of plans for a national convention and for petitioning parliament, the council found the task of maintaining the alliance too much for them, and the union collapsed in 1839. Of more importance for the future of the town was the passing of the Municipal Corporation Act (1835), which at last led to Birmingham's acquiring a charter and hence a municipal corporation in 1838.[25] It was only achieved after a lengthy controversy, opponents of incorporation arguing that the town was already well-governed by the commissioners, who had more power than a corporation would have under the Act, quite apart from the fact that incorporation would be an unnecessary expense.[26] Eventually the Liberal advocates of the scheme had their way, and a council consisting of a mayor, sixteen aldermen, and forty-eight councillors was established. The first mayor was William Scholefield, William Redfern was the first Town Clerk and R. K. Douglas, the editor of the *Birmingham Journal*, became Registrar of the Mayor's Court. As it happened, all three were veterans of the BPU.

What can be said of this participation of the middle-class employers of Birmingham in both national and local politics in the 1830s? Certainly it was not unique; the middle classes in other towns found themselves similarly involved at the time. The national excitement over the reform of the electoral system, itself a sign of the increasing importance of the urban middle classes, inevitably manifested itself among the provincial bourgeoisie. In one sense, it was for their benefit that the Act was passed, even though it brought no immediate and significant shift of political power to the middle classes. Again, once the Reform Act had been passed, other reforms had to follow, including the reform of local government. Thus it is hardly surprising that Birmingham should become involved in both the struggle over the Reform Bill, and the grant of incorporation.

There is no reason to suppose that this involvement indicates any great change in the political outlook of the town's middle classes. As we have already seen, in the eighteenth century they were both skilled and experienced in the lobbying of parliament, and of the Government itself. It will be recalled that they promoted their own legislation to acquire the Assay Office, and later on, the Proof House. They also made representations regarding trade treaties affecting their interests. In 1812 Attwood, Spooner and others presented evidence very effectively against the Orders in Council and against the monopoly of the East India Company, which monopoly was subsequently modified then abolished. So it can be argued that Birmingham employers had always been quick to advance and if necessary to defend their enterprise and initiative. Hence, the common description of Birmingham at this time as a radical town is correct in so far as it is taken to be a description of the willingness of the middle classes to entertain change and reform, though this was undertaken in a spirit of enlightened self-interest rather than from philanthropic motives.

One example of something more like altruism , however, may be found in the support given to the opening of Owen's Equitable Labour Exchange in Birmingham in 1833.[27] The membership of both the preliminary committee and the management committee was dominated by manufacturers, retailers and professional men. In Birmingham, Owen planned to involve, as he put it 'the Attwoods, the Scholefields, the Muntzes, the Joneses and many others who had been long labouring in the public vineyard'.[28] Undoubtedly the motives of those helping to organize the Exchange were largely philanthropic and directed in the main to the relief of poverty. Some, like William Hawkes Smith and William Pare, were committee members of the Birmingham Co-operative Society. The idea of the labour notes to be used by members of the Exchange may well have attracted those supporters of the BPU primarily interested in currency reform. At all events, at least ten of the sixteen men on the preliminary Exchange Committee were members of the BPU, and the chairman was G. F. Muntz, one of the union's most active leaders. By the end of 1834, the Exchange had closed down, but its brief life is certainly an indication of the interest in bettering the lot of the poor which was to be found among some, at least, of Birmingham's leading middle-class figures, an interest which is similarly to be found in the participation in the early days of Chartism of members of the BPU such as William Hawkes Smith.

To turn to leisure activities: it has already been pointed out at the beginning of this chapter that it would be wrong to portray the middle classes of Birmingham as narrow-minded industrialists and business-men, quite without interest in intellectual matters. In fact, the dozen or so members of the famous Lunar Society (already mentioned in chapter 5) constituted perhaps the most distinguished group of thinkers in the country in the mid-eighteenth century. There can be no doubt of the high intellectual level of men such as Erasmus Darwin, Joseph Priestley and Samuel Galton, though in some ways Matthew Boulton is the most interesting of the society's members, in that, in spite of a modest educational background, he seems to have acquired a wide general knowledge and culture and must have been a voracious reader. In particular, he appears to have had a pronounced technical flair, and his notebooks and correspondence reveal an impressive ability to engage in the intricacies of the steam engine and to calculate the costs and profitability of its installation in the Cornish mines.[29] In the early nineteenth century, the list of Birmingham thinkers becomes less striking, but there is still a good deal of evidence of serious and high-minded thinking among reformers such as Thomas Attwood, and religious leaders such as John Angel James. The Philosophical Institution (established 1800) provided another intellectual forum, the interests of which were largely scientific. Its building in Cannon Street (opened in 1814) contained a newsroom, a lecture room for 200, a reading room, museum, library and laboratories.[30]

As for political clubs, the two most important in the second half of the eighteenth century met at Freeth's Leicester Arms (or Coffee House) in Bell Street and at Joe Lindon's Minerva Tavern in Peck Lane. The former was a centre for Whiggery, Freeth himself being well known for his verses on local contemporary issues, while the latter was a centre for Toryism. It is said that over the fireplace ran the inscription 'No Jacobin admitted here'. Another club of a different nature was the Bean Club, founded after the Restoration as a loyalist dining club, but in the course of time developing a wider membership. Its members included Henry Clay, who became High Sheriff of the county in 1790, Samuel Aris, the founder of the *Gazette*, and his successor as publisher and printer, James Rollaston, together with members of the Street Commissioners and of the Hospital Committee. By the beginning of the nineteenth century, its membership was widespread among the middle classes, including (according to Dr Money) magnates of the county, gentlemen and tradesmen of the town, clergy and officers from the barracks, and even principal actors from the theatre. Thus it served as a useful social meeting place for both the town and county – the merchants and manufacturers of the town, and the larger landowners of the surrounding countryside. In this way its interests included both municipal and county affairs. Although it was a conservative institution, Dr Money considers that it was by no means reactionary in outlook, and through its membership it was closely associated with the whole development of Birmingham.[31]

Several other clubs must be mentioned. The Freemasons were organized into two lodges in the second half of the eighteenth century. One was known as St Paul's Lodge, its best-known members being John Freeth, James Rollaston and James Sketchley, the auctioneer and publisher of one of the earliest town directories. The other lodge, St Alban's, included as a member James Bisset, the author of the rhyming directory for Birmingham, *The Magnificent Directory* (1800), and an active mason in other lodges outside Birmingham. Another club, the Bucks, appears to have copied the Freemasons, though presumably without adopting their distinctive rituals. After an early rakish reputation, the Bucks became more respectable as a social club. James Rollaston was among its members, and so was Myles Swinney, publisher of the *Birmingham and Staffordshire Journal*.[32] One other club, the Anacreontic Society, had a total membership of 1,505 in 1814, mostly of local tradesmen, but with some members from outside Birmingham.[33]

As for the arts and recreation, the first playhouse opened in Moor Street in 1740, but later declined in the face of the opposition of a rival theatre in King Street. The Moor Street theatre was eventually converted into a Methodist chapel, much to the satisfaction of John Wesley, who would have liked to have seen all theatres so converted. The King Street theatre closed down in 1786 when another theatre opened in New Street. The first application of this theatre for a royal licence was rejected, but it was finally granted in 1807, the theatre becoming known as the Theatre Royal. The town lacked resident companies of its own in the eighteenth century, and was visited by London companies. It is hard to say what quality of performance was achieved by the 1840s, though one foreign visitor was very unfavourably impressed by a performance of *The Merchant of Venice* which he witnessed, declaring that although Birmingham might be a paradise as far as the useful arts were concerned, with respect to the fine arts, 'it is a very desert'.[34] However, he did refer to the great music festivals held in Birmingham, and these were highly praised by another visitor later in the 1840s:

> No town of its size in the Empire spends more time and money in concerts and music festivals than Birmingham; no small proportion of its people are amateur performers; almost all are musical critics; and the organ in its great Hall, the property of the town, is, with the exception of that at York, the largest in the Empire, and the finest, it is said, without any exception.[35]

Early on, concerts were held in St Philip's, and there was an emphasis on sacred music, especially oratorios, but from the 1830s onwards the Town Hall could be used, as it is today. It was said to provide the largest hall in England, with seats for 3,600 or 9,000 standing when the seats were removed.[36]

Other social activities in the eighteenth century included the weekly assemblies for cards, dancing, and conversation which were held in the Royal Hotel, Temple Row (erected 1772), as the town lacked grand assembly rooms of the kind to be found in York. Outdoor pleasures included the eighteenth-century practice of promenading in pleasure gardens such as the grounds of Duddleston Hall (renamed the Vauxhall Gardens), where there were bowling greens, a billiards table, and fortnightly concerts.[37] The indoor pleasure of reading was catered for from 1779 onwards with the establishment of the Birmingham Library, founded by nineteen subscribers, of whom all but one were Dissenters. They were joined by Dr Priestley, who took charge of the library, but after the riots it split in 1794 into two sections, the Old and the New Libraries. Even then, the Old Library still had 437 members, and about 20,000 volumes in 1814. In addition, there were eight or nine commercial libraries.[38] Lastly, the visual arts were catered for by the Academy of Arts, founded 1814, which was replaced by the Society of Arts in 1821. It held its first exhibition in its New Street premises in 1828.

In this general survey of the outlook and *mores* of the middle classes, two major points require final comment. The first relates to the composition of the middle classes as a whole. No attempt has been made here to define precisely which occupations qualify for the description of 'middle class', simply because the boundaries between middle class and working class were probably more blurred and indefinite in Birmingham than in any other major industrial town. The term 'working class' was relatively new in the early nineteenth century,[39] and it is hard to know how far the small master would consider himself to be of the lower middle class because he was an employer, or working class because he was an artisan who worked at the bench with his men. In all probability labels of this kind had little relevance for him, especially in a society where class barriers were always considered to be low. There were really no sharp dividing lines between the life-style of the small master and that of the white-collar worker or small shopkeeper (who all the same might think themselves socially superior to the working classes as a whole). In this chapter, attention has necessarily focused on those attitudes and activities which were clearly middle-class in nature and easily distinguished from working-class characteristics, for example, membership of the Freemasons or of the Bean Club as opposed to membership of a sick and draw club, but it should not be assumed that class divisions across the board were always as simple as this.

The second major point concerns the extent to which middle-class attitudes may be said to have changed over the period 1760–1840. It would be a caricature to suggest that increasing industrialization in Birmingham in the second half of the eighteenth century produced a new race of hard-faced, exploiting profiteers. Undoubtedly there were some harsh employers, but there was nothing new in this, and at the same time older, paternalistic practices persisted well into the 1830s and beyond. The traditional so-called moral economy had a long life in Birmingham and to suppose otherwise is to ignore much of the evidence given before the House of Commons in 1812 in connection with the petitions against the Orders in Council, and to assume that it is mostly mere eyewash and sanctimonious rubbish; this does not seem very likely, though of course inevitably it was coloured by middle-class assumptions and prejudices.[40]

Perhaps the most interesting question is why middle-class opinion should have taken such a radical turn in the 1830s. It has been suggested earlier in this chapter that there is no contradiction between approaches to the Government by the Birmingham middle classes in the second half of the eighteenth century and their later radicalism of the early nineteenth century. It could be argued further that this radicalism came naturally to an entrepreneurial class whose town had grown so large by then that they had become impatient at the restraints imposed by subservience to the traditional county authorities; they wanted their own MPs, their own magistrates, and their own municipal charter.[41] This is not to imply, of course, that their radicalism had anything revolutionary in it. It was in fact a very conservative form of radicalism. Attwood himself was an Ultra Tory, and significantly the BPU aimed to unite the forces of the middle and working classes. Significantly, too, the most active of Birmingham middle-class leaders, with the exception of Attwood, were prepared to support Robert Owen's Equitable Labour Exchange not merely because of the benefits it might bring to the working classes, but also because Owenism was based on communitarianism and not on the class struggle (which Owen rejected), that is, it was predicated on community reform of the kind which involved class collaboration. This is very much in keeping with the prevailing middle-class opinions in Birmingham at this time. As for the Evangelicalism which continued to prevail throughout the 1830s, it is hard to say whether it had much influence on middle-class attitudes, but it must, to some extent, have served to reinforce ideas of conciliation, co-operation, and reform.

Thus, there are good grounds for supposing that intensified industrialization in Birmingham did not produce any fundamental discontinuities in middle-class outlook. A belief in profit-making and individual enterprise, already strongly evident in the mid-eighteenth century continued into the nineteenth century, but does not appear to have been accompanied by the development of a new class outlook among employers or a sharpening of class conflict. Paternalistic attitudes, of varying degrees of sincerity, continued as a real element in Birmingham middle-class society well into the 1830s and beyond.[42]

9

The Culture of an Industrial Society: (2) the Working Classes

It is difficult to define precisely the nature of working-class culture at any time in the past, and particularly so during a period of such rapid social change as that of the Industrial Revolution. Birmingham workers witnessed an unprecedented expansion of their town and of its industry. Its physical appearance was subject to drastic change as green and open spaces in the town centre were submerged beneath a flood of bricks and mortar in the shape of new workshops and working-class housing. Against this changing background, Birmingham industrial workers became more truly urbanized than ever before, so that in addition to the familiar workshop scene there developed a new townscape which included newly built turnpikes, canals, schools, churches and chapels, municipal buildings like the new workhouse and town hall, and at the end of the period, the railway stations. In what ways did this new environment affect the outlook and life-style of Birmingham working people? How far were working-class habits and attitudes changed by increasing industrialization and urbanization by the mid-nineteenth century?

To begin with, an already familiar point must be emphasized. The typical male Birmingham worker had always been noted for his skill in metal-work, and his wages had always been relatively high and certainly far superior to those of the agricultural labourer in the surrounding countryside. This is not to ignore the large numbers who were mere labourers and on much lower wages than the skilled or semi-skilled, but it remains true that a substantial proportion of Birmingham workers earned good money throughout the period, and this enabled them to maintain a way of life which was well beyond the reach of the agricultural labourer. Not enough documentary evidence has survived to make it possible to trace changes in the standard of living from 1760 to 1840, but there are enough contemporary references to confirm that the skilled man did well, in normal times at least.

Thus, Arthur Young pointed out in the Birmingham of the 1770s, no adults earned less than 7s per week, and that some earned up to £3 a week.[1] The latter figure is amply confirmed by the frequent references to wages in the evidence of employers appearing before the Committee of the House of Commons for Petitions against the Orders in Council in 1812. According to Attwood, the usual wages of labouring men in normal times were 30–40s per week, while Potter stated that the best wages were 40–50s a week in good times, and second-rate wages 25–30s. Thomas Messenger, the brassfounder, confirmed that his best men received £3 per week, while Henry Dunbar's button workers earned up to 50s. Platers might be paid 45s per week.[2] These figures represent the highest wages received by skilled men and are by no means average wages for adult men; they do, however, serve as an indicator of what the best-paid might receive, and have implications for their standard of housing, diet, dress and recreation. A survey of members of a provident society printed in Chadwick's Report (1842), probably gives a better idea of average earnings. An average wage for 134 men aged between twenty-one and seventy worked out at £1 4s 2d, with the men in the younger age range earning more than the older men. Below the age of twenty-one the wages were much less: seventy-four boys aged fourteen earned an average of only 4s 5d a week, but by the age of nineteen, seven boys averaged 12s 4d, and eight averaged 13s 9d. Clearly wages were at their highest when men were at their peak of physical efficiency in their twenties, at the time when they often had their heaviest family commitments in the shape of young children to feed and clothe (the survey gives the youngest age of wage-earners, both male and female, as seven). Female earnings were very much less at all ages than the male equivalents. For example, sixty-eight women between the ages of twenty-one and sixty earned only 7s 10d per week on average. However, in commenting on the figures Chadwick's Report suggests that although admittedly the workpeople surveyed were 'a more provident and better class of workpeople', in fact there was a very numerous class of workers whose earnings were 'very much greater', and a number of workmen earned 30–50s, and many young women 10–14s per week. We are also told (rather surprisingly) that the working classes of the town were generally very well-clothed, most of them possessing two suits of clothes.[3]

Although high wages were generally obtainable in Birmingham throughout the period, even the skilled worker might suffer hardship when the price of bread was high, as in 1766 and in 1806, or again when trade was at a low ebb, as in 1812. The evidence of employers in that year, which has already been quoted, is full of references to wages being cut to a half or less. The more benevolent employers tried to keep as many in employment as possible, but at reduced wages, merely making goods for stock and not for immediate sale. Thus, William Bannister, who usually employed about 120 in his plating firm, had cut his work-force down to about eighty, and could not afford (he said) to let the wages rise above 20s or 21s, though they were normally up to 45s per week.[4] Some employers were clearly moved by the condition of men formerly employed by them. Mr Ridout, a merchant engaged in the export trade to America, was asked by the committee, 'To what state are these poor men reduced, of whom you used to purchase?' He replied:

They appear very much distressed. I have seen people shed tears: I have confined myself behind the door as if I was afraid of a constable, for fear of seeing these people, less they should importune me to give them orders; they have told me they did not know what to do. A man of the name of Yates who lives near Blockswich, who was a workman, came to me: I refused to buy any more shoe tacks and awl blades of him: he said, 'What can I do? If I go to the magistrate, he will tell me to go for a soldier; I am a married man, and God knows, what must I do unless I steal, and then I shall go to Botany Bay.' I do not like to hear such words; I cannot bear it.[5]

Even if workmen were kept on, but at reduced wages, they might be near starvation. Henry Dunbar, the button manufacturer, testified that

On a Saturday night I really am obliged to get my foreman to pay, it is hurtful to my feelings to see people with such calamitous stories, people with large families, say that 15 shillings will not maintain them, when they were in the habit of receiving 50 shillings, and some I am obliged to lend money to; some have even been obliged to get redress from the parish . . . in short, the distress has been so

great that for the last two or three months I have not paid them, I
have sent them to my foreman to be paid.[6]

There was a limit, of course, to the amount of goods that could
usefully be made for stock. The gilt toy trade was worst of all for
laying goods by, because of the rapidity with which fashions
changed.[7]

The last two quotations are a graphic reminder of one striking
aspect of working-class life throughout the period: the irregularity of
employment and the sufferings of even highly-skilled workers in
times of severe depression or when the harvest was bad and bread
prices high. The reverse side of the coin was to be seen in times of
prosperity, but during the French wars and in the post-war years trade
was frequently subject to periods of slackness, so that if work was at
the centre of the working man's existence (and of the working
woman's and working child's), then lack of work or short-time
working was also a grim reality which had to be endured from time to
time, and something which the prudent and better-paid had to
provide for. The principal means of safeguarding against want in
times of distress was the provident or friendly society.

Such societies were common in Birmingham throughout the period
and took a variety of forms. The earlier types were simple sick and
draw clubs where payment of a few pence subscription was usually
accompanied by a much greater expenditure on drink. As Hutton put
it: 'As liquor and labour are inseparable, the imprudent member is apt
to forget to quit the clubroom when he has spent his necessary two
pence, but continues there to the injury of his family'.[8] Certainly these
clubs were known to encourage heavy drinking at their fortnightly or
monthly meetings, but their assistance was invaluable in times of
distress. Attwood told the House of Commons in 1812 that the help of
these clubs was very great, and that there was hardly any industrial
worker in Birmingham who did not belong to a club.[9] This must be an
exaggeration, for unskilled labourers would obviously find it difficult
to keep up regular payments. Nevertheless, the clubs were very
numerous, and the 1835 edition of Hutton estimated that there were
about 400 of them, with some 40,000 members. By this time, a newer
form of society seems to have emerged known as provident societies,
meeting in the vestries or school rooms of the chapels or churches to
which they were attached; according to Hawkes Smith, these societies
were without the defects of the older type of club meeting in the public

house, being 'more scientifically conducted' and 'based on superior calculations'.[10]

Although the purpose of most clubs was simply to provide insurance against sickness and death, some had more limited objectives such as breeches clubs, watch clubs, clock clubs and even book clubs. Another type of club was the building club. According to Hutton, societies of this kind might be started by a bricklayer, and the subscriptions were very substantial: 'every member perhaps subscribes two guineas per month, and each house, value about one hundred pounds, is ballotted for as soon as erected. As a house is a weighty concern, every member is obliged to produce two bondsmen for the performance of covenants.'[11] Clearly, only a small minority of workmen could afford to support clubs of this sort, but Birmingham was well-known for its building societies and the type of house they built was commented on in chapter 7.

By the 1840s the number of friendly societies was increased by the establishing of local branches of national societies. By 1848 the Manchester Unity of Oddfellows had as many as seventy-two lodges with 4,246 members, while the Ancient Order of Foresters had sixteen courts.[12] When reporting on the conditions in the town in 1849, Rawlinson listed a total of 213 societies registered under the recent Act, of which about 159 met in inns, public houses or beershops. They generally met once a month, and had an annual dinner and Whitsun procession. The 213 societies had at least 30,000 members. In addition, there were thirteen building societies registered, and Rawlinson notes that the ladies had their own female friendly societies. He also gives the names of some of the societies which range from the Sick Man's Friendly Society, Abstainers Gift, Society of Total Abstinence, and Rational Sick and Burial Society to the even more colourfully-named True Blue Society, the Honourable Knights of the Wood, the Modern Druids, the Royal Dragoons, and the Society of Royal Veterans.

Obviously enough, the majority of these clubs had the dual function of providing succour when times were hard and of serving as centres of conviviality. As such, they illustrate an important and well-known aspect of working-class culture: the perceived need to stand together in times of adversity and to provide mutual help; but it was the association with conviviality that attracted criticism from middle-class observers. Thus Rawlinson remarked:

> Vast sums of money are expended by these clubs on unmeaning, gaudy and childish show. Once a year, usually in Whitsun week, they hold processions. More money is spent in processions, in loss of labour and in attendant expenses of the day, than would pay the rent-charge of a full supply of water, and perfect sewerage.

He concluded that 'the present clubs have been the means of doing some good with some evil'.[13] It is unlikely that most members of the societies would have viewed their activities in this critical and grudging way.

Where else would the unemployed man turn to when in need of help? Once the family resources were exhausted, friendly society benefit run out and everything pawnable had gone to the pawn-broker's, the only thing left was to apply to the Poor Law authorities. Hatred of the workhouse is more commonly associated with the harsh administration of the Poor Law after the Poor Law Amendment Act of 1834 than with the Poor Law of the eighteenth century, but it appears that in Birmingham there was a cordial dislike of going on the parish long before the reforms of the 1830s and the attempted abolition of outdoor relief. Thus, in 1812 Attwood observed that 'multitudes would rather perish than apply for parochial aid'.[14] By the mid-nineteenth century, this attitude was probably strengthened by the passing of the 1834 Act – it was said in the 1860s that the genuine Birmingham artisan hated and dreaded the parish[15] – though the Act had no direct effect on the Birmingham workhouse system. This was because a Board of Guardians was set up in 1783 following the passing of Gilbert's Act (1782), which encouraged the incorporation of urban parishes and the erection of a union workhouse. Birmingham already had a workhouse, built in 1733 for 600 paupers, and extended in 1766 by a wing to provide an infirmary, and again in 1779 by a wing on the other side of the building to give working space for able-bodied inmates. A plan to build an entirely new workhouse in 1783 fell through, no doubt to the satisfaction of William Hutton, who opposed the plan in the first edition of his work as an unnecessary expense.

It might be that the sheer size of the relief system under the 1783 Act led to an impersonal approach which antagonized applicants from the start: there were 108 guardians elected by ratepayers paying at least £12 a year in rates, together with twelve overseers appointed by the magistrates. The guardians themselves had to pay at least £20 in rates, and were drawn from the wealthier classes.[16] However, outdoor relief was given to large numbers; certainly more were relieved outside the workhouse than within. For example, in 1795 – a year of depression – 2,500 were relieved outside the workhouse as compared with 473 relieved inside. Again, in 1817 (another bad year) 5,240 were given outdoor relief, and 1,000 relieved inside. Relief might also be given in aid of wages, and Hutton gives an example of this in his 1809 edition.[17] Inside the workhouse, the able-bodied were taught trades such as spinning and weaving, and were also hired out to farmers. Children were accommodated in a separate Asylum for the Infant Poor, and were also taught trades.

By the 1830s national attitudes towards the poor were hardening, especially against the high cost of poor rates and against grants in aid of wages, and in Birmingham the giving of help to those already employed but at low wages was discontinued by the 1830s. There were also efforts to deal more systematically with the poor. A District Visiting Society was founded in 1830, and a Society for the Suppression of Mendicity, in the same year, to investigate the plight of beggars, and either to relieve them or to prosecute them for vagrancy.[18]

It is understandable that by the 1840s there was a long tradition of hostility to the Poor Law authorities in Birmingham. It was not because they were particularly harsh or unsympathetic, and indeed employers themselves might show considerable understanding of the feelings of unemployed workmen, as has already been seen; and it must be said further that manufacturers set up relief committees in times of distress, and helped organize soup kitchens. Yet at the same time there was a strong middle-class belief that much poverty was due to idleness or drunkenness rather than to genuine unemployment, and many working-class men and women were themselves not untouched by this belief and felt ashamed of having to go to the parish for help. Consequently the relieving officers were the last persons to be approached in times of need. When distress was deep and persistent, however, it might be unavoidable. Chadwick's Report (1842), noted how the number of applicants for relief went up and down from year to year, and that in the previous seven years it had varied from 5,818 to 10,222. Applications were made for different reasons, of course, but chiefly on account of sickness or want of work. Other applications were made by men whose trades had declined, or who were too old to learn new trades; or by women whose husbands were in prison, or whose children were ill.[19] Thus, misfortune drove men and women to the overseers as a last resort, and for both skilled and unskilled, the workhouse must have remained a feared and dreaded prospect throughout their working lives and into old age.

With working-class life centred relatively so strongly on life at work there was little time given to cultural activities. In particular, attitudes to education and schooling were less than enthusiastic. Probably the most important reason for this was the simple economic fact (noted in chapter 6) that it was traditional for children to go to work as soon as they were physically strong enough, and their earnings were an important supplement to the family income. Moreover, the employment of children was widespread in Birmingham industry, much of the work being especially suitable for children and young women, and not subject to the Factory or Workshop Acts until the 1860s. There is the further consideration that education in itself was not thought valuable to the individual boy or girl.[20] The ability to read and write might be useful, but anything beyond was regarded as mere trimmings and of doubtful utility. Education was not thought of as an agent for social mobility, success in life was rather a matter of self-help, hard work and the display of initiative – virtues especially esteemed in a town with so many small businesses where it was relatively easy to set up on one's own. Whatever the practical realities, the general belief in the possibilities of self-advancement was genuine enough, and this militated against any general drive towards popular education at least until the 1830s. The only qualification here is that a minority of thoughtful working men did place some value on self-education, and provided support for the adult education movement in the town, as will be seen later.

At the beginning of the period, the extent of schooling available was very limited. In the 1780s the major educational establishment was the King Edward vi Free Grammar School (see chapter 8) which had a sprinkling of boys from artisan families, but was predominantly middle-class. A further six English schools had been established by 1780 as off-shoots of this Anglican foundation, and were intended to supply an education suitable for sons of the working classes; but they catered for no more than 300 boys in all. There were two further Anglican schools in the shape of the Blue Coat School, founded in 1724 to provide apprentices for industry (something over a hundred boys and girls), and the very small Crowley's Charity, with about a dozen girls. All in all, it has been calculated that about one child in twenty-one in Birmingham in 1781 attended school.[21] This figure includes all the middle-class boys at the grammar school, but excludes the quite numerous private schools. Since these were patronized very largely by middle-class families, the 1781 estimate remains a reasonable indicator of the clearly very limited working-class attendance.

However, the establishment and growth of the Sunday School movement in Birmingham in the 1780s supplied a useful supplement to the existing day school provision. The movement started in Gloucestershire in 1783; by 1786 there were fifty-nine Sunday Schools in Birmingham. At first the Dissenters seemed to take the initiative, and founded rather more schools than the Church of England, but by the late 1820s the Anglicans began to expand their provision. The numbers of children involved were quite impressive: in 1791 about 13.5 per cent of working-class children in Birmingham were attending Sunday Schools, and by 1821 the figure was 39 per cent. It peaked at 40 per cent in 1831, declining to 35 per cent in 1841. However, it must be remembered that of the fifty-six Sunday Schools in 1838, less than half taught writing as well as reading. Arithmetic was taught in only seven schools, geography in five, and grammar and history in four. Thus the curriculum was severely restricted and was based for the most part on Bible reading. This narrowness would have been of less consequence had the children also attended day school during the week, but in 1838 only a quarter did so – 4,141 out of a total of 16,757 on the books. Further, the average Sunday School day was not long – on average, including prayer and singing, it lasted up to four hours.[22] Thus, however beneficial the work done in Sunday Schools, it could scarcely be the equivalent of full-time instruction in a day school.

Meanwhile, from the 1790s onwards, the number of day schools was increased by additional schools provided by the Church of England and by the Free Churches, and in 1809 the first non-denominational Lancasterian school was opened, to be followed by the first school of the National Schools Society (the Anglican society). Most of the new Anglican schools founded up to 1851 were National Schools, while the Wesleyans founded about ten schools, the Independents seven, and the Roman Catholics eight.[23] The 1830s appear to have been an important decade for the provision of additional school places, not only in the form of church schools, but also by the establishing between 1837 and 1852 of four new elementary schools by the King Edward Foundation for the sons of tradesmen and artisans, shopkeepers, clerks and small manufacturers. In addition, the Grammar School (now housed in new buildings), set up a new English or commercial department, so that of the total of 465 pupils, 250 were in the classical school, and 215 in the English school, among the latter being a few sons of clerks and tradesmen.[24]

In spite of this expansion, there were still more places available in 1838 in private schools than in schools provided by the churches, charities, or the King Edward Foundation. So far as the working classes were concerned, private schools fell into two major groups – the dame schools, and the common day schools. The former hardly deserve to be dignified by the name of school: they consisted of small groups of children instructed by the teacher in her living room between bouts of housework. She was usually poor, unqualified and near illiterate herself. One mistress interviewed in a survey of schools in Birmingham in 1838 complained how unprofitable the work was, and when asked why then she did it, she replied: 'Bless you, I would not continue school another day, but I can do nothing that pays me better. I am sure I have prayed every day since I began, that it may do, but it's no use. I can't get my prayers answered, instead of that it gets worse.' As the interviewer calculated that the average weekly receipts of dame school teachers amounted to only 4s 3½d each, her complaints are not surprising. There were 267 dame schools in Birmingham in 1838, with an average of 14.6 pupils each.[25] Children from such schools might go on to common day schools, of which there were 177, with an average of 31.9 boys and 20.4 girls to a school.[26] Here the instruction was often in the hands of a retired soldier, and similarly indifferent in quality. There were other kinds of private schools, of course, but they were for the middle classes and were described in the previous chapter.

All in all, it appears that provision for working-class education was still very meagre in Birmingham by the mid-nineteenth century. Whereas nationally one in 8.36 was in a day school in 1851, in Birmingham the figure was 11.02. Among West Midland boroughs only Wolverhampton (11.96) and Coventry (12.90) had worse figures, while Walsall, Stafford, Lichfield and Kidderminster all had better figures.[27] Moreover, it must be remembered that it was not usual for children to stay at school for more than a short period – up to two years was common, and many stayed for less than this. This does not necessarily indicate parental indifference to education, but attendance at school meant a loss of earnings, and this was a powerful disincentive. Further, going to school meant paying school fees – 2d to 6d a week in dame schools, 2d to as much as 1s 3d in common day schools. Church schools usually charged 2d per week, but sometimes charged fees dependent on the occupation of the parent; St Paul's charged 9d per week for children of manufacturers and shopkeepers, 6d for journeymen families, and 3d for children of other working men.[28] For simple economic reasons, therefore, sending children to school for anything other than a short period was not an attractive proposition for working-class parents, quite apart from the suspicion entertained by many that lack of education was no barrier to advancement if a boy was sufficiently determined. This is in spite of the fact that a number of Birmingham employers believed in education for the working classes, and preferred to employ workmen with some schooling, principally because it made for respectfulness and good behaviour. Samuel Turner, the button manufacturer with a large work-force of over 500, declared in 1840 that 'the educated workman was unquestionably of much greater value to his employer than the uneducated'.[29] Not many workmen appeared to agree with him, or if they did, they still failed to keep their children at school for any length of time. The consequence of all this was a low literacy rate in Birmingham in the 1840s. In 1846, 29 per cent of bridegrooms were still making their mark in marriage registers in Birmingham, and 47 per cent of brides. In Palmer & Holt's pin factory in 1843, among children aged seven to twelve, 67 per cent of the boys and 58 per cent of the girls could not read, while 81 per cent of the boys and all the girls were unable to write at all.[30] Hence the ability to read books and newspapers, or to write a letter or shopping list, scarcely formed an important element in Birmingham working-class culture in the mid-century. Naturally, exceptions could be found to working-class indifference to education, but they were confined on the whole to the best-paid, skilled workers, and they were the parents of working-class boys at the grammar school and in its elementary schools.

These same parents doubtless contributed to the limited numbers of the working classes in Birmingham who regularly attended church or chapel. The establishing of new places of worship in the town has already been traced in outline in the previous chapter, and the point has been made that in common with other large industrial towns, church and chapel attendance in 1851 was relatively low. The question is, what proportion of the attenders recorded in the religious census of that year was working-class? The simple fact that only about a third of all those able to attend on Census Sunday did in fact go to church or chapel, gives some indication of the low level of working-class attendance, for obviously a substantial proportion of attenders must have been middle-class. One can only guess what proportion; if a half, then the remaining half were working-class – an estimate erring perhaps on the side of generosity. On this basis, the total number of working-class attenders would be 29,084. If the working classes constituted about three-quarters of the population at the time, their numbers would be 174,631. Applying Mann's rule that up to 70 per cent of the population were available to worship at *some* time during the course of Census Sunday, then 121,241 working people could have gone to church or chapel. In fact, only 29,084 appear to have done so – roughly 24 per cent, or one in four. On the other hand, if the proportion of attenders who were working-class is estimated at nearer a quarter than a half, the 24 per cent falls to 12 per cent, or only one in more than eight.[31]

All this is highly speculative, of course, but in the absence of detailed information as to the constitution of individual congregations, it is not possible to go very far beyond this. Whether it is one in four or one in eight, or some figure in between, it is manifest that attendance by the working classes was very limited. Further, the one dissenting sect which in the Black Country and elsewhere in the Midlands had a substantial working-class membership – the Primitive Methodists – had only three places of worship, with a total attendance of 1,053, that is, about 702 actual attenders. A remark made some thirty years later seems to sum up the mid-century scene very well: 'Birmingham, for Primitive Methodism, has been like the seed sown on hard and rocky places.'[32] Further, although a substantial working-class presence might be expected in Roman Catholic churches, in fact the number of Roman Catholics in Birmingham in 1851 was relatively small, a far smaller proportion than in Manchester or Liverpool, and smaller even than in Bristol or Wolverhampton.[33] Total attendance for the Roman Catholics numbered only 5,107 – about 3,404 attenders. All in all, the bulk of working-class attenders was probably to be found among the Primitive Methodists, the Roman Catholics and possibly the Wesleyan Methodists (total attendance 8,383), rather than in the more middle-class denominations of the Church of England (total attendance 29,521), the Independents (total attendance 7,651), the Baptists (total attendance

8,803), or the Unitarians (total attendance 2,483). Among the Unitarians, Quakers and Baptists there was a sprinkling of self-employed craftsmen, but their numbers must have been comparatively few.[34] Although, as already noted, Birmingham was famous for Dissent, the population as a whole was not particularly Nonconformist as compared with that of other large towns, and Dissent did not go far down the social scale.

The low church and chapel attendance was not at all exceptional for a large industrial town, and it was one of the reasons why the compiler of the Religious Census, Horace Mann, observed gloomily that 'the masses of our working population . . . are never or but seldom seen in our religious congregations', while in 1860 Lord Shaftesbury said that not 2 per cent of working men in London attended church. Birmingham certainly had a better record in 1851 than this. Nevertheless, attendance was distinctly lower than in Coventry or in the Black Country townships, the biggest of which, Wolverhampton, had an attendance-to-population figure of 53.1 per cent, while Dudley's figure was 55.3 per cent. The comparable figure for Birmingham was 36.1 per cent.[35] The reasons for this are various: among them must be the sheer anonymity of life in a large industrial town which made it easy for immigrants to lose the habit of church attendance which had prevailed in their native villages. Another reason is the payment of pew rents: they were beginning to disappear by 1851, but more than half (36,485) of the total number of sittings (66,714) in that year were still subject to rent – even the Primitive Methodists levied rents on about a third of their seats. Although these rents in the free churches were usually small, they still acted as a disincentive to the poor. Then again, there were other social considerations. For the poorly-paid, it was not only a matter of having to occupy the free seats (itself a sign of their lowly status), but the simple need to have a suit or dress different from their working clothes could be an additional problem. For others, the sense that church and chapel were for the better-off and not for them, provided another reason for non-attendance. This was perhaps the greatest obstacle of all, and the feeling of social segregation was accentuated by some churches which held separate services for working men, sometimes in a tent pitched in a working-class area. There were few chapels in the poorer districts because all except the Methodists were dependent on the voluntary congregational system.[36] Further, the sense of social alienation might be increased rather than reduced as a result of the efforts of well-meaning missionaries among the poor who were often thought patronizing and interfering. In the opinion of one Chartist correspondent in the *Birmingham Journal* in 1839, the church parties

> would undoubtedly force the people to attend their place of worship by law; and their objects were to collect funds and send their booby-missionaries about the town, or maintain that other most pestiferous and annoying nuisance, the delivery of tracts at the houses of the poor. The rich man is not molested in this way.[37]

Another working-class writer considered visiting the poor to be something exceptional, the more usual attitude of ministers being one of indifference and distain: 'We have even heard of some preachers who have visited the poor in their own humble dwellings . . . but far more often we have seen preachers display the lofty look, cold neglect, and total disregard to the wants and claims of those around them.'[38]

Any final judgement as to the importance of religion in Birmingham working-class culture at the mid-century should not be determined by the statistics of church attendance alone, or even by the occasional expression of hostility to church or chapel. Nevertheless, attendance figures cannot be ignored. For example, the fact that in Merthyr Tydfil attendance was as high as 88.5 per cent surely provides some indication, at least, of the fervour with which the local community regarded attendance at chapel.[39] But what has to be taken into account in Birmingham is the relatively high attendance at Sunday School, and the existence of church schools which together must have given many working-class children some degree of understanding, however muddled, of the basic tenets of the Christian religion. Then again, attendance on Census Sunday would not have included all those who attended only from time to time, or only at Easter or Christmas. As for week-day contact, both churches and chapels supported charities providing food, clothing and fuel in times of distress, and ran savings clubs which met in their vestries or church halls.[40] Day-to-day contact was thus common enough for both the poorer and the better-off sectors of the working classes. The artisan was most likely to be the active participant in church and chapel activities, including regular attendance, while the labourer was more likely to encounter the representatives of church or chapel when times were bad and relief was being offered.

For all these reasons it is not possible to reach any precise conclusions as to the state of religious feeling among the Birmingham working classes. All that can be said is that the artisan class probably provided the bulk of working-class support for the churches and chapels and were most affected by the strength of Evangelicalism in the town; though even here it has been said that Birmingham was notoriously inhospitable to revivalist religion.[41] It may well be overestimating the strength of religious feeling to argue that Evangelicalism actively penetrated the life of the community, or that it was the cement which attached the artisan class firmly to the middle classes, as Dr Tholfsen has put it:[42] given the Census Sunday figures, it is hard to see how Evangelical belief was transmitted to more than a minority of the working classes. On the other hand, it is tolerably clear that in one way or another the fundamentals of Christian thinking filtered through to many working-class children and adults. Of course, it is possible that, in the words of one recent commentator: 'The majority of the working classes . . . by accident or design were lost to organized religion and were scarcely ever seen in the churches or chapels. If religion was strong, so was religious indifference.'[43] But this may be to place too much emphasis on organized religion and the bare statistics of attendance, and not to give sufficient weight to the more informal transmission of religious beliefs.

There remains the subject of leisure activities. Naturally, much depended here on individual taste, time available, and spending money. Most activities took place on weekday evenings (especially Saturday evenings), on Sundays and on St Monday, and this applies generally throughout the period 1760–1840. Only in the second half of the nineteenth century was St Monday replaced by the Saturday half-day off. Broadly speaking, the period up to the 1830s was one in which a variety of pursuits, sports and amusements was available, some of them of a traditional and cruel nature, while the succeeding decades saw the decline of cruel sports and the growth of rather more civilized forms of entertainment. As is well-known, the early Victorian era witnessed an increasing stress on rational recreation and seemly amusement in contrast to the boisterous sports of earlier years.

In the second half of the eighteenth century, the more serious-minded among the working classes in Birmingham could join one or more of a number of libraries or debating societies. For example, a library for the working classes was founded in 1797 by two Sunday School teachers which was known firstly as the Bristol Street Society and later as the Artisans' Library. By 1811 it had settled in Edmund Street, and in 1825 it was still in existence with a book stock of 1,500 volumes. Another Artisans' Library was established by James Belcher & Sons in 1816 with premises in Edgbaston Street, Deritend, the Bull Ring and High Street. Subscriptions for libraries of this kind were between 12s and one and a half guineas a year, so that their appeal was obviously to the better-paid working man.[44] Debating societies presumably also appealed to the more literate and articulate. In 1774 they included the Free Debating Society (or Robin Hood Free Debating Society), meeting at the Red Lion, and the Amicable Debating Society, which met at a coffee house. They were joined in 1789 by the Society for Free Debate.[45]

Another aspect of leisure activities pursued by the serious-minded is the desire for self-improvement seen in the field of adult education. The Birmingham Sunday Society was founded in 1789 by some of the teachers in the dissenting Sunday Schools to give instructions after Sunday School in writing, arithmetic, geography and other subjects. Some of the leading pupils were selected to qualify as teachers and formed a new Brotherly Society in 1796 to teach useful subjects: there were forty-five members in 1817. This has been described as the first mechanics institute in Britain, preceding the founding of Birkbeck College, London, by thirty-five years.[46] The Sunday Schools themselves, as already noted, were attended by young adults as well as by children.

No doubt the more intellectually-minded constituted only a minority among the working classes, even though it has been said that the superior Birmingham artisans were renowned for their interest in cultural as well as technical matters.[47] For the majority, the public house, open all day from early in the morning till late at night, was the great social centre. This was not only because of the company, the clubs and the friendly societies, but also because of the games available there: according to Hutton, they included fives, quoits, skittles, cards, dominoes, bagatelle and marbles. Gardening was also popular on the famous guinea and half-guinea gardens – these were plots of an eighth, and sometimes a sixteenth of an acre which were still plentifully available at the turn of the century. Others in search of livelier entertainment might attend the theatre in the gods, where they were known for their disruptive behaviour. As George Davis puts it, somewhat inelegantly, in his *Scenes from Low Life* (1790):

Oft when a brilliant thought is being spoke
a loud horse-laugh or clap will intervene
Destroying all the beauty of the scene . . .

Circuses and other shows included acrobats, conjurors, dwarfs, giants and even a learned dog who 'reads, writes, and casts accounts'. But the most popular and brutal sports were cockfighting, bull-baiting, badger-baiting and bear-baiting.[48] Cockfighting was sometimes organized on a large scale two or three times a year in the form of matches between counties lasting several days, or on a smaller scale on Monday nights, especially in winter. In both cases, bets were laid on the results. Bull-baiting was usually a feature of Easter, Whitsuntide and the wakes, one bull often being baited in three or four successive weeks. Birmingham was said to be the most notorious place in England for bull-baiting, and the practice was actually made illegal in the town in 1773, though it continued illegally until the last bull was baited in 1811. Badger-baiting was almost as common as cockfighting, the badger being put into a hole in the ground and dogs set on it. Bear-baiting seems to have been indulged in rather less than the other sports, presumably because bears were in shorter supply than cocks and bulls, though a famous bear, 'Old Nell', put in weekly appearances for several years in the yard in Coleshill Street.

In the first half of the nineteenth century these cruel sports began to die out, especially from the 1830s onwards. Martin's Bill forbade bull-baiting and bear-baiting in London, and was extended to the whole country in 1835, though cockfighting in particular continued illegally for some time after. The more intellectual interests of the working classes were furthered in 1825 by the establishing, with strong middle-class support, of the Birmingham Mechanics Institute. Richard Spooner was president, Thomas Attwood treasurer and Joseph Parkes one of the two secretaries. In its earlier days, it had a membership of a thousand and a library of 3,000 books, but by 1840 the membership had dropped to 487, and the Institute suspended operations in June 1842, and closed down shortly after. Other societies which flourished briefly at this time, but later failed, included the Athenaeum and the People's Instruction Society, founded in 1846, with 500 working-men members. The People's Hall of Science, an Owenite foundation, opened its own building in 1846, but after three years the Hall was sold. The Polytechnic Institute, founded in 1843, was built on the ruins of the Mechanics' Institute, and in turn gave birth to the Birmingham Midland Institute in 1854.[49] Thus, there was no lack of effort to provide institutions for the more thoughtful working man, but they did not prosper in the 1840s, possibly because of the rival attraction of Chartism from 1839 to the late 1840s.

Meanwhile, more frivolous entertainment continued to be available in the theatre and in gin shops and taverns. Gin shops sometimes provided music in the form of a fiddler or two, while some of the larger public houses had their own stages, one of them with room for more than a thousand customers who were charged 3s 6d admission, the same amount being returned in beer, spirits and tobacco. On Sundays, when no dramatic entertainment was allowed, psalms and hymns were sung, to the rather odd accompaniment of drinking and smoking.[50]

Open air entertainment continued in the form of football and cricket, which in the past had always been less popular than cockfighting and bull-baiting, but were played more and more by the mid-century; though it was not until later when the Saturday half-day had been established that professional football could develop as a spectator sport. In the 1840s cheap excursion trains became available at holiday times for trips to beauty spots in Warwickshire, Shropshire, Wales and even to the Liverpool docks.[51] In the same period local expeditions, termed gipsy parties, in the form of works outings to places like the Clent Hills became very common,[52] while annual works dinners and treats continued from the earlier period; even Julius Harvey gave a dinner to his workmen on his birthday in September 1789, though he left early on account of the rough behaviour of some of the men present as the drink circulated. (It may be, too, that his piles were troubling him; he complained of them some time afterwards.)[53]

Two forms of jollification indulged in during the middle years of the eighteenth century were still in existence a hundred years later; these were the wakes and the fairs. Wakes were local holidays lasting three or four days, originally being church festivals. In Hutton's time, there were three wakes, the Deritend, Bell and Chapel Wakes, while later on new wakes were started at Ashted, Erdington, Smethwick and Moseley.[54] Wakes were often crude and violent affairs, characterized by much drinking, bull-baiting, dogfighting and so on. Hutton had a very low opinion of them: 'a church festival turned into riot, drunkenness, and mischief. . . we may safely pronounce the wake the lowest of all low amusements, and completely suited to the lowest tempers'.[55]

By the mid-nineteenth century, wakes had become increasingly unpopular for a number of reasons. They were disliked by Evangelical employers, the new police found them a great nuisance, and even the more responsible and respectable artisan class was turning against them. Fairs, on the other hand, were less disliked by the middle classes. They combined traditional market stalls with entertainment booths, and were again the scene of working-class pleasures such as much drinking and eating (hot sausages, and tripe and onions were very popular), but apparently were rather more peaceful than wakes. Two fairs were held annually, one in spring and the other in autumn, and they continued up to 1914 and even beyond, long after the wakes had died out.[56] Both wakes and fairs were held in the open streets, there being no public park in Birmingham till Adderley Park was opened in 1856, followed by Calthorpe Park in the following year. There were commercial parks, however, such as the Vauxhall Gardens in Ashted, opened in 1758 for the middle classes, but becoming more available to the respectable working classes as the cost of admission was lowered. By the 1830s, entrance cost 1s 6d, and after 1842, only 1s.[57]

This survey of working-class leisure activities inevitably raises two questions. First, how many of the inhabitants of Birmingham actually participated in them, and to what degree? Obviously, this can be answered in only the most general terms, but it is clear that the more skilled and the better-paid would have money to spend on leisure, in the public house or elsewhere; they would be the most welcome customers anywhere. Yet, at the same time, money was not necessary to attend some outdoor spectacles, though it would be needed for betting purposes. The sheer variety of amusements leaves no doubt as to the reality of leisure activities among the working classes throughout the period. Earlier on, in 1767 there were 294 publicans in Birmingham and thirty-two maltsters. By the mid-nineteenth century, there were 717 brewers (i.e. publicans), 204 maltsters, 718 male and female licensed victuallers and beershop keepers, 565 inn servants, and 721 persons connected with shows, games and sport.[58] All these people formed part of a long-established and profitable leisure industry, and it is thus difficult to argue that the first half of the nineteenth century saw the destruction of old forms of recreation among the industrial working classes, in Birmingham, at least.[59]

The second question is: what changes occurred in leisure activities over the whole period 1760–1840? The two main changes have already been described – the gradual decline of the cruel sports towards the end of the period, and the beginnings of railway excursions in the 1840s. The former change took time, and indeed the activities of the Royal Society for the Prevention of Cruelty to Animals (founded 1824) were positively resented by some working men who objected to the society's interference with their care (or rather, lack of care) of working animals.[60] The latter change coincided with the increasing emphasis on outings and excursions typified in the works outing or gipsy party. Indeed, one contemporary observer in 1849 suggested that gipsy parties as much as anything had tended to diminish the importance of the wakes, which he thought might become extinct within the next few years.[61] Be this as it may, the wakes continued throughout the period and so did the fairs. St Monday was also observed throughout, both in small workshops and in some of the larger establishments, so there is nothing to show any appreciable change in the amount of time available for leisure. Whatever happened in the new textile towns of the North, there appears to have been no fundamental changes in leisure patterns of the working classes in Birmingham during the main years of the Industrial Revolution.[62]

Despite the variety of spare-time amusements and pastimes available to Birmingham workers, work inevitably remained the central fact of their existence, colouring their whole lives and culture. Why else were they called the working classes? Leisure activities, whether for the serious-minded or for the frivolous, had to fit into the pattern of the working week, and much would depend on the family income when it came to ways of spending spare time. With so much work available for women and children, it was the skilled man with working wife and children who had the largest income, though this does not necessarily mean that his house would be the largest or best furnished, or his diet better than others. Indeed, after commenting on the extravagent working-class way of purchasing food from hucksters (small shop-keepers) in small quantities at high prices, and on the prevalence of drunkenness, Chadwick's Report goes on to suggest that

> It [drunkenness] most generally prevails among that class of workmen who obtain the highest wages, but who are often found in the most deplorable and abject condition. The improvidence of which we are speaking is to be traced in very many instances to extreme ignorance on the part of the wives of these people. The

females are from necessity bred up from their youth in the workshops, as the earnings of the younger members contribute to the support of the family.

There follow the familiar Victorian animadversions on the evils of married women working away from home, a consequence of the widespread belief that women's place was in the home, and not in paid employment: 'To the habit of married women working in manufactories may also often be traced those jealousies and heart-burnings, those quarrels and that discontent which embitter the home of the poor man.'[63] This kind of criticism is to be found throughout the rest of the century, and it obviously stems from the conception of women as essentially home-makers and mothers, ignoring the fact that not all married women went out to work, and that many who did so went out of necessity rather than choice, as they had always done. Nevertheless, it is worth considering that there might have been substance in the often-expressed beliefs of this sort given that the need to combine the roles of mother, housewife, and industrial worker must have placed great strains on the married woman worker, as of course it still does today.

To attempt to trace the evolution of working-class culture in an expanding industrial town during the period 1760–1840 is not easy, but the fact that Birmingham was already heavily industrialized in 1760 has meant that few fundamental changes in working-class life-style are to be seen over the period. No doubt for those immigrating into the town from the countryside, the change from agricultural work to the routine of the workshop and to urban life must have been dramatic; but for those born into the industrial environment, no massive changes can be discerned in the way of life of the average industrial worker by 1840. The new work discipline of the larger establishments affected some, but not the majority, St Monday still bulked large in many workers' lives, and the public house remained the leisure centre of the early Victorian era. An increasing moral earnestness resulting from the Evangelical revival affected some, but relatively few compared with other nearby industrial areas. Increasing numbers of children went to school, and adult self-improvement became more noticeable, though adult literacy rates were not high in the 1840s. Women's literacy rates were lower than men's, as they were elsewhere, and women were very much the drudges of working-class society, much put-upon and exploited. Prostitution flourished, as it does today. In the 1840s, most prostitutes were aged from fourteen to eighteen (according to the superintendent of the 1st division of the Birmingham police force) and their clients were usually young men between fourteen and twenty. In one district which could be walked round in fifteen minutes there were 118 brothels, and forty-two other houses of ill-fame; the average number of prostitutes per brothel was three, making 354 in that district in all.[64] Working-class sports became less cruel, but drink rather than religion remained the opium of the people – the habit of drinking foreign wines was growing among the better class of workmen, according to Chadwick's committee – while opium itself and other hard drugs appear to have been rarely used.[65]

Comments and Reflections

The extraordinary expansion of industry and commerce in Birmingham during the period 1760–1840 does not fit easily into traditional accounts of the Industrial Revolution. These accounts emphasize, again and again, technological advance in the textile and iron industries, together with the development of steam power and railways. Yet Birmingham became a massive manufacturing centre in the eighteenth century, of greater importance even than Manchester in the early days of expansion, but without the aid of that wave of gadgets which characterized the Industrial Revolution in the schoolboy's essay described in Professor Ashton's famous story. Birmingham's success was based very largely on hand technology and, as we have seen, steam power played little part until the 1830s at the earliest. How then can its remarkable advance be put into perspective?

Much depends, of course, on how the Industrial Revolution is defined. Older views naturally stressed the expansion of the textile industry and in particular the triumphs of King Cotton, together with the gloomier aspects of social change. More recent attempts to penetrate to the heart of the matter have concentrated on specific aspects of economic change, such as the growth of real income per capita; one historian has it that the central defining characteristic must be the growth of real incomes substantially and progressively over many decades to levels above those found in pre-industrial economies.[1] This opens up interesting prospects of arguments over the trend of real incomes, and over what constitutes a pre-industrial economy. More conventionally-minded historians would be content to regard the Industrial Revolution as a suitable term for a period of unprecedented technological innovation, coupled with a change in the basis of the economy from agriculture to industry. Clearly it is this second aspect to which the Birmingham experience may be most directly related, and to which it made a major contribution.

In this, Birmingham was by no means unique. Many other towns and areas, apart from those engaged in textile, iron and coal production, played their own part in establishing Britain as the first industrial economy. It has been stressed that much of industry was still unmechanized by 1840, in the sense that it still had not adopted steam power or the factory system. Birmingham should then be seen as being typical of this other kind of industrial development, this other Industrial Revolution, as it has been called, a revolution based on the greatly extended use of a basic hand technology. Viewed in this light, Birmingham is an outstanding example of industrial growth flowing from an earlier period of expansion in the first half of the eighteenth century. In many ways it constitutes the economic norm, the archetypical city of the Industrial Revolution; whereas Manchester and the other textile towns, though of great importance to the growth of the economy, are really the exceptions in the story of industrial development as a whole, and possibly exceptional in their social development too. For the traditionally-minded, this is an interpretation which turns the familiar story on its head. For such people, Manchester, textiles, the factory and steam power must necessarily occupy the centre of the stage; but this view can no longer be reconciled with what is known about the persistence of handicraft industry and the late development of steam power. The list of occupations in 1851, together with tables showing the size of firms in that year, which are to be found in most modern text-books, tell their own story in this respect.[2]

Two important qualifications must be made to this suggestion that Birmingham is the typical case of urban industrial development during the Industrial Revolution. The first is that it would be wrong to give the impression that industry in Birmingham somehow grew without significant changes in its methods of production from, say, Tudor times until well into the nineteenth century. Although its progress from 1760 for the next half-century is unmarked by significant technological innovation, this could be misleading because important changes in hand technology had already taken place before then. As was made clear in chapter 1, by 1760 the stamp, press, lathe and drawbench were already in use. It might be going too far to say that by 1760 a technological revolution had already occurred in

Birmingham, but certainly the use of these machines was widespread and vital to the town's industrial success. It is difficult to over-emphasize the importance of mechanical aids in the toy and button trades, and their operation was freely commented on both locally and nationally. Here is an example of technological advance which permitted a high degree of skilled, specialized work without the aid of the water power which drove so much of heavy industry into the countryside. Too little attention has been paid to relatively sophistic-ated forms of machinery in the so-called pre-industrial era which continued in use until the mid-nineteenth century and beyond. It was not all simple hammer and file, spindle and shuttle before the Industrial Revolution.

Closely coupled with the use of these basic machines was the division of labour, which was so prominent in the Birmingham of the mid-eighteenth century. Contemporary comment on the division of labour was quoted in chapter 1, and there is no doubt that Birmingham was the place to visit at the time to see efficient hand production based on this and on the use of machines. It is significant that when Adam Smith wished to illustrate the principle of the division of labour in *The Wealth of Nations* it was pin-making which was chosen as an example. Thus, the kind of hand manufacture which saw Birmingham through most of the classic period of the Industrial Revolution was no antiquated survival of an earlier age; it was the constantly improving version of a state of the art technology which called on considerable skill from its operators.[3] Machinery did not lead to de-skilling in Birmingham in the eighteenth century, though it necessarily employed large numbers of relatively unskilled child assistants, as did machinery in the textile industry.

Another important qualification to be borne in mind is that the structure of industry and the size of the manufacturing unit were constantly changing. Some indication was given of this in chapter 3, but the problem remains of assessing what degree of change actually took place. The evidence is overwhelming for the survival of the small firm, and even the garret master in the 1860s, but it is hard to make out with any precision just how many large or medium-sized enterprises there were in the mid-nineteenth century as compared with the number of smaller establishments. It is not known exactly when the larger firms increased in number although this could have been before the French wars, when the Soho factory and Taylor's works already dominated the scene. Very large firms were certainly not entirely unknown at this time, but it must be remembered that a large firm in Birmingham before the French wars was not necessarily a single unified concern. Boulton's Soho manufactory certainly gathered together a large number of workmen under one roof, but many worked under sub-contract, and there were five or six firms operating there under Boulton's aegis.[4] The Soho foundry was a different and separate establishment. It may be that the larger work unit did not appear in any significant numbers until after the wars, especially in the 1830s, when steam power was increasingly used. If so, how far was this at the expense of the medium-sized and small master firms? It has been said that in the pre-war period the typical firm in the toy trade was a 'medium-sized' firm, but as the only evidence adduced for this takes the form of newspaper advertisements by defunct or bankrupt firms of machinery for sale,[5] it is by no means conclusive, and seems unlikely; smaller firms also went out of business without necessarily advertising in *Aris's Gazette*. Further, there does not seem to have been any minimum size imposed on firms in the toy trade, either by the nature of production methods or by competition within the trade which would have made the smaller firm non-viable.

Another suggestion is that the early nineteenth century saw both the proliferation of small-scale firms generally in industry *and* of larger work units; the reasons for the growth of small-scale firms was 'frequently an expression of depression, or "industrial involution" '.[6] It is not clear what this means, though it was alleged at the time (and has already been touched on) that artisans thrown out of work by depressed trade would often set up on their own as an alternative to going to the Poor Law overseers for relief. This last contemporary suggestion is surprising, since it was the skilled worker who was supposed to be protected against unemployment by membership of a friendly society (though admittedly support from the society would not last indefinitely). In any case, it can scarcely be the sole reason for the increased number of small firms in the early nineteenth century. As for the idea that the numbers of both large and very small firms increased in size after 1815, this is at least an interesting departure from the simple linear Marxist model of large firms getting larger and swallowing up or destroying the smaller firms; but there is very little evidence to show how it came about. We are left with the undisputed fact that Birmingham industry by 1840 included both large-scale and innumerable smaller workshops. There is little to show that this was at the expense of the medium-sized firm. Smaller firms certainly appear to have been alive and kicking when evidence was given before parliament in 1812, and again they feature in both Horner's Report (1833) and Grainger's Report (1843). As might be expected, they appear in Dr Eversley's analysis of firms in the Victoria County History for Warwickshire and in Professor Allen's categorization of firms at the mid-nineteenth century (see chapter 3). On the face of it, the idea that the medium-sized firm should have become less important after 1815 seems unlikely – without medium-sized firms, how was the transition from small to large to be achieved? However, without direct contemporary evidence of a kind which permits a detailed survey of the structure of Birmingham industry over the period 1760 to 1840, the question should perhaps remain open.[7]

Another difficulty is tracing the developing role of the factor with any precision. In chapter 1, figures were given for the increase in numbers of factors as shown in the directories of the time, and it is clear that one function of the factor was to serve simply as a wholesaler or middleman in the home trade. When selling at a distance from Birmingham, his role was very similar to that of a firm's traveller or representative. Thus, Drake (1825) says: 'Factors travel the country with *specimens* if portable, or *pictured representations* where they are too bulky or numerous.' And he describes them as 'visiting with their succinct and universal but portable showrooms'.[8] Drake has an odd turn of phrase, but presumably he means that they took round samples and illustrations of goods for sale. This picture of the factor on his rounds must be modified when he is seen as a supplier of raw material to the small master, and thus virtually a putter-out and employer when he also markets the finished goods. As such he might drive a hard bargain by discounting his prices and forcing the artisan to accept lower remuneration, or by shortening the period for credit. In this way, it has been argued, the position of the smaller producer deteriorated markedly after 1815.[9] Once more, the argument would be more convincing if more evidence were forthcoming to show how widespread this deterioration really was.

However, a different kind of economic function is performed by the factor who actually organized the production of a finished article, the constituent parts of which came from separate firms. Reference was made to this in chapter 3 in connection with the gun trade. The details of this operation remain obscure, yet it is clearly fundamental to the trade. The need for co-ordination of the many different manufacturing processes is obvious, but why were they not all carried on together under the same roof? It may have been that it was cheaper to have the parts made in the homes of the workers, as in the domestic putting-out system, but the final assembling of the guns had to be carried out somewhere. Meanwhile the various functions and roles undertaken by the Birmingham factor remains a subject for further research.

A last comment might be in order on the economic development of Birmingham. Just why industry expanded so vigorously in the second half of the eighteenth century has been examined in some detail in chapter 2. It might be worth while to look at the whole process from a slightly different angle, and to observe that there was a certain inevitability about economic growth in Birmingham after 1760, given the energetic developments of the previous half-century. This is especially so after the national quickening of the economy in the 1780s, and given the healthy state of trade and industry in Birmingham at that time, all predicated on the availability of cheap iron and fuel, the presence of a skilled work-force and of thrusting entrepreneurs, the efficient state of hand technology and the division of labour. Indeed, Professor Court has laid emphasis on this last factor, calling the division of labour 'an astonishingly fruitful economic conception' which he says obviously throws floods of light on the evolution of the Midlands trades.[10] Given all these favourable circumstances, it is not surprising that the Birmingham economy flourished after 1760, and that large industrial works developed in certain trades – they were destined to come, according to Court, even if steam had never been invented.[11] The surprising thing is that progress received such a severe setback during the Revolutionary and Napoleonic Wars. It seems unlikely that contemporary reports exaggerate the severity of the depression of the war years, given the number of such reports and the evidence given before parliament in 1812. As suggested earlier, it is probably a testimony to the importance of foreign trade to Birmingham manufacturers that war on the Continent should have had such dire consequences.

To turn now to the social history of the period, and first to the middle classes; there are perhaps two major stereotypes to be considered here. The first portrays a thriving, energetic class, constantly recruiting from below, consisting of a great mass of small men, comfortably off, but with a relatively thin upper layer of the really affluent. Further, these men were politically active in the pursuit of their business interests before the French wars, and very noticeably so thereafter as supporters of the Birmingham Political Union. This representation of the middle classes seems to be largely true, and to need little qualification. Upward social mobility appears to have been a reality in Birmingham, though its extent can be exaggerated, and we know little of those who failed in business, and who made the reverse journey into the ranks of the working classes. (It would be helpful if we knew more about local bankruptcy proceedings and the way in which they were conducted, especially the spirit in which the creditors sought to obtain a settlement. There are one or two interesting comments on this in Julius Harvey's diary.)[12] Businessmen could be crudely materialistic in their attitudes to business rivals and also to their own workers, but, as has been argued in chapter 8, the leaders of the community were not without a degree of culture, and Birmingham middle-class society did not lag markedly behind urban communities elsewhere in this respect. If the Industrial Revolution raised up a new breed of hard-faced businessmen, they did not form a conspicuous element in Birmingham society. How far the Evangelical movement in the first half of the nineteenth century affected class relationships is hard to say, but in some cases it undoubtedly influenced employers' attitudes towards their workers.

The second stereotype concerns relations between the middle classes and the working classes. These tend to be represented as being more amicable in Birmingham than elsewhere, largely owing to the close contact between employer and worker in the multitude of small workshops, and the relative ease with which a worker could start up on his own. In this connection, Birmingham is often contrasted favourably with Manchester. This view of class relationships has been widely held by historians of Birmingham, and owes much to the writings of Asa Briggs, Trygve Tholfsen and others.[13] In theory, this interpretation has much to recommend it – there is no gainsaying the fact that the small workshop was ubiquitous in Birmingham, whereas the average mill in Manchester was a much larger place, with a wider social gap between proprietor and workpeople – but what of the reality? As was seen in chapter 6, a recent reassessment has suggested that this emphasis on class co-operation is misplaced, in view of the pressures on the small master resulting from intensified competition and also of the numbers of strikes which took place. However, enough new evidence does not seem to be forthcoming to make necessary such a drastic revision, or to overturn the mass of evidence to the contrary contained in a parliamentary papers and elsewhere. As was seen in chapter 5 (and also in chapter 9), paternalism of the traditional kind was still strong among Birmingham employers up to 1840, the Birmingham Political Union attracted much working-class support, Owen's Equitable Labour Exchange was strongly supported by middle-class radicals (significantly, Marx and Engels were bitterly opposed to Owenism),[14] while Chartism also attracted some middle-class supporters, especially in its earlier phase.

It is true that violent disturbances broke out in 1839 in the form of the Bull Ring riots, and that the Priestley Riots of 1791 constituted very serious disorders, but it is difficult to show that either set of riots was the obvious result of sustained and developing class conflict. Of course, class conflict is to some extent in the eye of the beholder: for the Marxist, it has a basic reality, even though the participants may be unaware of its existence (and the same may be said perhaps of theories of social control). However, contemporary attitudes to Birmingham in the early nineteenth century are very different from those relating to Manchester, which city was regarded with a mixture of awe, fascination and fear: 'the shock city of the Industrial Revolution', as Asa Briggs calls it.[15] Though Birmingham had its moments of unease, there is nothing in its history at this time to match Peterloo, and the actions of the Manchester magistrates which precipitated it. Peterloo has been characterized by E. P. Thompson as an example of class war, but it is hard to see how any events in Birmingham can be similarly interpreted. Even Thompson considers that class antagonism was less acute in Birmingham than in Manchester, Newcastle or Leeds (though he does not say that it did not exist).[16] De Tocqueville, visiting Manchester in 1835, drew very unfavourable comparisons between that city and Birmingham, and noted 'separation of classes much greater in Manchester than in Birmingham'.[17]

The stereotyped picture of Birmingham as a scene of class co-operation rather than class conflict seems to be substantially accurate. This does not mean, however, that employers did not sometimes exaggerate the degree of co-operation existing between them and their workers – it often suited them to make such claims. But the weight of evidence pointing to class co-operation cannot be explained away simply in terms of middle-class ideological bias both then and now on the part of historians.[18] On the whole, Birmingham employers knew their men, and the dividing line socially between the small producer and the journeyman was very thin. At the other end of the scale, there was no resident leisured class within the town to serve as exemplars for the larger manufacturer who remained essentially an industrialist, actively engaged in carrying on his business, rather than an absentee employer living on profits.

Lastly, the Birmingham workers for whom the familiar horror stories of the Industrial Revolution do not apply: they were not employed in textile factories or down the coal mines (though presumably some children were sent up chimneys), nor did they all live in universally filthy slums amid scenes of disgusting squalor. This does not mean that hardship was not experienced both at work and in the home: long hours were worked often under harsh conditions, especially by women and children, and the standard of living of the lowest paid workers must have been wretchedly low. But it does mean that life in Birmingham was qualitatively different from life in Manchester, where Engels chose to set the scene for his famous study of the condition of the working class in England. According to Asa Briggs, had Engels lived not in Manchester but in Birmingham, his conception of class might have been very different (and Briggs adds teasingly that in this case Marx might have been not a communist but a currency reformer).[19] Yet descriptions of life in the cotton mills, working on (or under) the machines, or down the pits, carrying coals or dragging trucks, together with descriptions of sanitary conditions of the worst parts of Manchester in 1844, persist as typical illustrations of working and living conditions during the Industrial Revolution. The realities in Birmingham took different forms, though they were often grim enough.

However, there is more to it than this. It is not merely that life at work in Birmingham was different from life in the cotton mill or down the pit: rather it must be emphasized that it was far more typical of working life in other parts of the country than the new disciplines of the factory system. If, as was indicated earlier, Birmingham constitutes the norm in urban industrial development in the second half of the eighteenth century and after, then it follows that working conditions there were far from being an isolated and outmoded survival of the pre-industrial era. St Monday was still a reality in other regions of the country, and where it was observed, the working week consisted of five days not six. Hence working life in Birmingham was by no means exceptional in character.[20] As for the more recently expressed view that in spite of St Monday and the relatively modest working day of twelve hours (including meals), hours had actually become longer and work discipline intensified, there is little or no evidence for this, and we await further proof. It would be surprising, of course, if the mass of contemporary evidence somehow failed to mention such developments, had they been well-known at the time. Workmen might complain of unfair treatment, but rarely if at all about the length of the working day or the harshness of the work discipline; and strikes were usually centred on pay rather than hours or working conditions. In all probability a greater source of anxiety for most workmen was short-time working, and the loss of pay which resulted. Short-time working is difficult to quantify, and hence has received very little attention so far by historians, but it could cause great hardship, even among the highly-skilled, once their friendly society support ran out (see chapter 8). It was subjected to government enquiry in 1830 (see chapter 6), and the Report of the Select Committee is a significant indication of the importance attached to the subject at the time.

Only the employment of women and children in the pin workshops requires further comment here, for the working conditions of the children certainly invite comparisons with the cotton mills. It has been said that manufacture outside the factory system was based on extensive exploitation of labour, particularly of women and children, at least equal to that suffered under the factory system.[21] This is a questionably large assertion, but it has some truth in it as far as Birmingham children in the pin workshops are concerned. It is true that their pace of work was not determined by steam-driven machinery, but undoubtedly they were made to work very hard, and they were at times subjected to physical violence, as we have seen. This is perhaps the blackest side of life at work in Birmingham in the first half of the nineteenth century, and hitherto has not been discussed in any detail by Birmingham historians.

As for living conditions, little remains to be said. Although Birmingham is well-known for its terminating building societies in the first half of the nineteenth century, neither the number of society houses nor their quality seems at all remarkable, so that their principal significance appears to be the simple fact that the pay of skilled workers was high enough for some of them, at least, to own their own houses. Given that housing overall was somewhat better than in other large industrial towns, major questions still await an answer: what proportion of the housing stock was taken up by the roomier and better-built houses, and exactly how numerous were the older, more filthy courts compared with the newer courts? Was the back-to-back housing actually better than one would expect from its generally evil reputation? Only a very detailed study of housing development, based perhaps on maps and enumerator books, could provide answers to these questions.[22] The basic difficulty lies in the sheer size of the urban area, and the disappearance of so much nineteenth-century housing which makes field work so difficult.

Lastly, we are left with the broad general question of how workers spent their time away from work. For those who wish to emphasize the exploitation of labour during the Industrial Revolution, the very existence of working-class leisure activities (other than of a political nature) presents some difficulties: surely the workers had little or no time to relax or even to enjoy themselves? One answer here has been to suggest that social control practised by the middle classes in such fields as those of education, religion and leisure conditioned the working classes into an acceptance of the capitalist work ethic.[23] In Birmingham, however, as we have seen, only a minority of children spent any time at school before 1840, partly because the children's wages formed an important part of the family economy, and partly because education in itself was not thought to be of much importance by many parents. It was H. S. Tremenheere's view, as a former H.M. Inspector of Schools, that it was difficult to surmount the barrier of parents' ignorance of the true worth of education because it required a certain amount of education to know the true worth of education.[24] So there was not a great deal of moulding of children's attitudes through the agency of the schools before 1840. As for religion, religious observance was restricted, as we have seen, though it is as well to repeat here that the figures for attendance in chapter 9 are highly speculative. The situation was probably no better and rather worse in the second half of the eighteenth century, in spite of John Wesley's frequent visits to the town; it was said in 1788 that 'the great mass of people give themselves very little concern about religious matters, seldom if ever going to church.'[25] It may well be that after the Evangelical revival, the situation in 1851 was actually better than at the end of the previous century.

Leisure activities, on the other hand, were certainly widespread, and took many forms. There is little to show that time off for holidays, such as fairs or wakes, was restricted or controlled by the middle classes. St Monday, time off for the principal religious festivals, the closing of the works for stocktaking, the wakes and fairs, all continued, though by 1840 wakes were certainly frowned upon by the new police and the middle classes. One cannot fail to be impressed by the sheer variety of leisure activities, and by the amount of money spent on them – perhaps most of all in the ale-house. These leisure activities do not seem to have changed much over the years in their essential nature, except that as already remarked upon, they became more civilized by the beginning of the nineteenth century. Towards the end of his life (he died in 1809) Matthew Boulton considered that

> Birmingham was as remarkable for good forgers and filers as for their bad taste in all their works. Their diversions were bull-baiting, cock-fightings, boxing matches, and abominable drunkenness with all its train. But now the scene is changed. The people are more polite and civilized, and the taste of their manufactures greatly improved.[26]

This may be to ante-date the growth of more civilized tastes. Certainly in the 1790s, rowdy behaviour after closing-time was not unusual. George Davis's *Saint Monday or Scenes from Low Life* (1790) makes this amusingly clear. The apprentice, we are told, is taught in the ale-house 'to drink pint bumpers, and to swear; To smoke – to circulate the jest impure'. When time is called, he reels out in search of excitement:

> He sallies out to seek – what he calls *fun*.
> First, with a holly-stick, a lamp is broke
> To show his taste, and prove himself a *buck*.
> And if a *watchman* interrupts the deed
> He beats him if he can; then flees, with speed
> By mad intoxication led astray
> In a vile brothel to complete the day.

So, vandalism and assaults on the police after closing time are obviously no new thing in the Birmingham of the present day.

What can be said in conclusion about changes in Birmingham society during the eighty years surveyed in this book? The most striking characteristic perhaps is its simple cohesiveness and lack of dramatic change. It is true that throughout the period, industrialization and all that that implies for trade and the service sector of the town's economy dominated social relationships; nevertheless it was not as something imposed from outside, but rather a product of indigenous growth. Industrial evolution, not revolution, dominated the scene; old-style relationships, for good or ill, continued – especially old-style paternalism, often tinged with new-style Evangelicalism. Was Birmingham society more class-divided in 1840 than in 1760? The answer to this is, very probably, yes, but an increased class-consciousness among the working classes does not necessarily mean that class differences were sharpened or that class relations deteriorated. A thinking Birmingham working man (or woman) might well have been more aware in 1840 of the class structure of the society in which he lived, but might still have accepted it as part of the natural order of things, as indeed his forebears had done before him. Of course, this is not to ignore the reforming zeal of many Birmingham Chartists, who certainly aimed at some measure of political and social change, but there was still a deep conservatism in many Birmingham workers who contributed to the Tory vote in the 1860s and 1870s – Disraeli's angels in marble. Thus the social consequence of increasing industrialization in Birmingham in the period 1760–1840 was not a harsh division into mutually opposed social groups, but rather the development of tolerant class relationships. It was a different story elsewhere. What other large industrial town of the 1830s and 1840s could boast of such joint class enterprises as the Birmingham Political Union, the Equitable Labour Exchange, or the Complete Suffrage Union? The first manufacturing town in the world may well be proud of its social and economic achievements during the first century of industrialization in Britain.

Notes

Parliamentary Papers are abbreviated to P.P. throughout.

Chapter 1

1. John Leland, *Itinerary*, 2nd edn, 1745, Vol. 4, p. 108.
2. Camden's *Britannia* (1586), 1637 edn, p. 567.
3. Conrad Gill, *History of Birmingham*, Vol. 1 (1952), p. 57.
4. *Four Topographical Letters written in July, 1755 . . . from a Gentleman of London to his Brother and Sister in Town . . .*, (1757), p. 55.
5. William Hawkes Smith, *Birmingham and its Vicinity* (1836), Part II, pp. 4–5.
6. For further details of the Midlands iron industry in the early eighteenth century, see B. L. C. Johnson, 'The Foley Partnerships: the Iron Industry of the Midlands at the end of the Charcoal Era', *Economic History Review*, 2nd series, Vol. IV, No. 3, 1952, and 'The Midland Iron Industry in the early 18th century', *Business History*, Vol. II, No. 2, June, 1960.
7. Llewellyan Jewitt, *The Life of William Hutton* (1872), p. 133.
8. Gill, op. cit., p. 60. For a recent discussion of the connection between freedom from incorporation and economic growth, see P. J. Corfield, *The Impact of English Towns 1700–1800* (1982), pp. 91–3.
9. G. C. Allen, *The Industrial Development of Birmingham and the Black Country 1860–1927* (1929), pp. 28–9.
10. Gill, op. cit., p. 60.
11. R. A. Pelham, 'The immigrant population of Birmingham, 1686–1726', *Birmingham Archaeological Society Transactions*, Vol. LXI (1937).
12. Matthew Boulton Papers, Boulton & Fothergill Letter Book, 1757–65, letter 6 July 1763. A chape is the part of a buckle attaching it to the strap. Platina refers to an alloy composed of eight parts brass to five parts spelter: see R. B. Prosser, *Birmingham Inventors and Inventions* (1881), p. 55.
13. *Journal of the House of Commons*, XXVIII (1759), p. 496.
14. H. Hamilton, *The English Brass and Copper Industries to 1800* (1926), pp. 162–3.
15. *Four Topographical Letters* (1757), p. 63.
16. Lord Edmund Fitzmaurice, *Life of William, Earl of Shelburne* (1875), VOL. I, 1737–1766, p. 403.
17. Matthew Boulton Papers, Boulton & Fothergill Letter Book, 1771–3, letter 30 Dec. 1770.
18. Pearson & Rollason, *The Birmingham Directory* (1777), pp. XXV–VI.
19. For an illustrated account of these machines, see Hawkes Smith, op. cit., part III, pp. 11–16.
20. Gill, op. cit., p. 93.
21. Samuel Schroeder, *Day Book 1748–1751*, Kungliga Biblioteket MS X303, Stockholm, f. 170. I am

greatly obliged to Professor J. R. Harris for references to this document.

22. Ibid., f. 170.

23. Ibid., f. 171.

24. Ibid., f. 170.

25. Hawkes Smith, op. cit., part III, p. 16.

26. Gill, op. cit., p. 96.

27. Schröderstierna, op. cit., f. 168.

28. Lord Edmund Fitzmaurice, op. cit., p. 400.

29. *Four Topographical Letters* (1757), pp. 62–3.

30. Boulton Papers, M. Boulton's Letter Book, 1768–73. Letters 2 Feb. 1771, 24 Oct. 1772, and Nov. 1772 to the Earl of Warwick.

31. Boulton Papers, M. Boulton's Letter Copy Book, 1766–8, letter 2 March 1768.

32. See chapter 3 for details of individual industries.

33. Boulton put it succinctly in a letter in August 1765: 'no water, no polishing'. Six weeks later he recorded that the mill was all to pieces, and that 'the millwright tells us that it will be next Wed or Thurs before it will be set to rights': Boulton Papers, Letter Book B, 1764–, letters 31 Aug. 1765, 5 Oct. 1765.

34. Eric Hopkins, 'Boulton before Watt: the Earlier Career Reconsidered', *Midland History*, Vol. IX (1984).

35. Boulton Papers, Letter Book B, 1764–, letters 22 Dec. 1764, 7 Jan. 1765, and June 1765.

36. Ibid., Boulton & Fothergill Letter Book, 1771–3, letters 7 Feb. 1771, 9 March 1771, and 25 Jan. 1772.

37. See A. W. Coates, 'Changing Attitudes to Labour in the Mid-Eighteenth Century', *Economic History Review*, 2nd series, Vol. XI, 1958–9. For a recent discussion of leisure preference, see John Rule, *The Experience of Labour in Eighteenth Century Industry* (1981), pp. 54–5.

38. H. J. Dyos and D. H. Aldcroft, *British Transport* (1974), p. 77.

39. *Journal of the House of Commons*, XX (1726), pp. 741, 768.

40. M. J. Wise, 'Birmingham and its Trade Relations in the Early 18th Century', *University of Birmingham Historical Journal*, II, 1949–50, p. 77.

41. Ibid., p. 79.

42. Ibid., pp. 72–5.

43. *Journal of the House of Commons*, XXVIII (1759), p. 497.

44. William Hutton, *History of Birmingham* (2nd edn, 1783), pp. 69–70.

45. E. Robinson, '18th Century Commerce and Fashion: Matthew Boulton's Marketing Techniques', *Economic History Review*, 2nd series, Vol. XVI, No. 1, 1963, p. 55.

46. M. J. Wise, op. cit., pp. 64–71.

47. Boulton Papers, Boulton & Fothergill Letter Book, 1757–65, letters 6 Nov. 1762 and 20 June 1764.

48. For the nature and use of the Bill Account, see J. E. Cule, 'The Financial History of Matthew Boulton 1759–1800', Birmingham M. Comm. thesis (1935), pp. 11–12.

49. Hutton, op. cit., p. 99.

50. Exchequer Bills and Answers, E112, in the Public Record Office.

51. Boulton Papers, Fothergill Box, undated letter.

52. W. A. Richards, 'The Birmingham Gun Manufactory of Farmer & Galton and the Slave Trade in the 18th Century', Birmingham M.A. thesis (1972), pp. 32, 62, 148, 150.

53. See in particular Boulton Papers, Boulton & Fothergill Letter Book, 1757–65, and M. Boulton Letter Copy Book, 1766–8, letter 10 July 1767.

54. *Victoria County History for Warwickshire*, Vol. VII. (1964), p. 91.

55. D. C. Coleman, *The Economy of England 1450–1750* (1977), p. 139.

56. Richards, op. cit., pp. 46, 112.

57. Cule, op. cit., p. 289.

58. Boulton Papers, M. Boulton Letter Book, 1781–83, letter 9 Aug. 1782.

59. Fitzmaurice, op. cit., p. 401.

60. *Journal of the House of Commons*, XXVIII (1759), p. 497.

61. London Guildhall Library, Sun Insurance Registers, MS/11936/158, Vols 157–64.
62. Ibid., policy no. 218160, dated 23 March 1765.
63. Ibid., policy nos 227643, 227644, dated 25 Nov. 1765.
64. Ibid., policy nos 220802, 220803, 220804, dated 22 June 1765, 22 June 1765, 24 June 1765.
65. Ibid., policy nos 217052 (dated 12 Feb. 1765), 221138 (28 June 1765), and 227190 (18 Nov. 1765).
66. Hopkins, op. cit., p. 49.
67. Sun Insurance Registers, policy no. 216423, dated 17 Jan. 1765.
68. Ibid., policy nos 221313, dated 2 July 1765; and 226998, dated 13 Nov. 1765.
69. Llewellyan Jewitt, op. cit., p. 184.
70. I owe this information to Professor J. R. Harris. The point is discussed further in his article, 'Michael Alcock and the Transfer of Birmingham Technology to France before the Revolution', *The Journal of European Economic History*, Vol. 15, No. 1, Spring 1986.
71. C. W. Chalklin, *The Provincial Towns of Georgian England* (1974), p. 22. It should be noted that Chalklin disputes the figure given by Hutton of 15,000 for the population of Birmingham in 1700, claiming that his own figure of between 5,000 and 7,000 is the result of a calculation based on the parish registers of St Martins.
72. *Birmingham and its Regional Setting* (1950), pp. 173, 180. See also generally the article by M. J. Wise referred to in note 40.
73. A. Clow and N. L. Clow, *The Chemical Revolution* (1952), p. 133.
74. C. M. Law, 'Some Notes on the Urban Population of England and Wales in the 18th Century', *The Local Historian*, Vol. 10, No. 1, 1972.

Chapter 2

1. Conrad Gill, *History of Birmingham*, Vol. 1 (1952), p. 87.
2. See chapter 1.

3. *Victoria County History for Warwickshire*, Vol. VII (1964), (hereafter *V.C.H.*), pp. 27–30.
4. William Hutton, *History of Birmingham* (2nd edn, 1783), p. 264.
5. *V.C.H.*, p. 27.
6. Pearson & Rollason, *The Birmingham Directory* (1777).
7. *Sketchley's Birmingham, Wolverhampton and Walsall Directory* (3rd edn), 1767; *Pye's Birmingham Directory*, 1785.
8. W. T. Jackman, *Development of Transportation in Modern England* (1962 edn), pp. 684, 690.
9. J. A. Langford, *A Century of Birmingham Life* (1868), Vol. I, p. 224.
10. Hutton, op. cit., p. 263.
11. Ibid., pp. 268, 266.
12. Ibid., p. 267.
13. For details of canal building in the Birmingham area, see *V.C.H.*, pp. 33–4, and Charles Hadfield, *The Canals of the West Midlands* (1966).
14. Jackman, op. cit., p. 370.
15. Hutton, op. cit., p. 83.
16. Humphrey Lloyd, *The Quaker Lloyds in the Industrial Revolution* (1975), pp. 169–71.
17. Ibid., pp. 175, 209.
18. L. S. Presnell, *Country Banking in the Industrial Revolution* (1956), p. 6.
19. Eric Hopkins, 'Boulton before Watt: the Earlier Career Reconsidered', *Midland History*, Vol. IX (1984), p. 47.
20. *V.C.H.*, p. 8. However, it should be noted that the total for 1801 includes Aston and Edgbaston, the figure for St Martins and St Philips being 60,822. Gill, *op. cit.*, pp. 120, 155, 183, employs figures ranging from 'nearly 70,000' to 'over 70,000'.
21. For details of the building boom, see chapter 7.
22. The potting and stamping method was patented by Wood Brothers of Wednesbury in 1761. The process was improved by John Cockshutt (1771), and by Richard Jesson and John Wright of West Bromwich (1773). Cort's process was patented in 1773 and 1774. See Charles K. Hyde, 'Technological Change in the British

Wrought Iron Industry, 1750–1815: a Re-interpretation', *Economic History Review*, 2nd series, XXVII, 2 May 1974, and Charles K. Hyde, *Technological Change and the British Iron Industry, 1700–1870* (1977), p. 114.

23. R. B. Prosser, *Birmingham Inventors and Inventions* (1881), p. 3.

24. Bisset, *The Magnificent Directory* (1800).

25. A list of patents for the years 1772–1852 is given in Prosser, op. cit., pp. 196–227.

26. The three mills upon the Rea near Digbeth are described in Lloyd, op. cit., pp. 104–5.

27. W. H. B. Court, *The Rise of the Midland Industries 1600–1838* (1938), p. 257; Clive Behagg, 'Custom, Class and Change: the Trade Societies of Birmingham', *Social History*, Vol. IV, No. 3, 1979.

28. *Factory Enquiry Commission* (P.P. 1833, XX), 1st Report, report on Birmingham by Mr Horner, Depositions, pp. 5–7.

29. Court, *The Rise of the Midland Industries*, p. 257.

30. Robert Rawlinson, *Report to the General Board of Health . . . on the Borough of Birmingham* (1849), p. 49.

31. Notably Eric Hobsbawm, who develops the theme in his *Industry and Empire* (1968).

32. Hutton, op. cit., p. 70.

33. Ibid.

34. Minutes of the Select Committee on Petitions against the Orders in Council, pp. 10, 25, 27.

35. B. R. Mitchell and Phyllis Deane, *Abstract of British Historical Statistics*, (1962), p. 294.

36. Elizabeth Schumpeter, *English Overseas Trade Statistics 1697–1808* (1960), pp. 25, 26.

37. François Crouzet, 'Towards an Export Economy: British Exports during the Industrial Revolution', *Explorations in Economic History*, 17, 1980.

38. Neil McKendrick, in Neil McKendrick, John Brewer, and J. H. Plumb, *The Birth of a Consumer Society* (1982), pp. 9, 69.

39. Ralph Davis, *The Industrial Revolution and British Overseas Trade* (1979), pp. 25, 94, 95.

40. For a recent reassessment of the national export figures which emphasizes the continuing importance of the home market in the eighteenth century and the early nineteenth century, see N.F.R. Crafts, 'British Economic Growth 1700–1831: A Review of the Evidence', *Economic History Review*, 2nd series, XXXVI, No. 2, May 1983. It should be noted that the extent of smuggling of British goods, including hardware, into the continent and especially into France, adds an additional element of uncertainty to the already somewhat unreliable export figures.

41. Derek Fraser has unearthed a striking quotation from Jean Paul Sartre's historian, Antoine Roquentin, in his *Nausea* (1962 edn): 'I am beginning to believe that nothing can ever be proved. These are honest hypotheses which take the facts into account: but I sense so definitely that they come from me and are simply ways of unifying my known knowledge . . . slow, lazy, sulky, the facts adapt themselves to the vigour of the order I wish to give them but it remains outside of them. I have the feeling of doing a work of pure imagination.' See Derek Fraser, 'Politics and the Victorian City', *Urban History Yearbook*, 1979, p. 36. It is not often that historians reveal such doubts about the nature of their art.

42. W. H. B. Court, *Society and Choice in History* (1970), p. 243; E. A. Wrigley, *People, Cities, and Wealth* (1987), p. 51.

Chapter 3

1. See chapter 1.

2. De Witt Bailey and Douglas A. Nie, *English Gunmakers: The Birmingham and Provincial Gun Trade in the 18th and 19th Centuries* (1982), pp. 12–13.

3. D. Goodman, 'The Birmingham Gun Trade', in S. Timmins (ed.), *Birmingham and the Midland Hardware District* (1866), p. 400.

4. Bailey and Nie, op. cit., p. 20.

5. Goodman, op. cit., pp. 392–3.

6. Bailey and Nie, op. cit., p. 17.

7. Goodman, op. cit., pp. 392, 393.

8. Bailey and Nie, op. cit., p. 20.

9. Keith Dunham, *The Gun Trade of Birmingham* (1955), p. 15.

10. Bailey and Nie, op. cit., p. 17.

11. Goodman, op. cit., pp. 412, 413

12. Bailey and Nie, op. cit., p. 21.

13. Ibid., p. 20.

14. Dunham, op. cit., p. 16.

15. H. Hamilton, *The English Brass and Copper Industries to 1800* (1926), p. 138.

16. W. C. Aitkin, 'Brass and Brass Manufacture', in Timmins, op. cit., pp. 239, 242.

17. For details of the range of brass goods manufactured, see Hamilton, pp. 264–9.

18. Hamilton, op. cit., p. 264.

19. Ibid., pp. 217–24.

20. Ibid., pp. 233–6.

21. Ibid., pp. 292, 296.

22. G. C. Allen, *The Industrial Development of Birmingham and the Black Country, 1860–1927* (1929), p. 359.

23. Aitkin, op. cit., p. 359.

24. Minutes of the Select Committee on Petitions against the Orders in Council, pp. 48, 59.

25. *Factory Enquiry Commission*, (PP 1833, xx), 1st Report, Depositions, p. 5.

26. Hamilton, op. cit., p. 273.

27. Allen, op. cit., pp. 123–4.

28. Hamilton, op. cit., pp. 260, 263.

29. Allen, op. cit., p. 34; Samuel Timmins, 'The Industrial History of Birmingham', in Timmins, op. cit., p. 222. The modes of classification of occupations adopted in the census returns make it difficult to demonstrate the primacy of the brass industry quantitatively, but the 1851 figures given later in this chapter support the statement in the text, if the test applied is the simple one of numbers employed.

30. Aitkin, op. cit., p. 229.

31. *Victoria County History for Warwickshire*, Vol. VII (1964), p. 103.

32. Robert K. Dent, *Old and New Birmingham* (1880), pp. 112–13.

33. Robert K. Dent, *The Making of Birmingham* (1894), p. 257.

34. Arthur Ryland, 'The Birmingham Assay Office', in Timmins, op. cit., pp. 501–4.

35. William Ryland, 'The Plated Wares and Electro-Plating Trades', in Timmins, op. cit., pp. 477–8.

36. W. Ryland, op. cit., p. 478.

37. W. Ryland, op. cit., p. 488.

38. R. B. Prosser, *Birmingham Inventors and Inventions* (1881), p. 54.

39. John P. Turner, 'The Birmingham Button Trade', in Timmins, op. cit., p. 433.

40. Turner, op. cit., p. 435, p. 436.

41. Census Returns for Warwickshire, 1841 and 1851.

42. Prosser, op. cit., pp. 77–8.

43. Ibid., p. 79.

44. Allen, op. cit., p. 109.

45. Ibid., p. 54.

46. J. S. Wright, 'The Jewellery Trade', in Timmins, op. cit., p. 453.

47. Ibid., p. 454.

48. Prosser, op. cit., p. 39.

49. William Hawkes Smith, *Birmingham and Its Vicinity* (1836), Part III, p. 19.

50. Dent, *The Making of Birmingham*, (1894) pp. 453–5.

51. Conrad Gill, *History of Birmingham* (1952), Vol. I, pp. 109–10.

52. Allen, op. cit., p. 64.

53. *Children's Employment Commission* (PP 1843, xiv), Appendix to 2nd Report, report by R. D. Grainger, at f.18.

54. Census Returns, 1851. These returns are given as they are somewhat fuller than those for 1841.

55. W. H. B. Court, *The Rise of the Midland Industries, 1600–1838* (1938), pp. 256–9.

56. House of Commons Committee Reports, x, p. 663.
57. Minutes of the Select Committee on Petitions against the Orders in Council, 1812, p. 19.
58. Factory Enquiry Commission (PP 1833, xx), 1st Report; report on Birmingham by Mr Horner, p. 2.
59. Grainger's Report, at fol. 18.
60. Ibid., at fols 126, 129, 136.
61. Ibid., at fols 146, 147. The figure of 540 for the Islington Glass Works may be suspect. Stourbridge was the leading flint glass district in the mid-nineteenth century, and the average size of its glasshouses was much smaller, about 100 hands: see Eric Hopkins, 'Changes in the Scale of the Industrial Unit in Stourbridge and District 1815–1914', *West Midland Studies*, Vol. 8, 1975, p. 32.
62. Grainger's Report, at fols 153, 154, 162.
63. C. G. Carus, *The King of Saxony's Journey through England and Scotland in the Year 1844* (1846), pp. 169, 170, 171, 174.
64. L. Faucher, *Etudes sur l'Angleterre*, Vol. I (1856), p. 502 *et seq.*
65. *Morning Chronicle*, 7 October 1850, 'Labour and the Poor'; *The Leisure Hour*, 3 February 1853, p. 88.
66. The use of the hand press was described in 1853 as being 'universal' in Birmingham at the time: *The Leisure Hour*, 3 February 1853, p. 86.
67. Thomas H. Kelly, 'Wages and Labour Organisation in the Brass Trades of Birmingham and District', Birmingham PhD thesis, 1930, pp. 18–19.
68. Timmins, 'The Industrial History of Birmingham', in Timmins, op. cit., p. 223.
69. Allen, op. cit., pp. 114–15.
70. Timmins, 'The Industrial History of Birmingham', in Timmins, op. cit., p. 211.
71. Index of Masters, Apprentices and Trades, Birmingham Central Library.
72. *Children's Employment Commission* (PP 1843 xiv), Appendix to 2nd Report, Report by Theophilus Richards on Apprentices, and answers to questions put by him, fols 170 and 171.
73. J. S. Wright, in Timmins, op. cit., p. 453; Thomas Middlemore, 'The Birmingham Saddlery Trade', ibid., p. 475.
74. Bailey and Nie, op. cit., p. 20. The reasons put forward for this are that skilled workers refused to train apprentices who might constitute future competition in lean times, and that workers were paid piece rates and would not waste their time on training others.
75. Richards' Report, fol. 171.
76. It should be noted that the view has been advanced that apprenticeship was still of considerable importance in the metal trades of the Black Country in the middle of the nineteenth century: Eric Hopkins, 'Were the Webbs Wrong about Apprenticeship in the Black Country?', *West Midland Studies*, Vol. 6, 1973.

Chapter 4

1. For fluctuations in trade in the eighteenth century, see T. S. Ashton, *Economic Fluctuations in England 1700–1800* (1959), especially the Conclusions and the Tables on pp. 172–3; for Birmingham trade in 1772, see op. cit., p. 157.
2. Matthew Boulton Papers, Boulton & Fothergill Letter Book B, 1764–.
3. J. A. Langford, *A Century of Birmingham Life: or a Chronicle of Local Events from 1741 to 1841* (1868), Vol. I, p. 215.
4. G. H. Wright, *Chronicles of the Birmingham Chamber of Commerce 1813–1913 and of the Birmingham Commercial Society 1783–1812* (1913) is the standard work.
5. Witt Bowden, *Industrial Society in England towards the end of the 18th Century* (1925), pp. 168–9.
6. Wright, op. cit., pp. 11–12.
7. Ibid., pp. 25–37.

8. Wright, op. cit., p. 12; Witt Bowden, op. cit., pp. 168–9.
9. Langford, op. cit., p. 114.
10. For a more extended account of changes in the trading and service sectors, see Eric Hopkins, 'The Trading and Service Sectors of the Birmingham Economy 1750–1800', *Business History*, Vol. XXVIII, No. 3, July 1986.
11. These policies are in the Social Science Research Council Archives, and are discussed in detail in the article mentioned above.
12. Hopkins, op. cit.
13. The Cheshire sums levied were about £250 per year: Ian Mitchell, 'The Development of Urban Retailing 1700–1815', in Peter Clark (ed.), *The Transformation of English Provincial Towns 1600–1800* (1984), p. 271. The amounts levied for Birmingham were: 1786–7, £475 10s 2d; 1787–8, £573 16s 2d; 1788–9, £524 15s 4d: Exchequer Records, E182/1062, part I.
14. Select Committee on the Shop Window Duty, Minutes of Evidence, 1819 (528), II, pp. 13, 16.
15. *Victoria County History for Warwickshire*, Vol. VII, p. 115.
16. Eric Robinson, 'Boulton and Fothergill, 1762–1782, and the Birmingham Export of Hardware', *University of Birmingham Historical Journal*, VII, 1959–60, p. 76.
17. Harry Hanson, *The Coaching Life* (1983), p. 64.
18. S. R. H. Jones, 'The Country Trade and the Marketing and Distribution of Birmingham Hardware, 1750–1810', *Business History*, XXVI, No. 1, March 1984, p. 39.
19. Diary of Julius Harvey 1788–1793, typescript copy in Birmingham Reference Library, BRL 669002, entries for year 1789.
20. George Yates, *An Historical and Descriptive Sketch of Birmingham* (1830), p. 227.
21. Neil McKendrick, John Brewer and J. H. Plumb, *The Birth of a Consumer Society* (1982), p. 69.
22. Diary of Julius Harvey. All references in this paragraph to this diary are to be found under the dates given.
23. For figures of production of guns during the French wars, see chapter 3.
24. Nemnich, *Account of Birmingham* (1802), pp. 98, 100–101.
25. Langford, op. cit., pp. 82, 83, 101–102, 109.
26. Minutes of Evidence, Select Committee on Petitions against the Orders in Council, 1812, Vol. III, p. 10.
27. Ibid., pp. 75, 80.
28. Journal of the House of Commons, 1812.
29. B. R. Mitchell and Phyllis Deane, *Abstract of British Historical Statistics* (1962), p. 311.
30. William Hutton, *History of Birmingham* (4th edn, 1809), p. 469.
31. Yates, op. cit., p. 72.
32. Samuel Timmins (ed.), *Birmingham and the Midland Hardware District* (1866), p. 223.
33. N. F. R. Crafts, *British Economic Growth during the Industrial Revolution* (1985), pp. 132, 142, 143.
34. J. M. Winter (ed.), *War and Economic Development* (1975), pp. 98–9.
35. William Hutton, *History of Birmingham* (6th edn, 1835), p. 82.
36. Wright, op. cit., p. 63.
37. Langford, op. cit., pp. 344, 348.
38. Wright, op. cit., pp. 77, 80.
39. Hutton, 6th edn, p. 86.
40. E. Edwards, *Personal Recollections of Birmingham and Birmingham Men* (1877), pp. 47, 48.
41. Wright, op. cit., pp. 95–7.
42. Wright, op. cit., p. 100; Langford, op. cit., pp. 532, 536.
43. Edwards, op. cit., pp. 60, 61.
44. Wright, op. cit., p. 116; Langford, op. cit., pp. 572, 577.
45. Wright, op. cit., p. 121.
46. Timmins, op. cit., pp. 222, 229; R. Floud and D. McCloskey (eds), *The Economic History of Britain since 1700* (1981), VOL. I, p. 89.
47. For a helpful sketch of the coming of

the railways to Birmingham, see
Conrad Gill, *History of Birmingham*
(1952), Vol. I, pp. 283–90.

48. Edwards, op. cit., pp. 55–61.
49. E. P. Duggan, 'The Impact of
    Industrialization on an Urban Labor
    Market; Birmingham, England,
    1770–1860', Wisconsin PhD thesis,
    1972, p. 226.
50. Peter Mathias, *The First Industrial
    Nation* (2nd edn, 1983), p. 224. See
    also François Crouzet, *The Victorian
    Economy* (1982), p. 70.
51. *Report on the Sanitary Condition of the
    Labouring Population of Great Britain*,
    (1842, Vol. XXVII), p. 194.
52. Ibid., pp. 211–12.
53. The testimony of the Birmingham
    witnesses in 1812 before the Select
    Committee on Petitions against the
    Orders in Council provides much
    evidence for this distress. Employer
    after employer gave details of the
    suffering of their workmen, and
    several emphasized that it was the
    lack of employment rather than the
    high price of bread which was the
    root cause. See, for example, the
    evidence of Mr Potter (p. 43) and of
    Mr Ridout (p. 71) on this point,
    which is discussed again in chapter 8
    in connection with the paternalistic
    attitudes of some employers.

Chapter 5
 1. Paul Mantoux, *The Industrial
    Revolution in the 18th Century* (revised
    edn, 1935), pp. 386, 387. Mantoux's
    views are examined in C. Wilson,
    'The Entrepreneur in the Industrial
    Revolution', *History*, LII (1957). See
    also P. L. Payne, *British
    Entrepreneurship in the 19th Century*
    (1974), pp. 13–16; R. H. Campbell
    and R. G. Wilson, *Entrepreneurship in
    Britain 1750–1939* (1975), pp. 14–19;
    Peter Mathias, *The First Industrial
    Nation* (2nd edn, 1983), pp. 136–40.
 2. François Crouzet, *The First
    Industrialists* (1985); D. C.
    McClelland, *The Achieving Society*
    (1961); E. E. Hagen, *On the Theory of*

Social Change (1964); Payne, op. cit.,
p. 25; Mathias, op. cit., pp. 142–5.
 3. W. Hutton, *History of Birmingham*
    (4th edn, 1809), p. 85.
 4. Ibid., p. 103.
 5. J. Drake, *Picture of Birmingham* (1825),
    p. 13; see also Nemnich, 'Account of
    Birmingham' in *Universal Magazine*
    (1802).
 6. Hutton, op. cit., p. 103.
 7. It was Hutton who claimed that
    Taylor had left £200,000, though as it
    was pointed out in chapter 1, this is
    not apparent on the face of his will.
 8. Crouzet, op. cit., pp. 97, 129 in
    particular.
 9. The emphasis is usually placed today
    on the social advantages of
    membership of a religious
    community rather than on religious
    convictions in themselves.
10. There is no recent biography of
    Matthew Boulton, but see H. W.
    Dickinson, *Matthew Boulton* (1937),
    and Samuel Smiles, *Lives of Boulton
    and Watt* (1865). See also Eric
    Robinson, 'Boulton and Fothergill,
    1762–1782, and the Birmingham
    Export of Hardware', *University of
    Birmingham Historical Journal*, VII
    (1959–60), and '18th Century
    Commerce and Fashion: Matthew
    Boulton's Marketing Techniques',
    Economic History Review, 2nd series,
    XVI, No. 1 (1963).
11. For a detailed discussion of Boulton
    as financier and works manager, see
    Eric Hopkins, 'Boulton before Watt:
    the Earlier Career Re-considered',
    Midland History, Vol. IX (1984).
12. Erich Roll, *An Early Experiment in
    Industrial Organisation, being a History
    of the firm of Boulton and Watt, 1775–
    1805* (1930), p. 116.
13. Watt's memoir of Matthew Boulton
    is reprinted in Dickinson, op. cit., as
    an Appendix.
14. Conrad Gill, *History of Birmingham*,
    Vol. I (1952), p. 107, repeats the oft-
    told story that when Dr Roebuck
    transferred his share in Watt's steam
    engine to Boulton, he suggested that

Boulton might sell engines in three
Midland counties, to which he replied
that it would not be worth while to
make engines for three counties only,
but that it would be very worth while
to make them for the whole world.
15. Roll, op. cit., pp. 225–6.
16. For a criticism of Boulton's
    judgement, see J. E. Cule, 'The
    Financial History of Matthew
    Boulton, 1759–1800', University of
    Birmingham M.Comm. thesis, 1935,
    pp. 302–3. As for Taylor's less
    fortunate ventures, he suffered losses
    in his export trade in 1755, putting
    part of the blame on James Farmer's
    partner in Lisbon, with whom he had
    done business. James Farmer was a
    principal in Farmer & Galton, gun-
    makers, and he went bankrupt in that
    year. Thereafter Taylor seems to have
    been deterred from exporting
    directly, for some time at least. See
    W. A. Richards, 'The Birmingham
    Gun Manufactory of Farmer &
    Galton and the Slave Trade in the
    18th Century', Birmingham MA
    thesis, 1972, pp. 62, 168.
17. Gill, op. cit., pp. 101–2.
18. Hutton, op. cit., p. 121.
19. Ibid., pp. 123, 124.
20. Gill, op. cit., p. 102.
21. Useful sketches of all those
    mentioned in this paragraph are to be
    found in Gill, op. cit., pp. 65–6 and
    pp. 105–6; for Garbett, see P. S.
    Bebbington, 'Samuel Garbett 1717-
    1803', Birmingham M.Comm. thesis,
    1938; for Murdock's house, see
    Joshua Field's *Diary of a Tour in 1821
    through the Midlands* (1821).
22. Minutes of Evidence, Select
    Committee on Petitions against the
    Orders in Council, 1812 (PP 1812,
    Vol. III), p. 19.
23. London Guildhall Library, Sun
    Insurance Registers, MS/11936/158.
24. For a detailed discussion of the range
    of the policies issued, see Eric
    Hopkins, 'The Trading and Service
    Sectors of the Birmingham Economy
    1750–1800', *Business History*, XXVIII,
    No. 3, July 1986.

25. Roll, op. cit., Introduction, p. xv.
26. For the career of Edward Thomason,
    see *Sir Edward Thomason's Memoirs
    during Half a Century*, Vol. I (1845),
    and Gill, op. cit., pp. 109–11.
27. E. Edwards, *Personal Recollections of
    Birmingham and Birmingham Men*
    (1877), pp. 89–100; Gill, op. cit., pp.
    300–2.
28. Edwards, op. cit., p. 93.
29. J. T. Bunce, *Josiah Mason* (1882); Gill,
    op. cit., pp. 300–2.
30. Edwards, op. cit., pp. 79–88 – a very
    frank character sketch; Gill has little
    to say about his industrial career.
31. Edwards, op. cit., p. 83.
32. See chapter 3.
33. Select Committee on Petitions against
    the Orders in Council, 1812 (PP
    1812, Vol. III), p. 74; Select
    Committee on Manufacturers,
    Commerce and Shipping, 1833 (PP
    1833, Vol. VI), pp. 180, 265–6, 268.
34. *Children's Employment Commission* (PP
    1843, Vol. XIV), Appendix to 2nd
    Report, Report by R. D. Grainger, at
    f. 135.
35. Ibid., at f. 144.
36. Ibid., at f. 136.
37. D. A. Reid, 'Labour, Leisure and
    Politics in Birmingham c. 1800 to
    1875', Birmingham PhD thesis, 1985,
    p. 238. Chapter 5, 'Employers,
    Workers and Leisure', in this thesis
    provides a very helpful and
    enlightening survey of the
    paternalism of the time. See also
    Trygve R. Tholfsen, 'The Artisan
    and the Culture of Early Victorian
    Birmingham', *University of
    Birmingham Historical Journal*, Vol. IV,
    No. 1, 1953, especially pp. 159–60.
38. *Aris's Birmingham Gazette*, 2 July
    1759 and 11 September 1780.
39. J. A. Langford, *A Century of
    Birmingham Life*, Vol. I (2nd edn,
    1870), pp. 316–30; G. H. Wright,
    *Chronicles of the Birmingham Chamber
    of Commerce 1813–1913 and of the
    Birmingham Commercial Society 1783–
    1812* (1913); Witt Bowden, *Industrial
    Society in England towards the end of the*

18th Century (2nd edn, 1965), Chapter 3, section 5, especially pp. 176–7; Drake, op. cit., p. 17.

40. For a detailed account of the development of town government in Birmingham, see Conrad Gill, op. cit., chapters VIII and IX.

41. See chapter 7 for a discussion of public health problems in Birmingham in the first half of the nineteenth century.

42. Crouzet, op. cit., p. 149.

43. Ibid., pp. 129, 139, 142.

44. For a suggested five-class model of society which so far has not been widely accepted, but at least raises some interesting questions, see R. S. Neale, 'Class and Class-Consciousness in Early 19th-Century England: Three Classes or Five?', *Victorian Studies*, Vol. XII, No. 1, September 1968.

45. Hutton, op. cit., p. 137.

46. Crouzet, op. cit., p. 38.

47. Hutton, op. cit., p. 136.

48. The standard work here is Robert E. Schofield, *The Lunar Society of Birmingham* (1963).

49. David E. H. Mole, 'Challenge to the Church: Birmingham 1815–1865', in H. J. Dyos and Michael Wolff (eds)., *The Victorian City: Images and Realities*, Vol. II (1973), pp. 819–20.

50. R. W. Ram, 'Influences on the Patterns of Belief and Social Action among Birmingham Dissenters between 1750 and 1870', in Alan Bryman (ed.), *Religion in the Birmingham Area: Essays in the Sociology of Religion* (1975).

51. Mole, op. cit., pp. 820, 828.

52. Religious attitudes are discussed further in chapters 8 and 9.

Chapter 6

1. For the problems facing employers and the methods adopted to solve their problems, see S. Pollard, *Genesis of Modern Management* (1965), p. 182 et seq.

2. E. P. Thompson, 'Time, Work-Discipline, and Industrial Capitalism', *Past & Present*, 38 (1967), p. 90.

3. *Factory Enquiry Commission* (PP 1833 XX), 1st Report: Report on Birmingham by Mr Horner, pp. 2, 7, 9.

4. Horner's Report, p. 7.

5. *Children's Employment Commission* (PP 1843, XIV), Appendix to 2nd Report, report by Mr Grainger, at fol. 17 and fol. 18.

6. Grainger's Report, fol. 23.

7. Ibid.

8. Horner's Report, p. 5.

9. Ibid., pp. 2, 7.

10. Grainger's Report, fol. 17 and fol. 19.

11. Ibid., fol. 17.

12. Ibid., fol. 131.

13. Ivy Pinchbeck, *Women Workers and the Industrial Revolution, 1750–1850* (1930), pp. 197–9; Margaret Hewitt, *Wives and Mothers in Victorian Industry* (1958), p. 290; Michael Anderson, *Family Structure in 19th Century Lancashire* (1971), p. 71; John Foster, *Class Struggle and the Industrial Revolution* (1974), pp. 96–7.

14. Grainger's Report, fol. 170.

15. Ibid., fol. 122.

16. Ibid.

17. Ibid., fol. 125.

18. Ibid.

19. Ibid.

20. Ibid., fols 17, 18; 119, 126; 24.

21. Diary of Julius Harvey, 16 May 1789 and 24 June 1789.

22. Matthew Boulton Letter Copy Book 1766–1768, Boulton Papers, letter, September 1768.

23. For a discussion of workshop practices, see Clive Behagg, 'Secrecy, Ritual, and Folk Violence: the Opacity of the Workplace in the First Half of the 19th Century', in Robert D. Storch, (ed.), *Popular Culture and Custom in 19th Century England* (1982).

24. Quoted in Clive Behagg, 'Custom, class and change: the trade societies of Birmingham', *Social History*, IV, No. 3 (1979).

25. Ibid., pp. 468, 474.
26. Ibid., table I, p. 459.
27. Samuel Timmins (ed.), *Birmingham and the Midland Hardware District*, (1866) blandly states that workmen were 'mostly untrammelled by trades unions' (p. 223), a somewhat misleading statement.
28. *Children's Employment Commission* (PP 1864, XXII), 3rd Report, p. xi.
29. Ibid., J. E. White's Report, p. 57.
30. Douglas A. Reid, 'The Decline of St Monday, 1776–1867', *Past & Present*, 71 (1976), pp. 77–84.
31. Grainger's Report, f.19, f.21. Fairs continued up to the mid-nineteenth century, and although wakes had become unpopular by then, their number actually increased in the mid-eighteenth century and later: Douglas A. Reid, 'Interpretating the Festival Calendar: Wakes and Fairs as Carnivals', in Robert D. Storch, (ed.), *Popular Culture and Custom in Nineteenth Century England* (1982).
32. White's Report, p. 57. See also chapter 9 for a further discussion of holidays.
33. *Report on the Sanitary Condition of the Labouring Population of Great Britain* (PP 1842, XXVII), Report on the State of the Public Health in the Borough of Birmingham, p. 216.
34. Grainger's Report, fol. 20.
35. Ibid., fol. 20, fol. 21.
36. Ibid., fol. 22.
37. Ibid., fol. 158.
38. Ibid., fol. 144.
39. Eric Hopkins, 'Working Hours and Conditions During the Industrial Revolution: A Reappraisal', *Economic History Review*, 2nd series, XXXV, No. 1, February 1982.
40. G. C. Allen, *The Industrial Development of Birmingham and the Black Country, 1860–1927* (2nd edn, 1966), pp. 166, 167, 169.
41. For an argument that the new discipline might be introduced into workshops on the basis of improved tools and/or a more systematic exploitation of labour, see Raphael Samuel, 'The Workshop of the World: Steam Power and Hand Technology in Victorian Britain', *History Workshop*, 3 (1977), pp. 49, 60.
42. For the detailed argument, see Clive Behagg, 'Radical Politics and Conflict at the Point of Production: Birmingham 1815–1845. A Study in the Relationship Between the Classes', Birmingham PhD thesis (1982), especially pp. 22, 59.
43. Report from the Select Committee on Manufacturers' Employment, 1830.
44. Select Committee on Agriculture, 3rd Report, PP 1836 (465) VIII, pt II, QQ16657–60.
45. See chapter 3 for discussion of these sectors of the Birmingham economy.
46. G. C. Allen, op. cit., pp. 314–43.
47. Grainger's Report, fol. 19.

Chapter 7

1. For population figures, see *Victoria County History for Warwickshire*, Vol. 7, City of Birmingham (1964), p. 8, (hereafter *V.C.H.*) and the printed Census Returns. See also chapter 2, note 20, for comments on the figure for 1801.
2. C. W. Chalklin, *The Provincial Towns of Georgian England* (1974), p. 22.
3. *V.C.H.*, pp. 8, 9.
4. *V.C.H.*, p. 8.
5. B. Faujas de St Fond, *A Journey through England and Scotland to the Hebrides in 1784* (Glasgow, 1907), Vol. II, pp. 348–9.
6. W. Hutton, *History of Birmingham* (4th edn, 1809), p. 59.
7. Ibid., p. 71.
8. Ibid., p. 77.
9. Chalklin, op. cit., p. 89.
10. George Yates, *An Historical and Descriptive Sketch of Birmingham* (1830), p. 72.
11. *V.C.H.*, pp. 9, 10.
12. David Cannadine, *Lords and Landlords: the Aristocracy and the Towns, 1774–1967* (1980), p. 111.
13. *Report on the Sanitary Condition of the Labouring Population of Great Britain*

(1842), commonly known as Chadwick's Report, p. 194.

14. Cannadine, op. cit., p. 206. Gillott moved to a house at 9 Westbourne Road, with six bedrooms, a library, wine cellars, two picture galleries, stables, an aviary, greenhouse and carpenter's shop.

15. Ibid., pp. 91–4, 98.

16. Ibid., pp. 118, 121, 122.

17. Ibid., p. 100.

18. J. A. Langford, *A Century of Birmingham Life: or a Chronicle of Local Events from 1741 to 1841* (1868), Vol. I, p. 102.

19. These are the *Report of the Health of Towns Select Committee* (1840), the *Report on the Sanitary Condition of the Labouring Population of Great Britain* (1842), (Chadwick's Report), and the *Reports of the Commissioners of Enquiry into the State of Large Towns and Populous Districts* (1844, 1845).

20. Report (PP 1840, XI), p. xii.

21. Ibid., pp. 136–7.

22. Ibid., pp. 176–9.

23. Ibid., p. 204.

24. Report (PP 1842, XXVII), p. 196.

25. Ibid.

26. Ibid., pp. 193, 194, 195.

27. Ibid., p. 197.

28. Ibid., between pp. 192 and 193. There is a photograph of a court in Bromsgrove Street in Chalklin, plate 6, but it is clearly of one of the newer courts. Both the entrance and the court itself are wider than in the court depicted in Chadwick's Report, and the two-roomed house shown on the left dates from 1791.

29. This street is presumably Russell Street, off Steelhouse Lane, which is shown on Hanson's 1795 map, but has long since disappeared completely.

30. Report (PP 1844, XVII), pp. 2–4; p. 28.

31. Robert Rawlinson, *Report to the General Board of Health . . . on the Borough of Birmingham* (1849), pp. 23, 95.

32. Ibid., p. 29.

33. Report, pp. 1–2, and Appendix, p. 2.

34. Chadwick's Report, pp. 203, 205, 206–7.

35. *Children's Employment Commission*, (PP 1843, XIV), Appendix to 2nd Report, Report by Mr Grainger, fol. 175.

36. Ibid., fol. 176.

37. Chadwick's Report, p. 213.

38. Ibid., pp. 211–13.

39. J. E. Vance, Jnr, 'Housing the Worker: Determinative and Contingent Ties in Nineteenth-Century Birmingham', in *Economic Geography*, XLIII, 1967.

40. Stanley D. Chapman (ed.), *The History of Working Class Housing: a Symposium* (1971), pp. 232–5.

41. Calculated from scale drawings in John Prest, *The Industrial Revolution in Coventry* (1960), pp. 74, 82.

42. Eric Hopkins, 'Working Class Housing in the Smaller Industrial Town of the 19th Century: Stourbridge – a Case Study', *Midland History*, IV, Nos 3, 4, 1978.

43. Langford, op. cit., pp. 302, 308. Chalklin considers that there may have been some multiple occupancy in the 1770s, but that this was overcome by 1801. In the 1780s building kept up with the population explosion and also with the subsequent population growth. Between 1750 and 1820, Birmingham builders faced a five-fold increase in numbers, but by 1820 the pattern of one family to a dwelling was the norm: Chalklin, op. cit., pp. 197, 305–6.

44. Though Rawlinson does say in his report that in addition to the private wells and pumps, and the several public wells and pumps, many private water carts traversed the town, charging ½d the canfull (3½ gallons), p. 48.

45. Ibid., p. 25.

46. Chalklin, op. cit., p. 313.

47. *Morning Chronicle*, 10 March 1851.

48. Chalklin, op. cit., pp. 196–200.

49. Sun Insurance Registers, policies nos

221,313 (dated 2 July 1765), 226,998 (dated 13 November 1765) and 223,850 (dated 23 August 1765), London Guildhall Library, MS 11936/158.

50. Rawlinson's Report, p. 31.
51. Ibid.
52. Ibid., p. 26.
53. Ibid., p. 83.
54. In London, the worst housing was occupied by the worst-paid and most irregularly employed, and living space increased roughly with the amount of wages and the regularity of employment: H. J. Dyos and Michael Wolff (eds), *The Victorian City: Images and Realities* (1973), p. 367.
55. The *Morning Chronicle*, 7 Oct. 1850, claimed that 'In Birmingham a labourer must be skilled to have the slightest chance of obtaining a livelihood. Accordingly, it is the mechanic, not the mere labouring man, that is in request.'
56. The *Morning Chronicle*, 14 Oct. 1850, gives an example of some houses with only *one* room. This room was on the first floor, and was reached by an external ladder, the ground floor being occupied by an ashpit, a privy, and a brewhouse. Such houses must have been exceptional. For interesting and rarely attempted definitions of ashpits, cesspools, and middens, see M. J. Daunton, *House and Home in the Victorian City: Working Class Housing 1850–1914* (1983), p. 248.
57. Daunton, op. cit., pp. 29–30.
58. The mines inspector, H. S. Tremenheere, was shocked at what he called the 'sensuality and extravagance' of the Staffordshire miners in the Black Country nearby: 'Poultry, especially geese and ducks; the earliest and choicest vegetables . . . occasionally port wine, drunk out of tumblers and basins; beers and spirits in great quantities; meat in abundance, extravagantly cooked; excursions in carts and cars are the well-known objects on which their money is squandered': Tremenheere's *Report on the Mining Districts of South Staffordshire* (1850), pp. 9–10. Birmingham metal workers are likely to have been little different in their eating and drinking habits when times were good.
59. For the state of rural housing of the period, see J. Burnett, *A Social History of Housing, 1815–1970* (1978), chapter 2. According to Dr Burnett, the agricultural worker was almost certainly the worst housed among fully employed workers (p. 31).
60. For a discussion of the reasons for workers immigrating into industrial towns, see J. A. Banks, 'Population Change and the Victorian City', *Victorian Studies*, XI, 1967–8.

Chapter 8

1. *Victorian County History for Warwickshire*, Vol. 7 (1964), (hereafter *V.C.H.*) p. 209.
2. Leonore Davidoff and Catherine Hall, *Family Fortunes: Men and Women of the English Middle Class 1780–1850* (1987), p. 42.
3. William Hutton, *History of Birmingham* (1809 edn), pp. 86–9. Hutton tells the story of how he was defrauded by a friend in the purchase of a horse, and of how, when he complained, he received the reply, made with some warmth, 'I would cheat my own brother in a horse', p. 88.
4. Julius Harvey, Diary of 22 Oct. 1789.
5. Hutton, op. cit., p. 172.
6. It is not intended here to detail the development of particular churches or chapels. For a good general sketch, including an account of the Priestley Riots, see C. Gill, *History of Birmingham*, Vol. I, (1952), pp. 141–7.
7. R. B. Rose, 'The Priestley Riots of 1791', *Past & Present*, 18 Nov. 1960.
8. David E. H. Mole, 'Challenge to the Church: Birmingham 1815–65', in H. J. Dyos and Michael Wolff, *The Victorian City: Images and Realities*, Vol. II, (1973), p. 822.

9. Barbara M. Smith, 'The Galtons of Birmingham: Quaker Gun Merchants and Bankers, 1702–1831', *Business History*, Vol. IX, Nos 1, 2 (1967), pp. 144–6.

10. Julius Harvey, Diary of 1 June 1793; 5 March 1790; and 2 Dec. 1790.

11. George Jacob Holyoake, *Sixty Years of an Agitator's Life* (1892), p. 21.

12. Mole, op. cit., pp. 820, 823–6; H. Mann, *Religious Worship in England and Wales* (1854).

13. Geoffrey Robson, 'The Failures of Success: Working Class Evangelists in Early Victorian Birmingham', in Derek Baker (ed.), *Religious Motivation: Biographical and Sociological Problems for the Church Historian* (1978).

14. Davidoff and Hall, op. cit., p. 93. This work contains a very useful survey of evangelical attitudes in Birmingham.

15. Gill, op. cit., p. 162.

16. Ibid., pp. 197–9.

17. Hutton, op. cit., pp. 366–7.

18. Gill, op. cit., pp. 130–1.

19. Dennis Smith, *Conflict and Compromise: Class Formation in English Society 1830–1914: A Comparative Study of Birmingham and Sheffield* (1982), pp. 108–11.

20. A good narrative account is to be found in Gill, op. cit., chapter 10. See also Michael Brock, *The Great Reform Act* (1973), and Carlos Flick, *The Birmingham Political Union and the Movement for Reform in Britain 1830–1839* (1978).

21. For a discussion of the economic problems of Birmingham in the late 1820s, see Asa Briggs, 'Thomas Attwood and the Economic Background of the Birmingham Political Union', *Cambridge Historical Journal*, Vol. IX, No. 2, 1948.

22. Quoted in Flick, op. cit., p. 65.

23. Quoted in Flick, op. cit., p. 87.

24. For a discussion of this point, see Flick, op. cit., pp. 12, 95–6, 178–9.

25. It has been argued that it was not so much the dislike of physical force which alienated the leaders of the BPU from Chartism, but the fact that incorporation provided a new outlet for their energies, converting them from radicals into supporters of the establishment: Clive Behagg, 'An Alliance with the Middle Class: the Birmingham Political Union and Early Chartism', in James Epstein and Dorothy Thompson, (eds), *The Chartist Experience: Studies in Working Class Radicalism and Culture, 1830–60* (1982), p. 79.

26. For a detailed account of the controversy, see Gill, op. cit., chapter 11.

27. A recent and informative account of the founding of the Birmingham Equitable Labour Exchange may be found in Linda J. Fletcher, 'Robert Owen's Equitable Labour Exchanges', Open University B.Litt. thesis, 1984, especially chapter 3, 'Organisers and Users'.

28. Fletcher, op. cit., p. 89.

29. See, for example, his Cornish notebooks in the Boulton & Watt Collection as evidence of his technical knowledge of the steam engine.

30. *V.C.H.*, p. 214.

31. John Money, *Experience and Identity: Birmingham and the West Midlands, 1760–1800* (1977), pp. 99–102.

32. For further information on the Masons and the Bucks, see Money, op. cit., chapter 6, 'Masons, Bucks and Books'.

33. *V.C.H.*, p. 217.

34. J. G. Kohl, *England, Wales, and Scotland* (1844), p. 12.

35. Hugh Miller, *First Impressions of England and its People* (1847), p. 231.

36. Kohl, op. cit., p. 9.

37. *V.C.H.*, p. 218.

38. Ibid., p. 211; *Beauties of England and Wales*, XV, Part II (1814); Hutton, op. cit., pp. 165–6.

39. See Asa Briggs, 'The Language of Class in Early Nineteenth Century England', in A. Briggs and J. Saville, *Essays in Labour History* (1967).

40. D. A. Reid, 'Labour, Leisure and Politics in Birmingham, c. 1800 to 1875', Birmingham PhD thesis, 1985, pp. 229–31, provides an interesting discussion of paternalist attitudes.
41. Clive Behagg, op. cit., p. 79.
42. In connection with this point, it should be noted that in 1842 another predominantly middle class body, the National Complete Suffrage Union, was set up in Birmingham, aiming at both electoral reform and the repeal of the Corn Laws. Its leader was Joseph Sturge, a local Quaker and reformer. Although it soon declined, in 1844 Complete Suffrage supporters on the Town Council carried a motion in favour of 'full and fair representation of the people in Parliament'. See Alex Tyrrell, *Joseph Sturge and the Moral Radical Party in Early Victorian Britain* (1987), Chapter 10; Dorothy Thompson, *The Chartists* (1984), pp. 261–8; John Ryman, 'Religion and Radical Politics in Birmingham 1830–50', Birmingham B.Litt thesis, 1979; *Birmingham Journal*, 18.5.1844.

Chapter 9

1. *Victoria County History for Warwickshire*, Vol. 7 (1964), (hereafter *V.C.H.*) p. 109.
2. Minutes of Evidence of the Committee for Petitions against the Orders in Council, 1812, Vol. III, pp. 6, 35, 64, 105.
3. *Report on the Sanitary Condition of the Labouring Population of Great Britain: Local Reports* (1842, Vol. XXVII), pp. 209–10.
4. *Minutes of Evidence*, 1812, pp. 106–7.
5. Ibid., p. 68.
6. Ibid., p. 106.
7. Ibid., p. 86.
8. William Hutton, *History of Birmingham* (4th edn, 1809), p. 210.
9. *Minutes of Evidence* 1812, p. 4.
10. William Hawkes Smith, *Birmingham and its Vicinity as a Manufacturing and Commercial District* (1836), p. 35.

11. Hutton, op. cit., pp. 210–12.
12. D. A. Reid, 'Labour, Leisure and Politics in Birmingham, c. 1800 to 1875', Birmingham PhD thesis, 1985, p. 197.
13. R. Rawlinson, Report to the General Board of Health on . . . the Borough of Birmingham (1849), pp. 44–6.
14. *Minutes of Evidence,* 1812, p. 6.
15. Samuel Timmins (ed.), *Birmingham and the Midland Hardware District* (1866), p. 687.
16. C. Gill, *History of Birmingham*, Vol. I, (1952), p. 149; Hutton, op. cit., p. 308; George Yates, *An Historical and Descriptive Sketch of Birmingham* (1830), p. 177.
17. Mary C. McNaulty, 'Some Aspects of the History of the Administration of the Poor Laws in Birmingham between 1730 and 1834', Birmingham MA thesis, 1942, Appendix D; Hutton, op. cit., p. 318.
18. Trygve R. Tholfsen, 'The Artisan and the Culture of Early Victorian Birmingham', *University of Birmingham Historical Journal*, Vol. IV, 1953–4, pp. 158–9.
19. Chadwick's Report, p. 210.
20. Similar attitudes prevailed in the Black Country, where it was thought that people who read and kept books – shopkeepers, lecturers, ministers of religion – were no more prosperous than those who did not. There was a well-known Black Country expression: 'The father went to the pit and made a fortune, his son went to school and lost it.' See Eric Hopkins, 'Working Class Attitudes to Education in the Black Country in the Mid-Nineteenth Century', *History of Education Society Bulletin*, No. 14, Autumn, 1974.
21. M. B. Frost, 'The Development of Provided Schooling for Working Class Children in Birmingham 1781–1851', Birmingham M. Litt. thesis, 1978, pp. 29–31.
22. Frost, op. cit., pp. 32, 48; Children's Employment Commission (PP 1843,

xiv), Appendix to 2nd Report, report by Mr Grainger, fol. 190.

23. Frost, op. cit., pp. 39–40.
24. Dennis Smith, *Conflict and Compromise: Class Formation in English Society, 1830–1914: A Comparative Study of Birmingham and Sheffield* (1982), pp. 109–11.
25. Grainger's Report, fol. 186.
26. Ibid., fol. 188.
27. Frost, op. cit., pp. 56, 57.
28. Ibid., p. 370.
29. W. B. Stephens, *Education, Literacy and Society, 1830–1870* (1987), pp. 136–7.
30. Smith, op. cit., p. 276, and see the table for illiteracy in Stephens, p. 35; Stephens, p. 159.
31. For Mann's calculations, see his *Religious Worship in England and Wales* (1854). Dr Mole suggests that in Birmingham, probably three-quarters of citizens regularly abstained from public worship in 1851, but this figure appears not to take into account (as did Mann) those unable to attend because of age, sickness, or employment. See David E. Mole, 'Challenge to the Church: Birmingham, 1815–65' in H. J. Dyos and Michael Wolff (eds), *The Victorian City: Images and Realities*, Vol. II (1973), p. 829.
32. David E. H. Mole, 'The Church of England and Society in Birmingham c.1830–1866', Cambridge PhD thesis, 1961, p. 18.
33. Mole, 'Challenge to the Church: Birmingham 1815–65', p. 831.
34. Attendance figures from Mole's thesis, p. 321; for the social composition of Unitarians, Quakers and Baptists, see R. W. Ram, 'Influences on the Patterns of Belief and Social Action among Birmingham Dissenters between 1750 and 1870', in Alan Bryman (ed.), *Religion in the Birmingham Area: Essays in the Sociology of Religion* (1975).
35. B. I. Coleman, *The Church of England in the Mid-Nineteenth Century: a Social Geography* (1980), p. 41.
36. David Mole, 'Challenge to the Church', p. 83; 'The Church of England and Society', p. 262.
37. Geoffrey Robson, 'The Failures of Success: Working Class Evangelists in Early Victorian Birmingham', in Derek Baker (ed.), *Religious Motivation: Biographical and Sociological Problems for the Church Historian* (1978), p. 391.
38. Mole, 'The Church of England and Society', p. 266.
39. Coleman, op. cit., p. 41.
40. Robson, op. cit., p. 385; Mole, 'Challenge to the Church', pp. 831–2.
41. Robson, op. cit., p. 381.
42. Tholfsen, op. cit., p. 148.
43. Mole, 'Challenge to the Church', p. 821.
44. *V.C.H. for Warks*, Vol. 7, pp. 216, 211.
45. Ibid., p. 216.
46. Ibid., pp. 215–16.
47. Ibid., p. 224.
48. For a detailed account of these sports in Birmingham, and all the sports in this and the following paragraph, see *The Morning Chronicle*, 25 December 1849, Letter XX, 'The Amusements of the People'.
49. *V.C.H.*, pp. 229, 230.
50. *The Morning Chronicle*, loc. cit.
51. Ibid.
52. Reid, 'Labour, Leisure and Politics', p. 243 *et seq.*
53. *Diary of Julius Harvey 1788–1793*, entries for 1 and 26 September 1789.
54. Douglas A. Reid, 'Interpreting the Festival Calendar: Wakes and Fairs as Carnivals' in Robert D. Storch (ed.), *Popular Culture and Custom in 19th Century England* (1982).
55. Hutton, op. cit., p. 205.
56. Reid, 'Festival Calendar', especially pp. 136–41.
57. Reid, 'Labour, Leisure and Politics', pp. 338–9.
58. Sketchley's *Birmingham Directory* (3rd edn), 1767: Printed Census Returns, 1851. By 1871, there were 683 public houses and 1,193 beershops within

the borough of Birmingham, that is, one establishment for every 174 inhabitants: William M. Bramwell, *Pubs and Localised Communities in Mid-Victorian Birmingham* (1984), Queen Mary College, Geography Department Occasional Paper No. 22, p. 9. This paper also contains an interesting section on pub facilities and social relationships.

59. For arguments which take a different view of the national scene, see E. P. Thompson, 'Time, Work-Discipline, and Industrial Capitalism', *Past & Present*, No. 38, 1967, pp. 56–97.
60. B. Harrison, 'Religion and Recreation in 19th-Century England', *Past & Present*, No. 38, 1967, pp. 116–17.
61. *Morning Chronicle*, loc. cit.
62. For an interpretation which stresses the loss of leisure in industrial towns, see James Walvin, *Leisure and Society, 1830–1950* (1978), especially chapters 1 and 2.
63. Chadwick's Report, p. 211.
64. Grainger's Report, fol. 172.
65. Chadwick's committee made enquiries on this point at almost all the retail druggists in town, and reported that 'we have not been able to discover 30 instances of customers who regularly purchase large quantities of opium or laudanum from all the druggists to whom our inquiries have extended', p. 212.

Comments and Reflections

1. E. A. Wrigley, *People, Cities, and Wealth* (1987), p. 3.
2. For example, see Peter Mathias, *The First Industrial Nation* (2nd edn, 1983), pp. 239–40.
3. The point has been made earlier that these machines required 'skill, and experience of head, hand, and eye' on the part of the workman: see William Hawkes Smith, *Birmingham and its Vicinity* (1836), Part III, p. 16.
4. Stebbing Shaw, *History and Antiquities of Staffordshire* (1798), p. 120.
5. Maxine Berg, *The Age of Manufactures 1700–1820* (1985), p. 292.

6. Ibid., p. 303.
7. For an attempt to establish the gap in size between large and small firms, see the tables in Clive Behagg, 'Radical Politics and Conflict at the Point of Production: Birmingham 1815–1845', Birmingham PhD thesis (1982), pp. 37–60.
8. J. Drake, *Picture of Birmingham* (1825), p. 17.
9. Behagg, op. cit., chapter I, especially Sections II and III.
10. W. H. B. Court, *Scarcity and Choice in History* (1970), p. 243. He is followed in this respect by Professor Wrigley in his article on Modernization and the Industrial Revolution in his *People, Cities, and Wealth* (1987), p. 51.
11. Court, op. cit., p. 244.
12. For details of bankruptcy proceedings in the eighteenth century, see Julian Hoppit, *Risk and Failure in English Business, 1700–1800* (1987), pp. 35–7.
13. See in particular Asa Briggs, *Victorian Cities* (1968), chapter 5, his *Collected Essays of Asa Briggs*, Vol. I (1985), and his article on Birmingham in the *V.C.H. for Warwickshire*, Vol. 7.
14. Karl Marx and Frederick Engels, *The Communist Manifesto* (1848) (Pelican edn, 1967), pp. 114–18.
15. Asa Briggs, *Victorian Cities* (1968), p. 116.
16. E. P. Thompson, *The Making of the English Working Class* (1968), pp. 753, 897.
17. Asa Briggs, op. cit. n. 15, p. 115.
18. For a revisionist view opposed to that suggested in the text, see Clive Behagg, 'Myths of Cohesion: Capital and Compromise in the Historiography of 19th-Century Birmingham', *Social History*, Vol. II, Jan. 1986.
19. Briggs, op. cit., p. 116.
20. For conditions in the Black Country, and comparisons with conditions in Birmingham, see Eric Hopkins, 'Working Conditions in Victorian Stourbridge', *International Review of*

Social History, Vol. xix, (1974), Part 3, and the same author's 'Working Hours and Conditions during the Industrial Revolution: a Reappraisal', *Economic History Review*, 2nd series, Vol. xxxv, No. 1, Feb. 1982.

21. Berg, op. cit., p. 19.

22. In the meantime, see the introductory sketch in Eric Hopkins, 'Working Class Housing in Birmingham during the Industrial Revolution', *International Review of Social History*, Vol. xxxi (1986), Part 1.

23. The concept of social control is perhaps no longer as fashionable as it was, but see A. P. Donajgrodzki (ed.), *Social Control in Nineteenth-Century Britain* (1977); and F. M. L. Thompson, 'Social Control in Victorian Britain', *Economic History Review*, 2nd series, Vol. xxxiv, No. 2, 1981.

24. For Tremenheere's interesting views on working-class education, see Eric Hopkins, 'Working Class Attitudes to Education in the Black Country in the Mid-Nineteenth Century', *History of Education Society Bulletin*, No. 14, Autumn 1974; and 'Tremenheere's Prize Schemes in the Mining Districts, 1851–1859', *History of Education Society Bulletin*, No. 15, Spring 1975.

25. Quoted in Roy Porter, *English Society in the Eighteenth Century* (1982), p. 297.

26. Ibid., p. 317.

Bibliography

Manuscript and Unpublished Sources

At the Guildhall, London
Sun Insurance Policy Registers for 1765, and for 1777–86: MS 11936/158.

At the Public Record Office, London
Chancery Masters Exhibits.
Exchequer Bills and Answers (E112).
Exchequer Taxes for Warwickshire 1786–8 (E182/1062).
Extents in Aid.

At the Birmingham Reference Library
Birmingham Poor Law Assessments for the Eighteenth Century.
Birmingham Town Books.
Diary of Julius Harvey 1788–93.
Index of Masters, Apprentices and Trades.
Matthew Boulton Papers.

At the British Library, London
Four Topographical Letters written in July 1755 . . . from a Gentleman of London to his brother and sister in Town . . . (1757).

At the Kungliga Biblioteket, Stockholm
Day book of Samuel Schroeder, 1748–51 (MS X303).

Official Publications
Census of England and Wales, Reports 1801–51.
Journals of the House of Commons.
Select Committee on Agriculture, 3rd Report, 1836, viii, pt. 2.
Select Committee of the House of Commons on Petitions against the Orders in Council, 1812, Minutes of Evidence.
Select Committee on Petitions respecting the Apprenticeship Laws 1812–13, Report.
Select Committee on the Shop Window Duty, 1819, Minutes of Evidence.
Select Committee on Artisans and Machinery, 1824, Minutes of Evidence.
Select Committee on Manufacturers' Employment, 1830, Report.
Select Committee on Manufactures, Commerce and Shipping, 1833, Report.
Factory Enquiry Commission, 1833, Report and Depositions.
Select Committee on the Health of Towns, 1840, Report.
Children's Employment Commission, 1842, Reports and Evidence.
Report on the Sanitary Condition of the Labouring Population of Great Britain, 1842 (Chadwick's Report).
Reports of the Commission of Inquiry into the State of Large Towns and Populous Districts, 1844 and 1845.
Report to the General Board of Health . . . on the Borough of Birmingham, by Robert Rawlinson, 1849.
Report on the Mining Districts of South Staffordshire, 1850.
Children's Employment Commission, 1862, Reports and Evidence.

Contemporary Published Sources (1760–c. 1840)

Newspapers and Periodicals
Aris's Birmingham Gazette.

The Birmingham Journal.
The Morning Chronicle Letters 1849–51.
The Leisure Hour, 1853.

Directories
Sketchley's Birmingham, Wolverhampton, and Walsall Directory (3rd edn), 1767.
Swinney's Directory, 1775.
Pearson & Rollason, *The Birmingham Directory*, 1777.
Pye's Birmingham Directory, 1785.
The Universal British Directory of Trade, Commerce, and Manufacture, 1791.
Bisset, *The Magnificent Directory*, 1800.

Other Publications
The place of publication is London unless otherwise stated.
Beauties of England and Wales, Vol. XV, (1814).
Bodmer, J. G., *Diary 1816–17* (reprinted in *Transactions of the Newcomen Society*, X).
Camden's *Britannia* (1586), 1637 edn.
Carus, C. J., *The King of Saxony's Journey Through England and Scotland in the year 1844* (1846).
Davis, George, *Saint Monday or Scenes from Low Life* (Birmingham, 1790).
Defoe, Daniel, *Tour through Britain* (Everyman edn, 1928).
Drake, J., *Picture of Birmingham* (Birmingham, 1825).
Field, Joshua, *Diary of a Tour in 1821 through the Midlands* (reprinted in *Transactions of the Newcomen Society*, VI).
Hawkes Smith, William, *Birmingham and its Vicinity as a Manufacturing and Commercial District* (Birmingham and London, 1836).
Hutton, William, *History of Birmingham* (Birmingham, 1781; 2nd edn, 1783; 4th edn, 1809; 6th edn, 1835).
Jaffrey, James, *Hints for a History of Birmingham* (Birmingham 1856–7).
Jars, Gabriel, *Voyages Metallurgiques* (Lyons, 1774).
Kohl, J. G., *England, Wales, and Scotland* (1844).
Leland, John, *Itinerary* (2nd edn, 1745).
Miller, Hugh, *First Impressions of England and its People* (1847).

Nemnich, *Account of Birmingham* (*Universal Magazine*, 1802).
Stebbing Shaw, *History and Antiquities of Staffordshire* (1798).
Thomason, E., *Sir Edward Thomason's Memoirs during Half a Century* (1845).
Yates, George, *An Historical and Descriptive Sketch of Birmingham* (Birmingham, 1830).
Young, Arthur, *Tours in England and Wales* (1791).

Later Published Sources (c. 1840 to present day)
The place of publication is London unless otherwise stated.
Aldcroft, D. H. and Fearson, P. (eds), *British Economic Fluctuations 1790–1939* (1972).
Allen, G. C., *The Industrial Development of Birmingham and the Black Country, 1860–1927* (1929).
Anderson, Michael, *Family Structure in 19th-Century Lancashire* (Cambridge, 1971).
Ashton, T. S., *Economic Fluctuations in England 1700–1800* (Oxford, 1959).
Bailey, De Witt and Nie, Douglas A., *English Gunmakers: The Birmingham and Provincial Gun Trade in the 18th and 19th Centuries* (1982).
Berg, Maxine, *The Age of Manufactures: Industry, Innovation and Work in Britain 1700–1820* (1985).
Birmingham and its Regional Setting: a Scientific Survey (published by the British Association) (Birmingham, 1950)
Bowden, Witt, *Industrial Society in England towards the end of the 18th Century* (New York, 1925).
Bramwell, William M., Pubs and Localised Communities in Mid-Victorian Birmingham (1984), (Queen Mary College, Geography Department Occasional Paper No. 22).
Briggs, Asa, *Victorian Cities* (1968).
Briggs, Asa, *The Collected Essays of Asa Briggs*, Vol. I (1985).
Brock, Michael, *The Great Reform Act* (1973).
Bryman, Alan (ed.), *Religion in the*

Birmingham Area: Essays in the Sociology of Religion (Birmingham, 1975).

Bunce, J. T., Josiah Mason (1882).

Burnett, J., A Social History of Housing 1815–1970 (Newton Abbot, 1978).

Campbell, R. H., and Wilson, R. G., Entrepreneurship in Britain 1750–1939 (1975).

Cannadine, David, Lords and Landlords: the Aristocracy and the Towns 1774–1967 (Leicester, 1980).

Carus, C. G., The King of Saxony's Journey through England and Scotland in the Year 1844 (1846).

Chalklin, C. W., The Provincial Towns of Georgian England (1974).

Chapman, Stanley D. (ed.), The History of Working Class Housing: a Symposium (Newton Abbot, 1971).

Clark, Peter (ed.), The Transformation of English Provincial Towns 1600–1800 (1984).

Clow, A. and Clow, N. L., The Chemical Revolution (1952).

Coleman, B. I., The Church of England in the Mid-Nineteenth Century: a Social Geography (1980).

Coleman, B. I. (ed.), The Idea of the City in 19th-Century Britain (1973).

Coleman, D. C., The Economy of England 1450–1750 (Oxford, 1977).

Corfield, P. J., The Impact of English Towns 1700–1800 (Oxford, 1982).

Court, W. H. B., The Rise of the Midland Industries 1600–1838 (Oxford, 1938).

Court, W. H. B., Scarcity and Choice in History (1970).

Crafts, N. F. R., British Economic Growth during the Industrial Revolution (Oxford, 1985).

Crouzet, François, The Victorian Economy (1982).

Crouzet, François, The First Industrialists (Cambridge, 1985).

Cunningham, Hugh, Leisure in the Industrial Revolution (1980).

Daunton, M. J., House and Home in the Victorian City: Working Class Housing 1850–1914 (1983).

Davidoff, Leonore and Hall, Catherine, Family Fortunes: Men and Women of the English Middle Class 1780–1850 (1987).

Davis, Ralph, The Industrial Revolution and British Overseas Trade (Leicester, 1979).

Dennis, Richard, English Industrial Cities of the 19th Century (Cambridge, 1984).

Dent, Robert K., Old and New Birmingham (Birmingham, 1880).

Dent, Robert K., The Making of Birmingham (Birmingham, 1894).

Dickinson, H. W., Matthew Boulton (Cambridge, 1937).

Dickinson, H. W. and Jenkins, Rhys, James Watt and the Steam Engine (2nd edn, Ashbourne, 1981).

Donajgrodzki, A. P. (ed.), Social Control in Nineteenth-Century Britain (1977).

Dunham, Keith, The Gun Trade of Birmingham (Birmingham, 1955).

Dyos, H. J., and Aldcroft, D. H., British Transport (1974).

Dyos, H. J., and Wolff, Michael (eds), The Victorian City: Images and Realities (1973), Vol. II.

Edwards, E., Personal Recollections of Birmingham and Birmingham Men (Birmingham, 1877).

Epstein, James, and Thompson, Dorothy (eds), The Chartist Experience: Studies in Working-Class Radicalism and Culture, 1830–60 (1982).

Faucher, L., Etudes sur L'Angleterre (1856).

Fitzmaurice, Lord Edmund, Life of William, Earl of Shelburne (1875).

Flick, Carlos, The Birmingham Political Union and the Movement for Reform in Britain 1830–1839 (Folkestone, 1978).

Floud, R. and McCloskey, D. (eds), The Economic History of Britain since 1700 (Cambridge, 1981).

Foster, John, Class Struggle and the Industrial Revolution (1974).

Fraser, Derek, and Sutcliffe, Anthony (eds), The Pursuit of Urban History (1983).

Gauldie, Enid, Cruel Habitations (1974).

Gill, Conrad, History of Birmingham (1952), Vol. I.

Hadfield, Charles, The Canals of the West Midlands (Newton Abbot, 1966).

Hagen, E. E., On the Theory of Social Change (1964).

Hamilton, H., The English Brass and Copper Industries to 1800 (1926).

Hanson, Harry, *The Coaching Life* (Manchester, 1983).

Hartwell, R. M., *The Industrial Revolution and Economic Growth* (1971).

Hennock, E. P., *Fit and Proper Persons* (1973).

Hewitt, Margaret, *Wives and Mothers in Victorian Industry* (1958).

Hobsbawm, Eric, *Industry and Empire* (1968).

Holyoake, George Jacob, *Sixty Years of an Agitator's Life* (1892).

Hoppit, Julian, *Risk and Failure in English Business 1700–1800* (1987).

Hyde, Charles K., *Technological Change in the British Iron Industry 1700–1870* (Princetown, 1977).

Jackman, W. T., *Development of Transportation in Modern England* (1962 edn).

Jewitt, Llewellyan, *The Life of William Hutton* (1872).

Lander, E., *The Birmingham Gun Trade* (Birmingham, 1865).

Langford, J. A., *A Century of Birmingham Life: or a Chronicle of Local Events from 1741 to 1841* (Birmingham, 1868).

Lloyd, Humphrey, *The Quaker Lloyds in the Industrial Revolution* (1975).

Malcolmson, R. W., *Popular Recreations in English Society 1700–1850* (Cambridge, 1973).

Mann, Horace, *Religious Worship in England and Wales* (1854).

Mantoux, Paul, *The Industrial Revolution in the 18th Century* (revised edn, 1935).

Marx, Karl, and Engels, Frederick, *The Communist Manifesto* (1848) (Pelican edn, 1967).

Mathias, Peter, *The First Industrial Nation* (2nd edn, 1983).

McClelland, D. C., *The Achieving Society* (1961).

McKendrick, Neil, Brewer, John and Plumb, J. H., *The Birth of a Consumer Society* (1982).

Mitchell, B. R., and Deane, Phyllis, *Abstract of British Historical Statistics* (Cambridge, 1962).

Money, John, *Experience and Identity: Birmingham and the West Midlands 1760–1800* (Manchester, 1977).

Payne, P. L., *British Entrepreneurship in the 19th Century* (1974).

Pinchbeck, Ivy, *Women Workers and the Industrial Revolution 1750–1850* (1930).

Pollard, S., *Genesis of Modern Management* (1965).

Porter, Roy, *English Society in the Eighteenth Century* (1982).

Presnell, L. S., *County Banking in the Industrial Revolution* (Oxford, 1956).

Prest, John, *The Industrial Revolution in Coventry* (Oxford, 1960).

Prosser, R. B., *Birmingham Inventors and Inventions* (Birmingham, 1881, republished 1970).

Razell, P. E. and Wainwright, R. W., *The Victorian Working Class* (1973).

Roll, Erich, *An Early Experiment in Industrial Organisation, being a History of the firm of Boulton and Watt 1775–1805* (1930).

Rule, John, *The Experience of labour in Eighteenth Century Industry* (1981).

St Fond, B. Faujas de, *A Journey through England and Scotland to the Hebrides in 1784* (Glasgow, 1907), Vol. II.

Schofield, Robert E., *The Lunar Society of Birmingham* (Oxford, 1963).

Schumpeter, E., *English Overseas Trade Statistics 1697–1808* (Oxford, 1960).

Smiles, Samuel, *Lives of Boulton and Watt* (1865).

Smith, Dennis, *Conflict and Compromise: Class Formation in English Society 1830–1914: A comparative study of Birmingham and Sheffield* (1982).

Stephens, W. B., *Education, Literacy and Society 1830–1870* (Manchester, 1987).

Storch, Robert D. (ed.) *Popular Culture and Custom in 19th-Century England* (1982).

Thompson, Dorothy, *The Chartists* (1984).

Thompson, E. P., *The Making of the English Working Class* (1968).

Timmins, S. (ed.), *Birmingham and the Midland Hardware District* (1866).

Tyrrell, Alex, *Joseph Sturge and the Moral Radical Party in Early Victorian Britain* (1987).

Urban History Yearbook (Leicester, 1979).

Victoria County History for Warwickshire, Vol. 7, 'City of Birmingham' (1964).

Walvin, James, *Leisure and Society 1830–1950* (1978).

Winter, J. M. (ed.), *War and Economic Development* (Cambridge, 1975).

Wright, G. H., *Chronicles of the Birmingham Chamber of Commerce 1813–1913 and of the Birmingham Commercial Society 1783–1812* (Birmingham, 1913).

Wrigley, E. A., *People, Cities, and Wealth* (Oxford, 1987).

Articles

Banks, J. A., 'Population Change and the Victorian City', *Victorian Studies*, XI, 1967–8.

Behagg, Clive, 'Custom, Class and Change: the Trade Societies of Birmingham', *Social History*, IV, No. 3, 1979.

Behagg, Clive, 'An Alliance with the Middle Class: the Birmingham Political Union and Early Chartism', in James Epstein and Dorothy Thompson (eds). *The Chartist Experience: Studies in Working Class Radicalism and Culture 1830–60* (1982).

Behagg, Clive, 'Secrecy, Ritual and Folk Violence: the Opacity of the Workplace in the First Half of the 19th Century', in Robert D. Storch, (ed.), *Popular Culture and Custom in 19th Century England* (1982).

Behagg, Clive, 'Myths of Cohesion: Capital and Compromise in the Historiography of 19th-century Birmingham', *Social History*, 11, Jan. 1986.

Briggs, Asa, 'Thomas Attwood and the Economic Background of the Birmingham Political Union', *Cambridge Historical Journal*, IX, No. 2, 1948.

Briggs, Asa, 'The Language of Class in Early Nineteenth Century England', in A. Briggs and J. Saville, *Essays in Labour History* (1967).

Chapman, S. D., and Bartlett, J. N., 'The Contribution of Building Clubs and Freehold Land Societies to Working Class Housing in Birmingham', in Stanley Chapman (ed.), *The History of*

Working Class Housing: A Symposium (1971).

Coates, A. W., 'Changing Attitudes to Labour in the Mid-Eighteenth Century', *Economic History Review*, 2nd series, XI, 1958–9.

Court, W. H. B., 'Industrial Organisation and Economic Progress in the Eighteenth-century Midlands', *Transactions of the Royal Historical Society*, 1946.

Crafts, N. F. R., 'British Economic Growth 1700–1831: A Review of the Evidence', *Economic History Review*, 2nd series, XXXVI, No. 2, May 1983.

Crouzet, François, 'Towards an Export Economy: British Exports during the Industrial Revolution', *Explorations in Economic History*, 17, 1980.

Cule, J. E., 'Finance and Industry: the Firm of Boulton & Watt', *Economic History*, Feb. 1940.

Fraser, Derek, 'Politics and the Victorian City', *Urban History Yearbook*, 1979.

Gale, W. K. V., 'Soho Foundry, some Facts and Fallacies', *Transactions of the Newcomen Society*, 34, 1961–2.

Harrison, B., 'Religion and Recreation in 19th-Century England', *Past & Present*, 38, 1967.

Hopkins, Eric, 'Were the Webbs Wrong about Apprenticeship in the Black Country?', *West Midland Studies*, 6, 1973.

Hopkins, Eric, 'Working Conditions in Victorian Stourbridge', *International Review of Social History*, Vol. XIX, 1974. Part 3.

Hopkins, Eric, 'Working Class Attitudes to Education in the Black Country in the Mid-Nineteenth Century', *History of Education Society Bulletin*, 14, Autumn 1974.

Hopkins, Eric, 'Tremenheere's Prize Schemes in the Mining Districts, 1851–1859', *History of Education Society Bulletin*, No. 15, Spring 1975.

Hopkins, Eric, 'Changes in the Scale of the Industrial Unit in Stourbridge and District 1815–1914', *West Midlands Studies*, Vol. VIII, 1975.

Hopkins, Eric, 'Working Class Housing in the Smaller Industrial Town of the 19th century: Stourbridge – a Case Study', *Midland History*, IV, Nos 3 and 4, 1978.

Hopkins, Eric, 'Working Hours and Conditions During the Industrial Revolution: a Reappraisal', *Economic History Review*, 2nd series, XXXV, No. 1, Feb. 1982.

Hopkins, Eric, 'Boulton before Watt: the Earlier Career Reconsidered', *Midland History*, IX, 1984.

Hopkins, Eric, 'The Trading and Service Sectors of the Birmingham Economy 1750–1800', *Business History*, XXVIII, No. 3, July 1986.

Hopkins, Eric, 'Working Class Housing in Birmingham during the Industrial Revolution', *International Review of Social History*, XXXI, 1986, Part I.

Hyde, Charles K., 'Technological Change in the British Wrought Iron Industry 1750–1815: a Re-interpretation', *Economic History Review*, 2nd series, XXVII, No. 2, May 1974.

Johnson, B. L. C., 'The Foley Partnerships: the Iron Industry of the Midlands at the end of the Charcoal Era', *Economic History Review*, 2nd series, IV, No. 3, 1952.

Johnson, B. L. C., 'The Midland Iron Industry in the Early 18th Century', *Business History*, II, No. 2, June, 1960.

Jones, S. R. H., 'The Country Trade and the Marketing and Distribution of Birmingham Hardware, 1750–1810', *Business History*, XXVI, No. 1, March 1984.

Law, C. M., 'Some Notes on the Urban Population of England and Wales in the 18th Century', *The Local Historian*, Vol. 10, No. 1, 1972.

Mitchell, I., 'Pitt's shop tax in the history of retailing', *The Local Historian*, Vol. 14, 1981.

Mole, David E. H., 'Challenge to the Church: Birmingham 1815–1865', in H. J. Dyos (eds.) and Michael Wolff, *The Victorian City: Images and Realities*, Vol. II, 1973.

Neale, R. S., 'Class and Class-Consciousness in Early 19th-Century England: Three Classes or Five?', *Victorian Studies*, Vol. XII, No. 1, Sept. 1968.

Norris, John Mackenzie, 'Samuel Garbett and the Early Development of Industrial Lobbying in Great Britain', *Economic History Review*, X, 1957–8.

Pelham, R. A., 'The Immigrant Population of Birmingham 1688–1726', *Birmingham Archaeological Society Transactions*, XVI, 1937.

Ram, R. W., 'Influences on the Patterns of Belief and Social Action among Birmingham Dissenters between 1750 and 1870', in Alan Bryman, (ed.), *Religion in the Birmingham Area: Essays in the Sociology of Religion* (1975).

Reid, Douglas A., 'The Decline of St Monday 1776–1867', *Past & Present*, 71, 1976.

Reid, Douglas E., 'Interpreting the Festival Calendar: Wakes and Fairs as Carnivals', in Storch, Robert D. (ed.), *Popular Culture and Custom in 19th Century England* (1982).

Robinson, Eric, 'Boulton and Fothergill, 1762–1782, and the Birmingham Export of Hardware', *University of Birmingham Historical Journal*, VII, 1959–60.

Robinson, Eric, '18th Century Commerce and Fashion: Matthew Boulton's Marketing Techniques', *Economic History Review*, 2nd series, XVI, No. 1, 1963.

Robinson, Eric, 'Matthew Boulton and the art of parliamentary lobbying', *Historical Journal*, 7, 1964.

Robinson, Eric, 'Matthew Boulton and Josiah Wedgwood, Apostles of Fashion', *Business History*, XXVIII, No. 3, July 1986.

Robson, Geoffrey, 'The Failures of Success: Working Class Evangelists in Early Victorian Birmingham', in Derek Baker (ed.), *Religious Motivation: Biographical and Sociological Problems for the Church Historian* (1978).

Rose, R. B., 'The Priestley Riots of 1791', *Past & Present*, 18, Nov. 1960.

Rose, R. B., 'The Origins of Working

Class Radicalism in Birmingham',
Labour History, 9, 1965.

Samuel, Raphael, 'The Workshop of the
World: Steam Power and Hand
Technology in Victorian Britain',
History Workshop, 3, 1977.

Smith, Barbara M., 'The Galtons of
Birmingham: Quaker Gun Merchants
and Bankers, 1702–1831', *Business
History*, IX, Nos 1, 2, 1967.

Tholfsen, Trygve R., 'The Artisan and
the Culture of Early Victorian
Birmingham', *University of Birmingham
Historical Journal*, IV, No. 1, 1953–4.

Thompson, E. P., 'Time, Work-
Discipline and Industrial Capitalism',
Past & Present, 38, 1967.

Thompson, F. M. L., 'Social Control in
Victorian Britain', *Economic History
Review*, 2nd series, Vol. XXXIV, No.
2, 1981.

Vance, J. E., Jnr, 'Housing the Worker:
Determinative and Contingent Ties in
Nineteenth-Century Birmingham', in
Economic Geography, XLIII, 1967.

White, D. P., 'The Birmingham Button
Industry', *Post Medieval Archaeology*,
II, 1977.

Williams, D. E., 'Midland Hunger Riots
in 1766', *Midland History*, Vol. 3, No.
4, 1976.

Wilson, C., 'The Entrepreneur in the
Industrial Revolution', *History*, LII,
1957.

Wise, M. J., 'Birmingham and its Trade
Relations in the Early 18th Century',
*University of Birmingham Historical
Journal*, II, 1949–50.

Theses

Bebbington, P. S., 'Samuel Garbett
1717–1803', Birmingham M.Comm.
thesis, 1938.

Behagg, Clive, 'Radical Politics and
Conflict at the Point of Production:

Birmingham 1815–1845. A Study in
the Relationship Between the Classes',
Birmingham PhD thesis, 1982.

Cule, J. E., 'The Financial History of
Matthew Boulton 1759–1800',
Birmingham M.Comm. thesis, 1935.

Duggan, E. P., 'The Impact of
Industrialization on an Urban Labor
Market: Birmingham, England,
1770–1860', Wisconsin PhD thesis,
1972.

Fletcher, Linda J., 'Robert Owen's
Equitable Labour Exchanges', Open
University B.Litt. thesis, 1984.

Frost, M. B., 'The Development of
Provided Schooling for Working Class
Children in Birmingham 1781–1851',
Birmingham M.Litt. thesis, 1978.

Immer, John R., 'The Development of
Productive Methods in Birmingham,
1760–1851', Oxford D.Phil. thesis,
1954.

Kelly, Thomas H., 'Wages and Labour
Organisation in the Brass Trades of
Birmingham and District',
Birmingham PhD thesis, 1930.

McNaulty, Mary C., 'Some Aspects of
the History of the Administration of
the Poor Laws in Birmingham
between 1730 and 1834', Birmingham
MA thesis, 1942.

Mole, David Eric Harton, 'The Church
of England and Society in
Birmingham, c.1830–1866',
Cambridge PhD thesis, 1961.

Reid, D. A., 'Labour, Leisure and Politics
in Birmingham c.1800 to 1875',
Birmingham PhD thesis, 1985.

Richards, W. A., 'The Birmingham Gun
Manufactory of Farmer & Galton and
the Slave Trade in the 18th Century',
Birmingham MA thesis, 1972.

Ryman, John, 'Religion and Radical
Politics in Birmingham, 1830–50',
Birmingham B.Litt. thesis, 1979.

Index